Acclaim for BARRY LOPEZ's

About This Life

"[Barry Lopez] can bring the light of an arctic summer's midnight to your living room."   —*The Columbus Dispatch*

"Lopez writes with a photographer's keen eye, a novelist's sure-handed way with detail and a biologist's attention to scientific accuracy."   —*Newsday*

"*About This Life* is a shimmering window on the richness of the world [and] the vagaries of memory."   —*Portland Oregonian*

"Whether he is visiting remote islands or sites closer to home, Lopez provides a sincere look at what is marvelous about his surroundings, and his book admirably adds to what he calls a literature of hope."   —*Chicago Tribune*

"Curiosity, fresh insight, and luminous, precise prose . . . is generously on display here."   —*The Philadelphia Inquirer*

"Lopez is a careful and caring writer . . . he truly shows us the world's magic."   —*Seattle Post-Intelligencer*

"[Lopez has] that rarest of keen eyes, the one that can home in on the face in the mirror and see truly."   —*The Denver Post*

BARRY LOPEZ

About This Life

Barry Lopez is the author of six works of nonfiction, including *Arctic Dreams* and *Of Wolves and Men*; six works of fiction, including *Field Notes* and *Winter Count*; and a novella-length fable, *Crow and Weasel*. His work appears regularly in *Harper's*, where he is a contributing editor, as well as in *The Paris Review, Orion, The Georgia Review, Outside*, and elsewhere. The recipient of numerous literary awards, including the National Book Award for nonfiction, he lives in western Oregon.

Also by
BARRY LOPEZ

About This Life

About This Life

JOURNEYS ON THE THRESHOLD OF MEMORY

BARRY LOPEZ

Vintage Books | A Division of Random House, Inc. | New York

VINTAGE BOOKS EDITION, MAY 1999

Copyright © 1998 by Barry Holstun Lopez

All rights reserved under International and Pan-American Copyright
Conventions. Published in the United States by Vintage Books, a division
of Random House, Inc., New York. Originally published in hardcover
in the United States by Alfred A. Knopf, Inc., New York, in 1998.

Vintage Books and colophon are registered
trademarks of Random House, Inc.

The Library of Congress has cataloged
the Knopf edition as follows:
Lopez, Barry Holstun, [date]
About this life / Barry Lopez. — 1st American ed.
p.   cm.
ISBN 0-679-43454-2
1. Lopez, Barry Holstun, [date]—Biography.
2. Authors, American—20th century—Biography.
I. Title.
PS3562.O67Z464 1998
813'.54—dc21
[B] 98-14257
CIP

Vintage ISBN: 0-679-75447-4

Author Photograph © Nancy Bennett Evelyn

www.randomhouse.com/vintage

Printed in the United States of America
10 9 8 7 6 5 4 3 2 1

For Mary Holstun Lopez

for Adrian Bernard Lopez and John Edward Brennan

for Sidney Van Sheck and Dara Emery

and for my brother, Dennis Holstun Lopez

CONTENTS

About This Life

Introduction

A VOICE

I WAS BORN east of the heights of New Rochelle in the watershed of New York's Mamaroneck River in the winter of 1945. In the spring of 1948 my father, a billboard advertising executive, would move us away, to a home in rural California at the foot of the Santa Susana Mountains in the San Fernando Valley, far from this suburban landscape just thirty miles from New York City. I would never know why. Perhaps the move was an effort to save a marriage gone awry, or maybe he hoped to capitalize on prospects in southern California after the war.

For a long time I thought of California as the beginning, the place where my life took a distinctive shape, but something had already begun. When I recall incidents from those first three years in New York, some still vivid as a bowl of oranges on a summer windowsill, several seem to bear directly on my later life, to be adumbrations. Or perhaps that is only how memory works.

3

We lived on the second floor of a six-story apartment building situated on Orienta Point in the town of Mamaroneck. It faced onto Mamaroneck Harbor, an embayment of Long Island Sound. My parents, avid sailors, had a membership in the Nanhook Yacht Club, which was affiliated with "The Orienta"—a primary attraction for people who chose to live there.

A great lawn sloped north from the building down to a seawall and a narrow beach, off which sailboats were moored. My earliest memories are of crawling off a blanket onto this cool, prickly turf under a huge elm. Flower beds had been planted along the building's east side, and I remember walking in them with my mother to pick flowers as tall as I was. I remember the aroma of the soil in summer and the way the bare earth puckered to a dry crust after an early morning watering.

The odor and the flowers' colors in the garden attracted me. To ensure visits there with Mother, I'd sometimes line my alphabet blocks up on a windowsill—our windows were right above the gardens—and push them out. She'd take me along to retrieve them while she gathered bouquets.

I also remember the glare of light on the harbor and the *snap* of white sails coming taut in a breeze. In warm weather I was closely watched like other children on the beach, but I recall wading out into the water as if I were alone, and wanting to go farther. I could see across to Shootfly Island and the estuary of Otter Creek. Away to the east, where Turkey Rock and Hen Island stood out, lowlying Peningo Neck protected the harbor from the open waters of the Sound.

Standing in seawater stirred to wavelets by the wind, my head thrown back, I'd turn slowly to gaze at the towering crown of the elm, backlit and twinkling in noon light, turn and catch the long horizon of the sound to the east, keep turning to follow scudding sailboats on that wind. On the hottest days I sought out the shade of the big elm, but I would go back in the water again to experience that peculiar yearning—to swim, to sail, to go. I would wait in the water for something to emerge, to appear in that empty space above its surface.

Shortly after my brother was born in 1948, my father drove out to California. My mother and brother and I flew west afterward in a Constellation. (I remember a living-room-like atmosphere at the rear of this plane, where couch seats were arranged in a horseshoe around a table, and going into the terminal at Love Field in Dallas with one of the stewardesses to eat dinner while my mother attended to my infant brother.) My parents divorced two years later, and my mother began raising us with a dedication I would not understand or appreciate for years. She taught home economics during the day at a junior high school; twice a week she taught night school at a junior college. She also worked at home as a dressmaker.

My images of our first house, when I was three or four and my father still lived with us, are of the way it sat apart, surrounded by alfalfa hay fields. Our street was a macadam-surfaced ditch meant to funnel heavy winter rains into the Los Angeles River. It also served as a corridor for heading sheep to summer pastures in the Santa Susanas. On different days we might be stuck in the car for either reason.

After my father left, not to be seen again, Mother bought a small one-bedroom house on a half acre of land in the town of Reseda. For boys my age growing up then in the northern San Fernando Valley, adventure unfolded in fruit orchards and wisteria hedges, in horse pastures and haylofts, and around farming operations, truck gardens, and chicken ranches. During these same years the Los Angeles River channel, another haunt, was floored and walled in concrete, so we saw the last of that river's natural days. We hiked in the Santa Monica Mountains and we caught rides on slow freights west from Reseda to Canoga Park and back. We rode our bikes out as far as Porter Ranch, the rural fringes of valley settlement where braceros worked the fields and where encounters with coyotes, jackrabbits, and even rattle-snakes were not unusual.

Mother frequently drove my brother, Dennis, and me into the Mojave Desert on weekends, or up to Antelope Valley or away to one of a dozen beaches from Zuma, west of Malibu, to Pismo, up north near San Luis Obispo. We spent summer weeks in camp at Big Bear Lake or with Mother's friends at Lake Arrowhead in the San Bernardino Mountains.

One advantage of growing up in a single-parent home (it wasn't called that back then, of course; "broken home" was the preferred term) is that if your mother is an interesting or handsome woman, she can attract the attention of interesting men. My brother and I knew several such men, all but one in my memory impeccable in their conduct and generous toward us. I remember picnics at the home of a movie stuntman who kept a rambling, jerry-built house in an unspoiled part of the Calabasas hills, where he'd dammed a creek to create a swimming hole. And picnics at the summer house of a man who was the gentlest person I ever knew, a horticulturalist at the Santa Barbara Botanic Garden whom for a long time I wished my mother would marry. With them and Mother I experienced the crash of Pacific storm surf on the deserted beaches of Los Angeles and Ventura Counties. I felt the hysteria that came with brush fires fanned by Santa Ana winds and caught the astringent smell of creosote bush after a desert rain.

In the middle of what was, for me, this intensely physical landscape, another man emerged who engaged a different part of my mind. He was an aeronautical engineer at Hughes Aircraft and also an artist. He'd taught my mother painting in college in Alabama and had been her first husband. After their divorce, he moved to California and remarried. When my father left he became like a father to me. He drove a blue-gray sports car, an Austin Healey convertible, and I rode with him swiftly along winding Mulholland Drive above the city and down the broad promenade of the Pacific Coast Highway with the top down. One Christmas he built a large layout for my trains, a landscape of papier-mâché mountains and tunnels with a handcrafted bridge and a scenic backdrop he'd painted.

For years I believed my childhood nothing out of the ordinary, but it was a sort of bohemian existence. Mother was strict with Dennis and me about table and social manners. She disciplined us and was conscientious about our schooling and protective of our emotional lives. But I remember no impatience, no indifference toward imagination. She embraced our drawings, our stories, and our Tinkertoy kingdoms, and she drove us to many intriguing places in our green 1934 Ford coupe—to Boulder (later, Hoover) Dam, the La Brea Tar Pits. And she invited engaging, independent men and women to the house for dinner.

The parents of some of my classmates and some of Mother's friends worked in the motion picture industry and in television, but I do not remember that their professions colored my life in any untoward way. Work in Hollywood, like work at Lockheed or other aircraft companies, didn't seem any more remarkable to us as children then than farming or teaching. I was more interested, actually, in farming and in what was done by people who worked astride a horse, a mysterious and magnificent beast, with its shuddering flanks and high nickers.

One unusual thing about those years was that I raised pigeons. Many of them were tumblers, a kind of bird that folds its wings and then plummets from a height, only to pull up sharply inches from the ground. A tumbler then beats its way back up into the sky from which it plummets again. Sometimes a dozen or more will tumble together, careening past each other as they fall.

Watching the pigeons fly was an experience so exhilarating I would turn slowly under them in circles of glee. They would spiral above the house before flying off every day, and the tumblers would fall toward an adjacent field. They'd disappear behind lofty banks of aging eucalyptus north and south of the house in flocks of thirty and forty. When they returned in the afternoon, I found that faithfulness, their soft cooing at dusk in the pigeon coop, as soothing as my mother's fingers running through my hair.

I could not have understood at this age of course, only eight or nine, what it might mean to have a voice one day, to speak as a writer speaks. I would have been baffled by the thought. The world I inhabited—the emotions I imagined horses to have, the sound of a night wind clattering ominously in the dry leaves of eucalyptus trees—I imagined as a refuge, one that would be lost to me if I tried to explain it. The countryside around me was a landscape full of small, wild animals. When I walked alone down windbreaks of Russian olives or up sandy washes and met them, I'd stand still until they went on. They did not seem to my mind animals that wanted to be known.

My future, as I vaguely pictured it then, would include going to high school in the valley, maybe Stanford University afterward, and then perhaps I would work toward owning a farm. Like my friends, though, I had few concrete thoughts beyond repairing my bike and being included at the periphery of the circle of older boys, the ones who possessed such gleaming, loud, extraordinarily powerful, and customized automobiles.

When I was eleven my mother married again, and we moved back East to an apartment in the Murray Hill section of Manhattan on East Thirty-fifth Street. I would live there for six years before going away to college. This change was wrenching: socially, economically, and geographically. I was bewildered by it—a penthouse apartment, Jesuit prep school, Saturday afternoon trapshooting at the New York Athletic Club's Travers Island range, debutant balls at the Plaza and the Pierre. Gone were the rural, agricultural, and desert landscapes to which I was so attached. They were replaced by summers on the Jersey shore and by visits to eastern Alabama, where my mother had grown up. But, for the first time, I had an allowance. And I began to grasp from my new classmates, all boys, what went with this new life with no cars, where no one bicycled alone at night to the sound of big sprinklers slow-chucking water over alfalfa fields.

I recall a moment that first eastern summer of 1956, a scene I've come back to often. My parents put Dennis and me in a summer camp on the North Fork of eastern Long Island for a few weeks. Among my bunkmates were Thom and John Steinbeck, the writer's two sons. On parents day, John and Elaine Steinbeck would come over from their home in Sag Harbor in a cabin cruiser. He would row a dinghy in to shore to fetch the boys and take them back out for the afternoon to the moored boat. I might have been reading "The Red Pony" or other stories in *The*

Long Valley then. What I most remember, though, was that this man had come here from California, like me, and that things seemed to be going well for him. I was having a difficult time that first summer adjusting to city life. I missed the open-endedness of the other landscape, with its hay fields and its perimeter of unsettled mountains. And what I missed was embodied somehow in this burly man, rowing the boat away with his boys. Before I left for college I read all of Steinbeck's books. I drew from them a sense of security.

Later that same summer my parents rented a house for a few weeks near Montauk Point, at the tip of Long Island. My father, as I would always refer to him later, took my brother and me fishing several times on charter boats. As it happened, Peter Matthiessen—a writer I would later come to admire and get to know—was captaining just such a boat out of Montauk that August. Thirty years later, crossing Little Peconic Bay to the west of Montauk with him, in a boat he was thinking of buying, we tried to determine whether it could have been his boat that my father had hired one of those times.

I thrived in the city in spite of the change in landscape. I focused on my studies—Latin, history, English literature, French, art (a class taught by the painter John Sloan's widow)—a standard Jesuit regimen, light in the sciences. I developed into a fast, strong athlete, and graduated with letters in three varsity sports and a scholastic average high enough to have gained me entry to almost any university.

I felt privileged rather than deserving of all this. I understood that my Jesuit education, my social and economic class, my good grades, my trained and confident young man's voice, my white skin, and the hegemony of my religion all pointed toward being well received in the world. In my private heart, though, thinking back to the years in California and forgetting those early days of privilege at Orienta Point, I felt I was dressed in borrowed clothes. How did I come to be here?

The summer after I graduated from high school I traveled to Europe with fifteen of my classmates. We flew to Lisbon and then spent two months being driven in a small Fiat tour bus with huge windows through Spain, France, Italy, Switzerland, Austria, and West Germany. Later we crossed the Channel and toured England and Ireland. Among hundreds of things I did, I remember laying my hand on the thigh of Agesander's statue of Laocoön in the Vatican Museums and feeling the sinew of muscle in the white marble; seeing a matador gored and then spun like a pinwheel on a bull's horn in the corrida in Pamplona; an ethereal light that seemed to bathe Napoleon's catafalque in blue in Paris; and a vast cemetery of identical white crosses, ranked over green hills in northern France, a bucolic landscape lovely, benign, and enormously sad.

In the fall of 1962 I entered the University of Notre Dame in northern Indiana with the intention of becoming an aeronautical engineer. Once I got my driver's license I began leaving school on weekends, camping out or sleeping in the cars I borrowed, whatever was necessary to see the surrounding country from Michigan's Upper Peninsula to West Virginia. I once drove to Mississippi and back with my roommate over a weekend—eleven hundred miles—just to see it, drawn by little more than the lure of the Natchez Trace.

During my sophomore and junior years I started writing stories that had nothing to do with classroom assignments. I understood the urge to write as a desire to describe what happened, what I saw, when I went outside. The book that engaged me most along these lines was *Moby-Dick,* which I read three times before I entered college.

Story, as I understood it by reading Faulkner, Hardy, Cather, and Hemingway, was a powerful and clarifying human invention. The language alone, as I discovered it in Gerard Manley Hopkins and Faulkner, was exquisitely beautiful, also weirdly and mysteriously evocative.

My attitude toward language and story crystallized on a single afternoon in my sophomore year. I cut a class to hear Robert Fitzgerald read from his new translation of *The Odyssey.* I'd heard the translation was brilliant; what was spellbinding about his reading, however, was the way the audience became galvanized in beauty by his presentation. History, quest, longing, metered prose, moral consternation, and fantastic image all came together in that room. The feeling broadened and calmed us. Whatever Fitzgerald did in that hour, that's what I wanted to do.

I was driven to write, but of course anguished over my efforts. Who was I to speak? What had I to say? As a college student of nineteen, I was being encouraged in the idea that if I spoke I would be heard. The privilege that ensured this, however, was the accident of my mother's third marriage. It was nothing I'd earned. And much of what seemed to me so worth addressing—the psychological draw of landscape, that profound mystery I sensed in wild animals (which reading Descartes had done nothing to dissuade)—was regarded as peculiar territory by other nascent writers at the university.

In my senior year at Notre Dame, at bat in an intramural baseball game, I took a high inside pitch that shattered the stone in my senior ring. I left the setting empty. The emptiness came to symbolize doubts I'd developed about my education. I'd learned a lot, but I had not learned it in the presence of women or blacks or Jews or Koreans. Something important, those refinements and objections, had been omitted.

When I departed the university in 1966 (with a degree in Communication Arts) I left in order to discover a voice and a subject, though this was not at all clear then. I floundered in two jobs for a year, married, finished a graduate degree with the thought that I would teach prep school, and then entered the master of fine arts program in writing at the University of Oregon. I left that program after only a semester, but matriculated at the university for more than a year, during which time I met a singular teacher in the English department, a man named Barre Toelken. He helped me frame the questions seething inside me then about how justice, education, and other Enlightenment ideals could be upheld against the depth of prejudice and the fields of ignorance I saw everywhere around me.

Toelken pointed me toward anthropological research which demonstrated that other cultures approached questions of natural history and geography in the same way I preferred. They did not separate humanity and nature. They recognized the immanence of the divine in both. And they regarded landscape as a component as integral to the development of personality and social order as we take the Oedipus complex and codified law to be.

As a guest in the Toelkens' home, I frequently met scholars and other insightful people from outside white, orthodox, middle-class culture. I didn't consider that these people spoke a truth no one else possessed; but, listening to them, I saw the inadequacy of my education. It lacked any suggestion that these voices were necessary, that they were relevant. Further, it became clear to me in the Toelkens' home that their stories, despite the skilled dramatizing of human triumph and failure, were destined for quarantine in the society of which I was a part. I was not going to find these voices in American magazines.

In the years after those first encounters with senior Native American men, itinerant Asian poets, black jazz musicians, and translators, I deliberately began to seek the company of people outside my own narrow cultural bounds. I was drawn especially to men and women who had not dissociated themselves from the passionate and spiritual realms of life, people for whom mystery was not a challenge to intelligence but a bosom.

The effect of these encounters was not a belief that I was now able to speak for such people—a notion I find dangerous as well as absurd—but an understanding that my voice, steeped in Jung, Dante, Heisenberg, Melville, and Merton, was not the only voice. My truth was not the one truth. My tongue did not compose a pinnacle language. These other voices were as indispensable to our survival as variations in our DNA.

In my earliest essays, I wanted to report what *others* were thinking, and I was driven by a feeling that these other voices were being put asunder by "progress" in its manifold forms.

Although I'm wary of pancultural truths, I believe in all human societies there is a desire to love and be loved, to experience the full fierceness of human emotion, and to make a measure of the sacred part of one's life. Wherever I've traveled—Kenya,

Chile, Australia, Japan—I've found that the most dependable way to preserve these possibilities is to be reminded of them in stories. Stories do not give instruction, they do not explain how to love a companion or how to find God. They offer, instead, patterns of sound and association, of event and image. Suspended as listeners and readers in these patterns, we might reimagine our lives. It is through story that we embrace the great breadth of memory, that we can distinguish what is true, and that we may glimpse, at least occasionally, how to live without despair in the midst of the horror that dogs and unhinges us.

As long as it took for me to see that a writer's voice had to grow out of his own knowledge and desire, that it could not rise legitimately out of the privilege of race or gender or social rank, so did it take time to grasp the depth of cruelty inflicted upon all of us the moment voices are silenced, when for prejudicial reasons people are told their stories are not valuable, not useful. Anyone educated in the existence and history of metaphorical expression—Schrödinger's or Li Po's—cannot help but recoil before such menace, such ignorance.

ONCE I WAS asked by a seatmate on a trans-Pacific flight, a man who took the liberty of glancing repeatedly at the correspondence in my lap, what instruction he should give his fifteen-year-old daughter, who wanted to be a writer. I didn't know how to answer him, but before I could think I heard myself saying, "Tell your daughter three things." Tell her to read, I said. Tell her to read whatever interests her, and protect her if someone declares what she's reading to be trash. No one can fathom what happens between a human being and written language. She may be paying attention to things in the words beyond anyone else's comprehension, things that feed her curiosity, her singular heart and mind. Tell her to read classics like *The Odyssey*. They've been around a long time because the patterns in them have proved endlessly useful, and, to borrow Evan Connell's observation, with a good book you never touch bottom. But warn your daughter that ideas of heroism, of love, of human duty and devotion that women have been writing about for centuries will not be available to her in this form. To find these voices she will have to search. When, on her own, she begins to ask, make her a present of George Eliot, or the travel writing of Alexandra David-Neel, or *To the Lighthouse.*

Second, I said, tell your daughter that she can learn a great deal about writing by reading and by studying books about grammar and the organization of ideas, but that if she wishes to write well she will have to become someone. She will have to discover her beliefs, and then speak to us from within those beliefs. If her prose doesn't come out of her belief, whatever that proves to be, she will only be passing along information, of which we are in no great need. So help her discover what she means.

Finally, I said, tell your daughter to get out of town, and help her do that. I don't necessarily mean to travel to Kazakhstan, or wherever, but to learn another language, to live with people other than her own, to separate herself from the familiar. Then, when she returns, she will be better able to understand why she loves the familiar, and will give us a fresh sense of how fortunate we are to share these things.

Read. Find out what you truly believe. Get away from the familiar. Every writer, I told him, will offer you thoughts about writing that are different, but these are three I trust.

IN THE PAGES that follow, you will see how this thinking has played out for me. My beliefs will be apparent, but not, I hope, obtrusive. And it will be obvious that I have left town, or tried to, and that I've wanted to put to work what I saw. I've chosen these essays to give a sense of how one writer proceeds, and they are reflective of my notion of what it means to travel. The order is not chronological, and I've not included all the work of recent years.

If I were asked what I want to accomplish as a writer, I would say it's to contribute to a literature of hope. With my given metaphors, rooted in a childhood spent outdoors in California and which take much of their language from Jesuit classrooms in New York City, I want to help create a body of stories in which men and women can discover trustworthy patterns.

Every story is an act of trust between a writer and a reader; each story, in the end, is social. Whatever a writer sets down can harm or help the community of which he or she is a part. When I write, I can imagine a child in California wishing to give away what he's just seen—a wild animal fleeing through creosote cover in the desert, casting a bright-eyed backward glance. Or three lines of overheard conversation that seem to contain everything we need understand to repair the gaping rift between body and soul. I look back at that boy turning in glee beneath his pigeons, and know it can take a lifetime to convey what you mean, to find the opening. You watch, you set it down. Then you try again.

PART ONE

Out of Country

I

SEARCHING FOR DEPTH
IN BONAIRE

I

THE LAST DAY I spent on Bonaire, a Catholic Sunday, I drove most of the small Dutch island's few dirt tracks and undivided asphalt roads. This short traverse—the island is only twenty-four miles long—took me south to rows of refurbished slave huts standing alongside towering, blistering-white mounds of sea salt; out to a windward Caribbean shore to look at pictographs made centuries ago by indigenous Caiquetío Indians; then to Gotomeer, a lake on the northwest coast where at dusk flamingos rise up in a billowing sheet of pink, flecked with carmine and black, and roll off south across the Bonaire Basin for the coast of Venezuela, sixty miles away.

That dependable evening Angelus of departing birds deepened

the architecture of the sky, and it resolved, for a moment, the emotional strain of my brief, disjointed conversation with this landscape. No longer Caiquetío land, no longer Spanish, provisionally Dutch, Bonaire has become an international hinterland. Five hundred years of complicated cultural history have produced a subtle, polyphonic rarity here, full of striking temporal hitches. At a fruit stall an elderly woman in a thirties-style print dress pops a button of dirt off a fresh cantaloupe with her thumb and waits for a young man in J. Crew casuals adjusting his earphones to see that he's in the way. Not long after deplaning, one easily feels embarrassed for having come here, as I had, with but a single idea: to dive the pellucid waters of the place Amerigo Vespucci named La Isla de Palo Brasíl.

BONAIRE IS the second largest of five islands in the seemingly indefinite Netherlands Antilles. Sint Eustatius, Saba, and Sint Maarten (which the Dutch share with the French)—three very small, densely populated islands clustered five hundred miles northeast of Bonaire, to the east of Puerto Rico—compose one geographical element. Bonaire and its larger neighbor, heavily populated Curaçao, compose the second. (Nearby Aruba, long a sixth member of this political archipelago, seceded from the Dutch Antilles on January 1, 1986, resolving a fractious sibling rivalry with Curaçao but sharply curtailing its own access to financial assistance and technical advice from Holland.)

Sophisticates on Curaçao regard lightly populated Bonaire as hopelessly bucolic; a promotional brochure says foreign investors will be pleased by its "progressive and cooperative political climate." Lying safely south of the track of Caribbean hurricanes, its mildly humid air cooled by persistent trade winds, the island is a rocky, desert place, crooked like a dog's hind leg. Its landscape rises gently from green, red, and lavender salt ponds in the south through a bush plain to low, brush-covered hills four or five hundred feet high at its northwest end. It is without a permanent river (residential freshwater comes from a desalinization plant and a few natural springs), although brilliant fair-weather clouds regularly stream west over the island, even at night, obscuring the Southern Cross and other familiar constellations.

Before an impatient eye, Bonaire appears stark and bony. Its early cover of brazilwood and lignum vitae forest is gone, sold to Europe piecemeal, centuries ago. Its dry, meager vegetation, rooted in bleached coral rubble, lies trampled and battered by generations of donkeys and bark-stripping goats. Its coarse headlands of volcanic ironstone, irradiated by a tropical sun, scorch and nick the hands.

Starkness of a different kind arises from a contrast between the genteel manner of Bonaire's residents, entering and exiting (light as sparrows) the innocent pastels of their stucco homes, and the island's two modern, rigid, metallic edifices: Bonaire Petroleum's brightly lit oil transfer terminal in the north and Trans World Radio's antenna park to the south, a powerful transmission facility operated by a fundamentalist Christian sect.

A fevered search for mineral wealth and the religious acquisition of souls, of course, form the beginning of Bonaire's engagement with the Old World; these subjects—spiritual salvation and the control of resources like oil—are old ones on Bonaire. In 1513, Diego Colón dismissed Aruba, Curaçao, and Bonaire as "*islas inútiles*" (useless, meaning without metals). The Caiquetíos were brusquely sold off to hidalgos in Hispaniola, where they soon perished working in Spanish "gold" mines. In 1634 Bonaire—the name apparently derives from a Caiquetío term, *bajnaj,* meaning "lowland"—was acquired by the Dutch in their search for sources of salt and wood. Two hundred years later slavery was abolished; open to settlement, Bonaire stabilized as a sort of sprawling hacienda. People independently grazed cattle and sheep, grew aloe vera and divi-divi pods, evaporated seawater for salt, burned coral to make chalk, raised horses, and made charcoal, all for export. This diverse subsistence economy, augmented later in this century with wage labor off-island—in oil refineries on Aruba and Curaçao, aboard fishing vessels, and in the cane fields of Cuba—persisted relatively unchanged until the 1970s, when real estate development and tourism began abruptly to alter the island's tenor.

This latest economic wind blows with a vaguely disturbing odor—the forcing pressure of big, fast money, the entrepreneur's heat to create wealth in "undeveloped" lands. (From an older Spanish perspective, perhaps it's only *plus ça change, plus c'est la même chose*.) A modern visitor from the United States like myself takes wry note of the fact that Bonaire Petroleum and Akzo Salt, the great bulk of the island's economy, are U.S.-owned businesses, as is the fundamentalist station. You see all this—a strangely beautiful landscape, attractive people, a kind of praying mantis economy—more or less quickly, in the first few hours. But I did not travel here to nurture a ready cynicism. I did not make the long flight through Denver and Miami to idealize whatever threatened virtue there might be in rural Bonairean life, or to feed any sense of irony over the fate of the Monroe Doctrine in postcolonial America. I came with a single intention: to become intimate with the island's undisturbed realm—its fringing coral reef.

Bonaire's reefs are among the most astonishing in the Americas. Patient divers can find nearly every one of the western Atlantic's seventy or so kinds of coral here. Schools of horse-eye jack, swift as tuna, bolt into the dimness. Starfish and white anemones pearlesce in the lugubrious shadows cast by Atlantic manta rays. Blizzards of tropical fish swarm over and through fields of exotically shaped sponges, some tall as barrels. Four-foot-long tarpon, predatory fish whose ranks of scales resemble chain mail, routinely rise at night from Bonaire's near depths to swim alongside divers in the dark. Most days, one can see farther than eighty feet in the limpid, sun-shot water. Among the rare local creatures I hoped to find were a cryptic, ambushing hunter called a frogfish; pistol shrimps; glowing fluorescent sponges; and an animal emblematic of the Jovian peculiarities of these waters, the ethereal sea horse.

I would eventually make seventeen dives, over eight days. I would lie awake those nights, a trade wind blowing through my room, trying to understand where I was. The contrast between a desiccated land and the rococo display of life in the sea, between hardscrabble existence on tenuous farming land holds and the burgeoning growth of condominiums to provide housing for divers like myself made sleep difficult. As we sometimes seek to hide ourselves in dreams, so I focused those nights on the beauty of the world into which, come morning, I would fling myself.

LIKE MANY scuba divers I had made my initial dives (after those for certification) in a tropical sea, in warm, clear, currentless waters on the Great Barrier Reef in my case, east of Cairns, Australia. In the years following I saw more of the tropics but dove, too, in steep-walled fjords in southeast Alaska, in subtropical Galápagos's shark-filled waters, in kelp forests off the coast of California, and under the sea ice in McMurdo Sound, in Antarctica. Diving regularly on the northwest coast of the United States, near my home, in strong currents and cold water and wearing a bulky dry suit has made diving in the tropics seem an unencumbered, almost rarefied experience. The ornate patterns and brilliant color of tropical reef life, displayed like Persian rugs in glycerin hues, and the sometimes overwhelming number of living forms in lucent, tranquil water, are enough to make some cold-water divers, like myself, speechless. The visual impact of Bonaire's reefs is further intensified by the fact that they have changed very little since Vespucci's ships passed overhead. Only large conchs and lobsters and the larger grouper have been hunted out. Here is a welter and diversity of life still comparable to what once stunned the first Europeans to enter the Americas.

In 1971, as a precaution, Bonaire closed its near-shore waters to spearfishers, to collecting for the aquarium trade, and to commercial fishing. The same terrestrial barrenness that once caused the island to be disparaged (and so left undeveloped) has, oddly, contributed directly to the preservation of its reefs. Elsewhere in the tropical world coral reefs are significantly endangered—a blight little known but comparable to that on tropical rain forests. (Because coral reefs occupy less than 1 percent of the ocean floor but harbor close to 25 percent of ocean species, marine scientists regard any threat to them as alarming.) An unspecified amount of reef destruction in the past decade, all over the world, has been attributed to a rise in ocean temperatures, one debated cause of which is global warming. Less debatable causes of coral-reef destruction include coastal logging and intensive agriculture. Sedimentation from eroded, clear-cut slopes and pesticide and herbicide runoff from farmlands may have damaged many coral reefs in Central America and Indonesia irreversibly. In the Philippines, cyanide flushing used to stun fish bound for pet shops and restaurant aquariums and fishing with dynamite are major problems.

One is not reminded of these troubles in Bonaire. Before coming here I had read several intriguing papers about Bonaire's healthy waters. One discussed the shelter offered by sea-grass beds and saltwater-tolerant mangrove swamps in an embayment called Lac Lagoon, a highly productive nursery for yellowtail snapper, great barracuda, stoplight parrotfish, schoolmaster, French grunt, and dozens of other species of fish. Another paper described cryptobiotic marine communities, so-called hidden neighborhoods established beneath natural coral rubble in Bonaire's shallow waters, ensembles of life in which the authors counted 367 species of sponges, tunicates, bryozoans, and other small aquatic creatures. These communities were vigorous, varied, resplendent.

Provoked by such wonder, or driven by curiosity, the ordinary diver in Bonaire finds this complex seascape nearly impossible to penetrate with any degree of certitude. With a concentrated effort (an enthusiasm admittedly at odds with the relaxed atmosphere of the resorts), one might sort out the differences among several dozen fish or learn to distinguish between corals and sponges. But even for a conscientious diver the task is enormous. The descriptive vocabulary—crinoids, ctenophores (ten-ah-fores), nudibranchs (nu-da-branks)—offers relatively few images or names easy to recall. Of the thirty-three or so body plans, or phyla, into which all life is routinely sorted, only two arrangements are at all familiar to land-habituated divers: arthropods (insects and spiders) and chordates (all fish, amphibians, reptiles, birds, and mammals). Representatives of *every* phylum are found in the ocean, arthropods and chordates minor among them. The specific arrangements of biological architecture, metabolism, and propulsion are so counterintuitive here, so strange to human senses, they seem extraplanetary. Moreover, many animals—sea fans, hydroids, wire corals, for example—look like plants. Other animals, such as encrusting corals and scorpionfish, look like rocks. Even fish, the easiest animals to identify, can be perplexing—juveniles of various species of reef fish frequently look nothing like their parents, and other species change shape and gender over time. And a *single* organism, such as a sea nettle, may look no different from a *colony* of animals, such as a Portuguese man-of-war.

A diver in sixty feet of water, checking to see how much air is left and how long she or he has been down and where dive partners may be, does not readily hit upon any good approach to these mysteries.

Most scuba divers at Bonaire's dozen or so resorts—about 29,000 a year fly in, more than double the island's indigenous population—anticipate balmy, hospitable weather and plan to make two or three dives a day for a week or so. Developing a refined sense of what one is actually looking at underwater doesn't seem called for; to be able to talk about it in any detail seems, for many, to run vaguely counter to the idea of a vacation. The experience, principally, is to be thrilled by. The reefs are to be genuinely appreciated and, perhaps over cocktails, are conceivably meant to provoke. One is prompted to wonder, for example, what's happened to this kind of profusion, this density of life, in the rest of the world? Aside from enclaves of birds in the jungles of Ecuador and Peru or wildlife in isolated parts of Congo, few undisturbed terrestrial spots remain for any late-twentieth-century observer. But then one might also be moved to wonder a little about Bonaire. Sections of its reefs have recently been closed to diving in order to "rest" them. They have begun to show the scrapes, breakage, and fatal smears of small animal life associated with intensive tourist diving. (Barely fifty years old, scuba diving has already had a marked effect at some localities. Reefs in the Florida Keys, for example, have been severely damaged in spots by thousands of dive-boat anchorings, by the snatching and impact of divers unable to control their buoyancy and drift, and by divers carelessly kicking out with their fins.)

When I emerged from Bonaire's waters each day, I would enter in my notebook the names of the fish I had seen on Leonora's Reef or in one of the other places where ten or twelve of us dove at a time: cornetfish, smooth trunkfish, yellowhead wrasse, long-spine squirrelfish, balloonfish, midnight parrotfish, honeycomb cowfish, whitespotted filefish, lizardfish—and then the crabs and snails, the eels, the sponges, the corals, until I was worn out, paging through the reference texts and inquiring among the dive-masters who supervised our excursions.

One afternoon, walking back to my room from the boat dock, I stopped next to a frangipani tree in which a single bird, a bananaquit, was singing. I imagined the dense thicket of the tree's branches filled with forty or fifty kinds of singing, energetic birds, and that I had only a few moments to walk around the tree, peering in, to grasp some detail of each to memorize. I had no paper on which to write down a name or on which to sketch. Then, I imagined, they flew away. Who were they? How could I know where I was, really, if I didn't know who they were? It was like that every day underwater—an unknown host, confounding and esoteric as the nine choirs of angels.

THE REFLEXIVE HABITS human beings must develop to stay alive underwater with scuba (self-contained underwater breathing apparatus) are inherently risky. They have largely to do with controlling the rate at which pressure on the body's tissues changes. Divers who are physically fit and diving under supervi-

sion in a benign environment like Bonaire, and who posses
amateur technical diving skills, rarely experience a problem
diving is dicey, strange. The stress the human body is subjec
by the change in pressure at a depth of only 16 feet compares with
the effect of a change in altitude of 18,000 feet on land. Releasing
the increase in pressure too quickly can be fatal. In holiday circumstances like those prevailing on Bonaire, one can be lulled
into thinking nothing will ever go wrong—with the salubrious
weather, the magnificent reefs, or one's own dive technique. It is
the feeling, of course, one vacations in search of.

The divemasters on Bonaire cautioned us repeatedly, in a
friendly way, not to dive deep, not to go below one hundred feet.
It is not only inherently dangerous (four atmospheres of pressure
at that depth is enough to precipitate nitrogen narcosis and disorientation), but for most, unnecessary—the density of marine
life drops off quickly after about sixty feet. As much as anything,
their cautions were a reminder to pay attention to air consumption, to the time you spent at each depth, and to your rate of
ascent to guard against decompression sickness, the so-called
bends.

Few scuba diving accidents occur at depth. Most happen at the
mysterious surface, a wafer-thin realm where air bounds water,
where light suddenly changes flux, ambient sound changes register, and the body passes through a membrane fraught with possibility or, coming the other way, with relief. When water closes
over a diver's head, a feat that once had seemed implausible, to
breathe underwater, seems suddenly boundless with promise.
There is often little indication at the undulating, reflective surface, the harrowing transition zone, of the vividness, the intri-
cacy, the patterns unfurled below.

Something, most certainly, happens to a diver's emotions
underwater. It is not merely a side effect of the pleasing, vaguely
erotic sensation of water pressure on the body. (Doctors sub-
jecting volunteers to greater atmospheric pressure in hyper-
baric chambers don't find the increased flow of plasma beta
endorphins—the "buzz" hormones—that divers frequently ex-

perience.) Nor is it alone the peculiar sense of weightlessness, which permits a diver to hang motionless in open water, observing sea life large as whales around him; nor the ability of a diver, descending in that condition, to slowly tumble and rotate in all three spatial planes. It is not the exhilaration from disorientation that comes when one's point of view starts to lose its "left" and "down" and gains instead something else, a unique perception that grows out of the ease of movement in three dimensions. It is not from the diminishment of gravity to a force little more emphatic than a suggestion. It is not solely the exposure to an unfamiliar intensity of life. It is not just a state of rapture with the bottomless blue world beneath one's feet, what Jacques Cousteau called *"l'ivresse des grandes profondeurs."*

It is some complicated run of these emotions, together with the constant proximity of real terror, exhilaration of another sort entirely. I have felt such terror underwater twice, once when I was swept away in a deep countercurrent in the Gulf of Mexico, and another time beneath the ice in Antarctica, when a piece of equipment froze and a sudden avalanche of events put me in a perilous situation. Afterward, I was not afraid to go back in the water, but I proceeded with more care. The incidents made me feel more tenderly toward anything at all managing, in whatever way, to stay alive.

II

ONE DAY, walking into town from the resort where I was staying, I saw a man making a wall of coral stone, three feet high, two feet wide, and hundreds of feet long. The wall would separate the grounds of a new resort condominium from the public road, Kaya Gobernador N. Debrot. He controlled the definition of this stretch of space by fitting randomly shaped stones in a ruler-straight wall with its edges perfectly square. We didn't speak. I did not stare while he worked but came back in the evening to appreciate the lack of error in what he'd engineered. He had the firmest grasp of this reality.

No such attentiveness marked the resort meals available where I was staying. They so lacked imagination in their preparation that after one or two dinners one had experienced the whole menu. Nothing was to be found under the surface. Seeking an alternative, I began to walk into town with my dive partner Adam Apalategui, an American Basque, to see what we could find. Kralendijk, meaning "the place of the coral dike" in Dutch, is the largest of Bonaire's two towns, and locally more often called Playa. We located a good spot there, a small pub and restaurant named Mona Lisa. One evening, after the chef had elaborated in English for us on his French-language menu of the day, he suddenly offered to make something special, a medley of local wahoo, barracuda, and dorado, brought in fresh only an hour ago. At an adjacent table he went over the same menu again, speaking Dutch. The meals he served were set out beautifully on the plate, distinctively flavored, punctuated and savory. His appreciation of the components of the meal that night intensified for me moving images of the three species of fish. As we ate I imagined one thread of succulence tying the Dutch chef, our dives, and the indigenous fishes together. The chef, lingering with us as he had in his initial description of the meal, meant the connection to be made, to enhance the experience of Bonaire.

In most every settlement or rural village I've visited in Africa, in China, in Australia, I've taken a long walk in the late evening air after such a pleasant meal. Sudden bursts of domestic noise, the sprawl of sleeping dogs under a yard light, the stillness of toys on pounded earth, the order in wash hung over a line—all compel a desire to embrace the unknown people associated with these things, as if all the unwanted complication had gone out of life. One evening, as Adam and I strolled north along the main road back to our resort and rooms, I ruminated silently, and quite presumptuously, on the Bonaireans.

In a book I was then reading called *Politics on Bonaire,* Anke Klomp describes the evolution of a system of political patronage that characterizes the island. (The Netherlands Antilles are autonomous within the kingdom of the Netherlands. The five islands form a parliamentary democracy, with parliament sitting in Willemstad, Curaçao. Each island also has its own legislative and executive bodies.) Among the more interesting things Klomp discusses is the curious history of egalitarian society here. Because it could never support banana, sugar, coffee, cotton, or tobacco plantations, Bonaire never developed either a class of gentlemen planters or an agrarian working class. As a result, social distinctions based on ownership of land, on race or ethnicity, remained relatively unimportant, as they did not in the rest of the Caribbean. (The building of oil refineries on Curaçao and Aruba early in the twentieth century brought an influx of North American and European managers and divided those previously analogous societies more sharply along racial and class lines.) Bonaire exports very little today save salt (much of it bound for the northeastern United States, for use on winter roads); and it is without an agricultural or manufacturing base. Since all goods must therefore be imported, and because government is the major importer, politicians on Bonaire are in effect, in Klomp's phrase, " 'gatekeepers' par excellence." Further, since Bonaire's population is small, the imposing personality of a single politician can have a major impact on political expression on the island.

Where this has led and how patronage operates on Bonaire are the central subjects of Klomp's book. Observations in her introduction, however, cause a reader to reflect on the ethnic and racial accord apparent today in the streets and shops of Kralendijk and Rincon, Bonaire's second town. And to wonder what changes have come since 1983, when *Politics on Bonaire* was written. The number of resorts and condominiums to accommodate divers has greatly increased since then; and, to hear local people tell it, the conspicuous wealth of North American and European visitors and their abrupt, suspicious public manner have subtly altered the unconscious atmosphere of equality that once characterized Bonaire.

The situation, of course, is more complex than this worry. One gains some insight into social subdivisions, and into the island's history, by listening to where and how people speak. English, the language of tourism, is spoken at the airport, in gift shops and resorts, and in many of the restaurants. In the schools and in banks and government offices it is Dutch. On the street and in homes throughout the island (as on Aruba and Curaçao) it is Papiamentu, a creole developed from the Portuguese pidgin of slave traders and influenced by Spanish, Dutch, and West African dialects. In the open-air vegetable market near the Kralendijk docks, and on a popular radio station, it is Venezuelan Spanish. Bonaireans politely and easily compliment each other by saying so-and-so speaks three or four languages, lending the island a cosmopolitan aspect, but this is rarely true. What some people learn in addition to the language they are born to, which of course they may speak poorly, is almost always the "supermarket idiom" of another language, a tropeless speech of commercial transactions and declarative conversation—unengaged, impersonal, pleasant. It is the language of international air carriers, phatic and anemic. To listen closely to its banalities, or to hear no other, fuller language spoken in place of it, is eventually to become terrified. It is the language that matches the meals served at my resort.

One evening, after Adam and I had walked back from town, after the silence of my room had replaced the night drift of human voices along the road, I grew restless and went out again. I stood on the resort's plank dock by the water, near an open-air restaurant where the last patrons were throwing pieces of bread to schools of fish racing frantically back and forth beneath the illuminated surface of the water. Forty miles to the west the lights of Willemstad glowed on the horizon. Above the penumbra of that glow, Venus sparkled in a deep Prussian-blue sky. Higher overhead huge cumulus towers scudded west.

I watched the enormity of the clouds for several minutes. What I wanted to experience in the water, I realized, was how life on the reef was layered and intertwined. I now had many individual pieces at hand; named images, nouns. How were they related? What were the verbs? Which syntaxes were indigenous to the place? I had asked a dozen knowledgeable people. No one was inclined to elaborate—or they didn't know. "Did you see the octopus!" someone shouted after a dive. Yes, I thought, but who among us knows what it was doing? What else was *there*, just then? Why?

I wanted to know in the way, sometimes, you want to know very much more than a person's name.

On the way back to my room, just as I was passing an open window, I unconsciously raised a hand to brush my forehead and glanced in. Moonlight filled the interior of a bedroom. A woman in a sleeveless cotton nightgown lay wide awake beneath a single sheet. She waved at me tentatively, as though I were someone walking by in a dream she was having.

III

OUR LAST DAY on Bonaire, Adam and I drove a small Japanese rental car south of Kralendijk to see the salt flats that had once drawn the acquisitive attention of the Spanish and then the Dutch. The salt ponds here were actively worked from about 1624 until 1863, when the Dutch abolition of slavery rendered the operation unprofitable. In 1972 a United States and Dutch concern began exporting salt again on a regular basis. A few of these shallow ponds also now serve as a fortuitous refuge for a once endangered population of greater flamingos. (Their numbers have increased tenfold since this nesting ground was closed to egg collectors, hunters, and low-flying aircraft.) The nearby rows of slave huts—each a carefully restored, peak-roofed, work-week domicile for two—are an anomaly, too comely a reminder of this malign human proclivity. Out of curiosity I began to sketch and measure the huts to see what I might learn. I didn't know whether they had been accurately restored, but standing inside them it was apparent they had been designed to take astute advantage of cooling trade-wind breezes, to shed downpours, and to insulate against tropical heat, like tile-floored adobes.

As is sometimes the ironic case with such shadowed places, they have attracted lovers in another age, people who have drawn hearts and scribed their initials or written their names in chalk and ink all across the whitewashed walls, inside and out. Here, also, was "The Criminal gang is the best so fock [sic] the rest," a sentiment about life on the island that hadn't yet registered at the resorts.

At a place called Onima, fifteen miles away on the east coast—because of heavy surf and strong currents there is no diving on this side of the island—we found several sets of Caiquetío pictographs in unprotected shelters. (Early chroniclers describe the Caiquetío as tall, honorable, *"una gente muy pulida y limpida,"* a clean people elegant in their manners and movement.) Many of the pictographs had been gouged by vandals or written over with graffiti. It took several minutes to spot, higher up on the undersides of overhanging rocks, other drawings in apparently perfect condition. Fascinated, I began to draw some of them, including a strikingly accurate rendering of a species of angelfish. As I did so, a woman approached in a rental car along the dirt road. Who was this? A companion, someone like us? Driving slowly, she rolled down her window and scanned the limestone bluff where I was standing, as though searching for an address; then, gathering speed, she drove quickly away. I imagined her indifferent to the site, to the history it contained. Then I realized she was alone, that two men were standing around, and that this was an unfrequented part of the island. We had closed it to her.

The paintings and drawings were similar to ones I had seen in northern Spain, in Arnhem Land in Australia, at Brandberg in Namibia, in canyons on the Colorado plateau. The evidence of humanity in each place is tantalizing, replete with meaning, but finally elusive, inscrutable.

An hour later, within Bonaire's relatively large Washington/ Slagbaai National Park, Adam and I located a watering hole called Poos de Mangel. Numerous birds flitted through the thicket of its trees crowding a small, dust-and-algae-covered pool. I got out of the car with my binoculars and a locally published guide. Whenever I visit a new country, I buy as soon as I can a guide to its birds. It often proves to be the most accurate and least political survey of life in the region. Its pages, frequently written in a tone of appreciation, urge a reader to do little more than share the author's regard. In Kralendijk I had found Peggy Boyer's *Birds of Bonaire,* a guide in English and Papiamentu with black-and-white line drawings by Carl James Freeman. Opening it, I immediately recognized a half dozen birds I'd seen around the resort but had not known names for, like the bananaquit.

I stood back in the trees by the pool for half an hour, watching red-necked pigeons, yellow warblers, smooth flycatchers, and black-faced grassquits angle in warily, branch to branch, finally hopping down to sip the water.

Turning back south, we stopped at several spots along the coast where Adam hoped to photograph flamingos and where we saw great white egrets, brown pelicans, and least terns. Late in the afternoon we halted for cool drinks at a small inn on a cove near the island's northwest tip, a place called Boca Bartól, a stunning dive site. Spokes of coral radiate seaward from the beach, the canyons between them floored with pale sand—a formation called spur-and-groove. Inviting as it is, few divers travel to this site. The currents are often strong and the drive up from Kralendijk can take more than an hour on a winding, pitching dirt road. Adam and I sipped our drinks and watched with mild envy as four divers prepared to go in. (Nitrogen gas remains in solution in a diver's tissues after he or she surfaces, the result of breathing normal air at depth. It may take twelve hours or more for this gas to completely diffuse into the bloodstream, the circulatory system carrying it to the lungs, where it is exhaled. Prudence dictates divers stay out of the water during the twenty-four hours before they fly to guard against decompression illness, the gas-bubble-related maladies that can set in when an aircraft gains altitude and cabin pressure drops.)

The four divers before us glinted like seals in sunlight glaring from the water and then were gone. We knew how ethereal, how quiet, how consolidating to the spirit such a stray king-dom as this could be. It might launch you past many forms of melancholy.

In Rincon, at a filling station across the street from a branch of Maduro & Curiel's Bank, we asked which road would take us back to Kralendijk via Gotomeer, the lake where flamingos mass in the evening. Rincon seems an amiable town. Its streets meet at casual angles, like footpaths in a mountain village, and many of its house doors stand ajar. With the heat of the day now past, a group of boys was changing clothes in an open field at the edge of town for a soccer game. As we merged with the main road I saw a statue briefly in the rearview mirror, a man in a suit and tie and hat, striding. I guessed at who it must be—José Gregorio Hernán-dez, a Venezuelan physician who died in 1919. Gregorio Hernán-dez is said to have ministered to his patients diligently and compassionately, often without charge. He is regarded by many today in Bonaire, Aruba, and Curaçao as an intercessor before God on behalf of the sick. You spot his picture in taxicabs. Statues of him in that black suit, a dark vest, and a fedora are found beside sickbeds.

The fact of Gregorio Hernández (his admirers continue to petition the Catholic Church to have him beatified), like the clouds that pass majestically over Bonaire each day, makes the ordinary venality and inevitable shallowness of so much in human affairs—the coarseness and greed of life, the failure of ideals, the withering of our aspirations—seem forgivable, even inconsequential. The memory of Gregorio Hernández's work on Bonaire, as his admirers describe it, filled Rincon in that moment with grace and made its every element—watchful dogs, paving stones, wild parrots—transcendent in the afternoon light.

I wanted to go back and look at the statue, but Adam hoped to see the flamingos gathering at dusk, so I drove on. As the car picked up speed, we passed a middle-aged man with hand tools walking home from his kitchen garden in trousers caked with mud. I wanted to see the vegetables washed and firm on his din-ner plate. I wished to know more about Gregorio Hernández.

I wanted to come back to dive between the pale green coral spurs at Boca Bartól. I wanted the exquisite flamingos just ahead to ferry each heart's anguished speculation about who we are, the knowledge of our beautiful and infernal complexity, across to the shores of Venezuela tonight, where, in another language, the endless deciphering of what we are up to would go on.

2

A SHORT PASSAGE IN
NORTHERN HOKKAIDO

E AST OF THE TOWN of Abashiri, the long shallow
curve of northern Hokkaido, northernmost of the Japanese islands, turns abruptly northeast to form the
high, uninhabited coast of the Shiretoko Peninsula. A heavy surf
breaks on light gray sand here on a fall afternoon, where I stand
looking out across waters most Western eyes are innocent of—
the Sea of Okhotsk. Russian waters.

Behind me, to the south, stretch maritime meadows and nearly
unbroken tracts of pine and spruce forest in which volcanoes
stand dormant. Brown bears walk in the wooded hills rising to
the east, beyond a trim pattern of small farms. Red foxes run
these beaches. I can see their prints and, beyond, the upright figure of my friend Naoki, now leaning over to pick up something.

This half-wild, bucolic landscape is not what one arrives in highly industrialized Japan expecting to experience. I'd been told that the people of northeastern Hokkaido, the side of the island opposite Sapporo, had a different bearing, that they were not so distant with strangers and that they were less formal in their day-to-day affairs than Japanese in cities on Honshu to the south— Osaka, Kyoto, and Tokyo, from whose hectic precincts Naoki and I had just come. I could easily see for myself upon arriving here that there is no headlong development in this region of Japan, no impetuous commerce. The people are proving to be as I have been told, shifting from acquaintance to something like camaraderie almost as quickly as some North Americans.

I had thought about the far reaches of Japan for years. The kind invitation of a Japanese novelist enabled me to travel to Tokyo and when I revealed a curiosity about Hokkaido he sent me north immediately with Naoki Nishibe, a friend of his and a native of that region.

Naoki's father, Kazumi Nishibe, met us at the airport at Memambetsu, south of Abashiri, and drove us north to the coast. Naoki, twenty-seven, is an intense, short, powerfully built man. His father is much more reserved. His hands and face are creased and seasoned by forty years of outdoor work. He wears a light gray suit and tie.

What Naoki has found is a perfect scallop shell, its delicate, unchipped edge like the crenulated rim of a Belleek porcelain dish.

We drive on along the wave-crashed shore to Lake Notoro, an embayment, actually, of the Sea of Okhotsk. Mr. Nishibe bargains with fishermen at a small dock for fresh salmon, scallops, and snails. (I'd asked Naoki to keep an eye out for an intact scallop shell on our beach walk, a gift for someone back home. Mr. Nishibe, though he speaks no English, quickly caught the drift of that conversation—it precipitated his parley with the fishermen for fresh scallops.)

With the shellfish and salmon secure in the trunk of the Honda, the three of us head down the coast to the Nishibe farm where Naoki grew up, a few miles outside the town of Koshimizu.

As we drive I can only stare in enchantment. I am reminded of the sparsely settled, agrarian countrysides of western North America, the coast plains of Washington State and lush green riverine valleys in the Coast Ranges.

I ask Naoki if many tourists ever come to this part of Hokkaido. My Japanese is rudimentary, his English halting. Very few *gaijin,* he says, very few foreigners, but a fair number of Japanese, especially in the spring, when wildflowers are in brilliant profusion; also in the summer, when warm weather makes a boat ride on one of the area's pristine mountain lakes or a walk in the evergreen forests very pleasant.

"Many honeymooners," says Naoki after a long pause, looking up from his Japanese-English dictionary with a smile.

When the road draws close to the beach I ask if we might stop again. I am astounded—*the Sea of Okhotsk,* I keep saying to myself. Siberia fronts these same waters. This ponderous storm surf, I reflect, will soon lie frozen on the sand in buckled plates of sea ice. Snow will fly, and the bears of Hokkaido will go into hibernation. It seemed as obdurate a coast as I imagined that of the Atacama Desert in Chile to be. Down the beach from where I stand, fifteen or twenty gray herons, birds that would come to my shoulder, strut all angular in the churning surf. What do they seek there?

The Nishibe house, set amid fields inland from the sea, is foursquare and plain. I offer Naoki's mother two small presents from home when I enter, a jar of my wife's pear marmalade, a jar of my neighbor's fireweed honey. I was made to understand before I departed for Japan that to be a guest in someone's home here would give me a completely new understanding of what welcome and cordiality meant. I was intent on reciprocity in these matters, however, and out of habit carry many small presents to convey my sense of pleasure at being brought in out of the indifferent world.

Mrs. Nishibe—a glance at the hand-polished surfaces of her kitchen tools and I can hope her judgment will be informed, not merely polite—samples both marmalade and honey immediately and pronounces each exquisite. And nothing will do now but that she must prepare a few presents for me to take home, just as soon as she prepares tea and a light meal for all of us. Her guileless courtesy is disarming. A well-mannered people, I conclude, watching Mrs. Nishibe later ironing *furoshiki,* the traditional wrapping cloths used with presents.

That evening Mr. Nishibe takes his son and me and a friend of his to a Japanese resort inn, a *ryokan,* where guests can soak in the steaming mineral waters of a hot spring. Before we do, the four of us enter a shoji-screened private dining room for the evening meal. We sit cross-legged on tatami mats, Naoki and I side by side with our dictionaries between us and facing his father and his father's friend, Minoru Taketazu, across small black lacquered tables. The meticulously prepared food placed before me is so carefully arranged—the half dozen dishes on the first of four trays, and the food itself, arranged on each dish according to line, color, and texture—that I am hesitant to disrupt the symmetry. I enjoy traditional Japanese food, but am hard-pressed here to distinguish among many varieties of raw fish and sea vegetables. I am also apprehensive that I might embarrass my host with failures of etiquette, but Mr. Nishibe only nods reassuringly at my adventurous appetite, and even compliments me on my use of the chopsticks. Speaking through Naoki and shaking his head in disappointment, Mr. Nishibe adds that the youth of Japan are sadly deficient in these skills. Too many forks, he says.

Mr. Taketazu, sitting directly across from me, full of gesture, loquacious and affable, seems oddly familiar. It's something in the drift of our conversation, which is turning on the habits of wild animals. He speaks very little English but, again with Naoki's help, we manage to exchange a startling amount of information. He is about the same age as Mr. Nishibe, and the two of them exchange the beaming looks of proud parents when, at several points during dinner, using my dictionary, I try to state my affection for the landscape of Hokkaido.

I knew before I came, I tell them, that it is possible to witness the elaborate courtship displays of the Japanese crane here and

to see other large birds unknown to most North Americans—
Blakiston's fish owl and Steller's sea eagle. The Kurile seals, I
continue, the brown bears, red foxes racing over the frozen sea—
such animals, encountered in the undisturbed wilds of Shiretoko
and Akan National Parks, could pull a disaffected visitor up out of
himself very quickly. Was it really true that few foreigners ever
came? The three men looked at one another. Mr. Nishibe made a
summary comment to Naoki.

"No Holiday Inn," said Naoki.

After supper Mr. Taketazu asks me to sign a book of mine, a
translation, and offers me a book of his in English, *Fox Family: Four
Seasons of Animal Life.* I try to compose words appropriate to the
moment, words that in the future may recall the memory of the
meal, our enthusiastic conversation, and the generosity of our
host.

Something hangs unresolved in my mind about this modest
Mr. Taketazu. When he hands me the fox book, I decide his name
must be familiar from a scientific paper I might have once read in
translation.

We return to our separate rooms, change into light cotton
kimonos, the summer *yukata,* and meet again outside the men's
ofuro (communal hot tub). Naoki explains the etiquette—a
small towel held over the genitals, a thorough scrubbing and
shampoo at one of the washing stations along the wall before
entering a large tiled tub sunk in the floor. The chasteness, clean-
liness, and orderliness of this ritual (my clothing rests folded
in its own small wicker basket, perfectly aligned with dozens
of other identical baskets on a white shelf in an adjoining
room) are in keeping with principles of behavior long observed
throughout Japan.

The steaming, sulphurous water is intensely calming. It encourages gentle and desultory conversation, not serious talk.
Nevertheless, Naoki successfully communicates something quite
abstract, that, traditionally, these circumstances did away with
the façades from behind which people might be inclined to speak
falsely. No one, he says, tells lies here.

A wall at the end of the room separates our *ofuro* from the women's, but it does not reach the vaulted ceiling of the building. From behind it come bursts of evocative, high-pitched laughter.

We retire an hour later. Before stretching out on my sleeping mat, or futon, an inviting envelope of ironed white sheets and cotton quilts, I glance through Mr. Taketazu's book. Staring at the many stunning photographs of foxes, I finally recall the connection. Several years before this Mr. Taketazu had made a film about the red fox, or Ezo fox, of Hokkaido. It virtually changed the attitudes of Japanese people toward this animal. I'd seen an edited version of the film in the States and been very impressed by the compassionate way Mr. Taketazu had suggested making provisions for wild animals within a settled but still rural land.

Tomorrow, I thought, I will have to pay my respects to Mr. Taketazu. I quickly make some notes about the day's events and get into bed. I am exhausted by the effort to understand and to be understood, and I know no moment so blissful at the end of such a daylong effort than repose between fresh sheets, one's skin bare and still puckered and tingling from a hot, soaking bath.

IN THE MORNING the four of us drive up to Mount Iō, a barren, jagged volcano on the periphery of a taiga plain. The wail of the ground vents, that violent escape of steaming air, and the pall of sulphurous fumes end our conversation along the footpath and send each of us off into private thought. The surface of the ground near the larger vents is coated bright yellow with sulphur deposits. Apart from these brilliant fumaroles, the volcano has a stern, prehistoric visage. It's a dark shoulder set against the melancholy taiga and denser forests to the west. The Hokkaido bear, the same species as the North American brown bear, lives out there in good numbers, but it is rarely seen by the automobile traveler. If you want that encounter you must hike up into the mountains. Standing on the volcano's steaming flanks, staring up into the moss-hung limbs of the pines and spruces, I could easily imagine bears watching the handful of visitors strolling here. Perhaps the bears have their own version of the *ofuro* rituals, and are waiting for nightfall, when all of us will have moved on.

Our next stop—the two-lane roads we are traveling all look as if they'd just been paved, and Mr. Nishibe contends that these sleek, new roads simply encourage visitors to Hokkaido to drive too fast, that they actually cause more accidents than the old roads—is at a caldera (the basinlike depression left after the collapse or detonation of a volcano), which Mr. Taketazu tells me holds the clearest water in the world and is called Lake Mashu. He also adds that we are most fortunate: the lake is almost always blanketed with fog, but today it glitters under a cloudless sky. The reflection of sunlight on the water is too dazzling for us to see anything beyond its surface from our vantage point on the rim. Mr. Taketazu assures me, however, that from the right angle it's possible to see the bottom contour at about 130 feet.

I've been trying all day to put my finger on an essential difference between Hokkaido and similar landscapes in western Oregon and maritime Washington. From the rim of this caldera I sense part of the answer. It's more domestic here. In the distance are family farms, herds of Holstein dairy cattle, and rows of windbreak poplars. The maples and beeches in the woods are beginning to turn. In all this the landscape more resembles the Berkshires or the Adirondacks: the individual setting of each farm, the pursuit of small-scale agriculture hard by the haunts of wild bears, and autumn spreading like fire across the forest.

Mr. Taketazu must leave—he's a veterinarian and has to attend to some animals at a nearby farm. But we'll all meet later for dinner. Naoki, Mr. Nishibe, and I continue the trip over a high pass, driving beneath the shelter of extended snowsheds along a sinuous road that clings to the mountainside to my left and affords a view to the right of great stretches of evergreen forest and steep-pitched mountains standing alone, a scene reminiscent of views in the American Cascade Range. We descend after little more than an hour to Akan-kohan, a tourist town at the edge of Lake Akan. The shop windows are filled with Japanese kitsch. A variety of watercraft stand ready to take visitors out on the lake.

But Mr. Nishibe has other ideas.

I should know by now that a thought offered only in passing might as well be a formal request as far as my host is concerned. I'd mentioned earlier that I was not eager to seek out remnants of the aboriginal culture of Hokkaido, that of the Ainu. I find their modern predicament painful to consider and believed witnessing the roadside scenes here—a few Ainu dressed in traditional costumes performing faux rituals for tourists—would be depressing. (The southwestern peninsula of Hokkaido, south of Sapporo, has been occupied by the Japanese for four hundred years. It was not until after the Meiji restoration in 1868, and with American help, that the Japanese settled the rest of Hokkaido, virtually destroying Ainu culture in the process. This extirpation of a native culture, for some attempt at conveying a sense of Hokkaido's atmosphere, prompts a comparison with the nineteenth-century American frontier. The presence of great bears in the mountains, unruly public celebrations in some of Hokkaido's small logging and fishing towns, and the freshly settled appearance of much of the countryside enhance the image.)

Mr. Nishibe parks the car and we begin walking through the streets of Akan-kohan. He asks for directions frequently and is finally able to locate the small curio shop he is looking for. The local carver who works there is out. We eat lunch and return an hour later. A man named Kazuo Sunazawa, burly and accommodating, has returned. What is arranged in the ensuing conversation I cannot guess. All Naoki says, rather cryptically, is "*Ainu eskashi*" (Ainu elder).

The three of us follow Mr. Sunazawa's car north out of town. Lush, nearly junglelike growth around Lake Akan gives way to evergreen forests as we climb the flank of Mount Oakan. In little more than an hour and a half we arrive at a small town at the edge of Lake Kussharo, where we are ushered into a small, unpretentious home. The only person present is an elderly man sitting on the floor in the central room, smoking a cigarette in a long cigarette holder. He wears white socks (the Japanese *tabi* with soles and sewn so as to separate the big toe from the others), black cotton pants, and a gray sweater with a black-and-white diamond pattern on the chest. His house coat is also black, with scrolled yellow threadwork designs, suggesting the ornate floral patterns done in beadwork that distinguish North American Indian clothing from around the Great Lakes. He has a long, narrow beard, bushy eyebrows that flare winglike above his eyes, and thin, gray hair. His eyes are blue. A cataract is prominent in the left one.

For once I am without any sort of present, but Naoki, seemingly always prepared, offers our host a box of delicacies and graciously indicates that it is from both of us.

Zenjiro Hikawa is seventy-six, an Ainu, the eldest of eight children. A long conversation follows, to which I mostly listen. Occasionally I am able to introduce a simple question, through Naoki, about Ainu home life or about the bear ceremony, the central religious celebration among the Ainu, or about the actual hunting of that animal. With hand gestures and pencil drawings I am able to participate somewhat more in the conversation, which is managed by Mr. Sunazawa, the only one present fluent in both Ainu and Japanese. It is Mr. Sunazawa who begins to make the first drawings in a notebook that moves around the wood-plank floor among us, part of his effort, it seems to me, to draw out a reluctant Mr. Hikawa. Some of the drawings show the placement of poisoned arrows used in bear hunts (the poison is derived from a species of *Aconitum,* a plant related to wolfsbane and monkshood). Other drawings depict the traditional arrangement of guests around an Ainu hearth and the patterns of facial and hand tattoos among Ainu women.

As the afternoon progresses, Mr. Hikawa takes up again the work we have interrupted, the carving of dry willow sticks about ten inches long and a half inch in diameter. The rhythm of his stroke gradually terminates our conversation. With the draw of his knife he creates thick bundles of thin shavings which remain attached to the stick at different points. He either gathers them in bunches like tresses and cinches them with one of the shavings or leaves them flared, a rampant array. He stops once or twice during his work to explain the two figures he's carving, one a hearth god, the other a house god. Beyond the supple movements of his long fingers, at his feet, is a birdcage in which two redpolls perch, watching him. They haven't made a sound.

Later, Mr. Hikawa brings out an aboriginal longbow, a present from someone who purchased it from Indians in the interior of Brazil. I am able, solely because of the coincidence of some of my own reading at the time, to say a few words about two of those tribes, the Kréen-Akaróre and the Yanomami; and to describe the great cedar logs carved into totem poles which still stand on British Columbia beaches before the abandoned villages of Tlingit and Kwakiutl people. But, to my obvious distress, true conversation is not possible. I must be satisfied with what I can see in the room, and with a few words and drawings. I feel I have offered nothing of substance to the conversation. As we are departing, Mr. Hikawa, with a hand at my shoulder, gently turns me around. He meets my eyes, smiling, and hands me the two figures he has carved.

On the road back to Naoki's farm I watch dusk descend over the countryside. A nearly full moon rises yellow-orange in a deep blue sky. Stout-legged horses graze in fields along the road and herds of Holstein cattle drift toward the milking barns before sharp-voiced dogs. Over long distances I am relieved of the urgent sense of time. So much of northeastern Hokkaido seems to stand quiet at the edge of human endeavor. Nowhere here is the scale of human enterprise large. It meshes easily with the land.

Time accelerates very suddenly as we turn into the driveway at the Nishibe farm. Mr. Taketazu is waiting there to take me to his home for dinner. (Though we know few words in common this strikes neither of us as a problem. He has also asked a translator to join us later.) It's a short drive. Raccoon dogs, Japanese hares, and red foxes reside in pens outside the two-story, log-frame house. Inside and upstairs in Mr. Taketazu's study we settle down across from each other at a low table, a *kotatsu,* that has a heating element underneath. We draw its quilted cover over our legs and around our waists and then open out a dozen or so large books in front of us, filled with pictures. For the next hour they serve as guides and references as we mimic the movements and sounds of various animals in order to frame our conversation.

Initially our two worlds are drawn together in a discussion of birds. At Lake Notoro, I ask, were those ravens or Japanese fish crows scavenging so artfully in the fishermen's nets? "Ravens," he says, smiling in an amused but disapproving way at the thought of them. The level of communication in our conversation is good; it occurs to me to try to convey something subtle. In Japanese folklore the fox, with which Mr. Taketazu is so familiar, plays a role similar to the one the coyote plays in Western American folklore—a trickster. I often think of ravens, also trickster figures in North America, as "flying coyotes." I wonder if it's possible to draw on Mr. Taketazu's understanding of the similarity between fox (*kitsune*) and raven (*watarigarasu*), and then to introduce the idea of air coyotes, of airborne *kitsune,* and make the joke carry. I page quickly through my English-Japanese dictionary. *Tondeiru* seems to do it for "flying" and I try, tentatively, *tondeiru kitsune.* For a moment there is nothing but consternation in his attentive face. Then a broad smile of recognition.

The translator eventually joins us, but Mr. Taketazu—he is very voluble, very passionate for a Japanese—and I are getting on well. To be sure, the translator allows us to be more precise. I ask the translator to inquire which bird, of all the ones he knows, Mr. Taketazu most looks forward to encountering. "The fish owl," he answers solemnly. I'm puzzled. In North America the owl has a contradictory image. It's seen as both a wise creature and a sinister animal, a night hunter. Among native peoples in North America the owl is generally associated with death. Mr. Taketazu elaborates when he notices my knitted brows. The fish owl, which once guarded the entrances to Ainu villages, has godlike qualities, he emphasizes. To meet it in the woods today, he says, is to rekindle the ancient relationship of interdependence between man and animal. The bird's aura is still imposing, he tells me, an encounter with it electrifying.

Ten of us—Mr. Taketazu, his wife, two of their children, two of his eldest son's friends, myself, the translator, and, later, Naoki and his father—all have supper in Mr. Taketazu's study on tables set up for the purpose. I fall out of the conversation. Early the next morning Naoki and I are to travel south across the Konsen uplands and along the Kushiro River past Lake Toro to a great marsh. On the northern fringes of that marsh we might see Japanese cranes, *tsuru,* in their first mating rituals of this season. That night we'll fly back to Tokyo from the city of Kushiro.

As I brought the pieces of fresh fish to my mouth, the crisp vegetables, I recalled the storm surf pounding in from the Sea of Okhotsk, the twirling descent of bright fall leaves along the road, the soles of my feet burning on Mount Iō. I imagined *kuma,* the brown bear, moving through forests on a path indicated by an older Ainu's expressive hand.

At the door where we stand to say good-bye, I try to make my gratitude to Mr. Taketazu clear, not simply for his hospitality but for his bearing as a human being, his compassionate attitude toward animals. When I finish speaking, Mr. Taketazu holds up a gift in the half-light of the hallway—a fish owl's speckled primary feather. I extend my hand toward the perfect form.

I follow Naoki and his father through the darkness to where the car is parked. The smells of farmed earth in the damp, cool air are familiar and comforting. I try to imagine the books I will send to Mr. Taketazu, ones with the wildlife drawings of Olaus Murie, or with stone lithographs of the polar bear and bearded seal from the Inuit at Cape Dorset, or the portraits Karl Bodmer made of Blackfeet men with the white fur of the ermine wound up in their hair. I imagine him finding all this in his mailbox one day, like a flock of birds.

I put my hand to the cold chrome of the door handle. For so many centuries, the exchange of gifts has held us together. It has

made it possible to bridge the abyss where language struggles.
One travels as far for this as one does to stand before a wild brown
bear, or to put hands on the enduring monuments of a vanished
culture. Here, in an owl's long flight feather, is the illiterate voice
of the heart. *Arigatō,* I say, quiet gratitude to the heavy night air of
Hokkaido.

3

ORCHIDS ON THE VOLCANOES

FOG, MELANCHOLY AS a rain-soaked dog, drifts through the highlands, beading my hair with moisture. On the path ahead a vermilion flycatcher, burning scarlet against the muted greens of the cloud forest, bursts up in flight. He flies to a space just over my head and flutters there furiously, an acrobatic stall, a tiny, wild commotion that hounds me down the muddy trail, until I pass beyond the small arena of his life. Soon another comes and leaves; and afterward another, tiny escorts on a narrow trail descending the forest.

I had not expected this, exactly. The day before, down below at the airstrip, I'd looked out over a seared lava plain at the thin, desultory cover of leafless brush and thought, In this slashing light there will be no peace. How odd now, this damp, cool stillness. Balsa and scalesia trees, festooned with liverworts and mosses, give on to stretches of grassland where tortoises graze. Blue-winged teal glide the surface of an overcast pond. The migrant fog opens on a flight of doves scribing a rise in the land, and then, like walls sliding, it seals them off.

Beneath this canopy of trees, my eyes free of the shrill burden of equatorial light, my cheeks cool as the underside of field-stone—I had not thought a day like this would come in Galápagos. I had thought, foolishly, only of the heat-dunned equator, of a remote, dragon-lair archipelago in the Pacific. I had been warned off any such refreshing scenes as these by what I had read. Since 1535 chroniclers have made it a point to mark these islands down as inhospitable, deserted stone blisters in a broad ocean, harboring no wealth of any sort. A French entrepreneur, M. de Beauchesne-Gouin, dismissed them tersely (and typically) in 1700: "*la chose du monde la plus affreuse,*" the most horrible place on Earth. Melville, evoking images of holocaust and despair in "The Encantadas," viewed the Galapagean landscape as the aftermath of a penal colony. A visiting scientist wrote in 1924 that Isla Santa Cruz, where I now wandered, "made Purgatory look like the Elysian Fields."

Obviously, I reflected, feeling the heft of the mist against the back of my hands and the brightness of birdsong around me, our summaries were about to differ. And it was not solely because these writers had never ventured far inland, away from the bleak coasts. Singularly bent to other tasks—commercial exploitation, embroidering on darkness in a literary narrative, compiling names in the sometimes inimical catalogs of science—they had rendered the islands poorly for a visitor intent, as I was, on its anomalies, which by their irreducible contrariness reveal, finally, a real landscape.

GALÁPAGOS, an archipelago of thirteen large and six smaller islands and some forty exposed rocks and islets, occupies a portion of the eastern Pacific half the size of Maine. It lies on the equator, but oddly; the Humboldt Current, flowing up from the

Antarctic Ocean, has brought penguins to live here amid tropical fish, but its coolness inhibits the growth of coral; and the fresh-water streams and sandy beaches of, say, equatorial Curaçao or Martinique are not to be found here. The Galápagos are black shield volcanoes, broadly round massifs that rise symmetrically to collapsed summits, called calderas. Their lightly vegetated slopes incline like dark slabs of grit to cactus-strewn plains of lava. The plains, a lay of rubble like a storm-ripped ocean frozen at midnight, run to precipitous coasts of gray basalt, where one finds, occasionally, a soothing strip of coastal mangrove. Reptiles and birds, the primitive scaled and feathered alone, abound here; no deerlike, no foxlike, no harelike animal abides.

The tendency to dwell on the barrenness of the lowlands, and on the seeming reptilian witlessness of the tortoise, as many early observers did, or to diminish the landscape cavalierly as an "inglorious panorama"—an ornithologist's words—of Cretaceous beasts, was an inevitability, perhaps; but the notion founders on more than just the cloud forests of Santa Cruz. Pampas below many of the islands' calderas roll like English downs serenely to the horizon. Ingenious woodpecker finches pry beetle grubs from their woody chambers with cactus spines. The dawn voice of the dove is as plaintive here as in the streets of Cairo or São Paulo. Galápagos, the visitor soon becomes aware, has a kind of tenderness about it; its stern vulcanism, the Age of Dragons that persists here, eventually comes to seem benign rather than aberrant. The nobility that may occasionally mark a scarred human face gleams here.

Biologists call Galápagos "exceptional" and "truly extraordinary" among the world's archipelagoes. They pay homage to its heritage by referring to it as "the Mount Sinai of island biogeography." But these insular landscapes give more than just scientific or historical pause. With flamingos stretched out in lugubrious flight over its fur seal grottoes, flows of magma orange as a New Mexican sunset percolating from its active volcanoes, towering ferns nodding in the wind like trees from the Carboniferous, and with its lanky packs of bat-eared, feral dogs some two hundred generations removed from human contact, Galápagos proves unruly to the imagination.

A departing visitor typically recalls being astonished here by the indifference of animals to human superiority. Sea lions continue to doze on the beach as you approach, even as you come to stand within inches of their noses. Their eyes open with no more alarm at your presence than were you parent to their dozing child. Mockingbirds snatch at your hair and worry your shoelaces—you are to them but some odd amalgamation of nesting materials. While this "tameness" is not to be forgotten, and while it is an innocence that profoundly comforts the traveler, Galápagos imparts more important lessons, perhaps, about the chaos of life. A blue-footed booby chick, embraceable in its white down, stands squarely before an ocean breeze, wrestling comically with its new wings, like someone trying to fold a road map in a high wind. An emaciated sea lion pup, rudely shunned by the other adults, waits with resolute cheer for a mother who clearly will never return from the sea. You extend your fingers here to the damp, soft rims of orchids, blooming white on the flanks of dark volcanoes.

SANTA CRUZ, in whose highlands I had gone to hike, lies near the center of the archipelago, some 590 miles west of Ecuador. Almost half of Galápagos's permanent population of 16,000 lives here, on farms, in two small villages, and in the large town of Puerto Ayora. The geography of this island is typical of Galápagos; the character of the vegetation changes, rather sharply, as one gains altitude. Candelabra and prickly pear cactus, dominating the lowlands, give way to a transitional zone of dry brush. Higher up, this scrubland turns to forest, then to heath and open country, where sedges, grasses, and ferns grow. It was while climbing up through these life zones on the slopes of an extinct volcano, hearing wet elephant grass swish against my pants, that I first became aware of my untempered preconception of Galápagos as desolate. And it was here, along a fence line meant to restrain cattle, that I initially encountered that immense and quintessential animal of Galápagos, the giant tortoise. In those first moments it seemed neither a dim nor a clumsy beast. In its saurian aloofness, in the wild shining of its eyes as it ceased its grazing to scrutinize my passage, I beheld a different realm of patience, of edification, than the one I knew. Tortoises hesitate and plunge across the highlands like stunned ursids. The spiritual essence of Galápagos clings to them.

It was also on Santa Cruz, in the streets of Puerto Ayora, that I first sensed the dimensions of something disturbingly ordinary—the difficulties the people of Galápagos confront today: an erratic economic development that has come with the growth of tourism, and the disaffection of local farmers, fishermen, and lobstermen with the distribution of wealth here.

Galápagos seduces the visitor with the complexity of its beauty; but, like any mecca of wonder in the modern era, its beauty, its capacity to heal the traveler from afar, is threatened by the traveler himself, and by the exigencies of modern society. In 1985 a huge, man-caused fire burned nearly a hundred square miles of forest and pampa on southern Isla Isabela. The fire began on the rim of Volcán Santo Tomás and burned for months before an international team of forest-fire fighters finally put it out. The press in North America and Europe exaggerated the havoc (penguins, for example, did not flee before the flames, nor did flamingos turn gray from a fallout of ash)—and the exaggeration precipitated an indictment. While the cause of the fire remains undetermined, it was widely assumed in the United States and Europe that it was started, accidentally but perhaps on purpose, by residents of the small village of Santo Tomás. The charred landscape was viewed, by some, as a dark statement of economic frustration, of the village's irritation with officials of Galápagos National Park, who will not allow them to extend their croplands and small-scale ranching operations into the—to them—"unused" interior of the islands, or to cut timber there.

Two extreme views about the future of Galápagos have since emerged. Some scientists, already aware of the extensive damage done in the islands by domestic animals gone wild—there are currently 80,000 feral goats on Isla Santiago alone—would like to see the resident population of Galápagos greatly reduced and most of the agricultural holdings bought out and incorporated into the park. Many colonists, on the other hand, want to see both tourism and town trade continue to expand, in order to supplement their relatively meager incomes from farming, ranching, fishing, and odd jobs. (Galápagos has no indigenous people with prior land claims. The first colonists arrived in 1832, when Ecuador took possession of the islands.)

But these are extreme positions. Economic hardship is evident to anyone walking the dirt streets of Galápagos's villages; but, on Isla Santa Cruz at least, the accommodation achieved among colonists, scientists, and national park personnel seems, to one who inquires, of a relatively high order. Considering how recently principles of conservation, let alone land-use planning, have become part of village life in South America, the acquiescence of many farmers to park-service demands for conservation is striking. (In a gesture of reciprocal understanding, park managers recently began planting teak trees on private land, to compensate owners for the saw timber they are not allowed to take from the park.)

Galápagos has two indisputable, interrelated problems: economic development (farming, fishing, tourism) without any overall plan; and non-native plants and animals, which continue to change the islands' ecology. The latter situation is dire, but no worse than it's been in recent memory. Programs to eliminate feral goats on some of the smaller islands have been successful, as have efforts to reintroduce tortoises to areas where their populations have been decimated by feral cats, dogs, pigs, and rats. (A new, current worry is that feral dogs may breach a rugged, waterless stretch of lava on Isabela called Perry Isthmus and begin to prey on the least-disturbed animal populations in the whole archipelago, those on northern Isabela.)

Galápagos National Park incorporates nearly 97 percent of Galápagos, a combined land mass half the size of Connecticut.

(Near-shore waters were recently declared a "marine resource reserve" by the Ecuadorian government. Tourism and commercial fisheries officials, the park service, and the Ecuadorian navy are currently working out a management agreement.) The other 3 percent of the land comprises about a hundred square miles of farmstead, a few small settlements, and three large villages— Puerto Ayora, a base for tourism and scientific research on Santa Cruz; Puerto Baquerizo Moreno, the islands' administrative center on San Cristóbal; and Puerto Villamil, a farming and ranching community on Isabela. Agriculture in Galápagos has always been marginal, because of a lack of fresh water, poor soils, and periods of drought. Fishing offers an economic alternative, but Galápagean fishermen increasingly are of the view that profit lies with converting their work boats to touring yachts.

Changes in the Galapagean economy are directly related to a sharp rise in tourism. During the 1960s only a few thousand tourists a year visited the archipelago. When the numbers increased in the 1970s, a park committee suggested a limit—12,000 per year, later raised to 25,000. By 1996 more than 55,000 were arriving, severely straining hotel and restaurant facilities at Puerto Ayora and more limited facilities at Baquerizo Moreno, the two communities connected to the mainland by air. Officials are now looking for specific answers to three separate questions: How many visitors can the park itself absorb? How many visitors can the park service manage? And how many people can simultaneously be present at a single location in the park before a visitor's sense of the magical remoteness of Galápagos is lost?

POINTS OF LEGAL DISEMBARKATION in the park—seabird colonies, cactus forests, saltwater lagoons—are limited, currently to fifty-four; the tour I joined, therefore, took us to the very same spots other visitors see. Occasionally we did encounter another group, but what we saw or heard at nearly every site was so uncommon, so invigorating, that the intrusion of others rarely detracted. We snorkeled amid schools of brilliant sergeant majors and yellow-tailed surgeonfish at a place called Devil's Crown, off Isla Floreana. At tide pools on the coast of Santiago, octopuses stared at us askance, and small fish called blennies wriggled past, walking peg-leg on their fin tips from pool to pool over the rock. At Isla Española we stepped respectfully around blue-footed boobies nesting obdurately in the trail. At Punta Cormorant we watched a regatta of ghost crabs scurry off up the beach, a high-stepping whirr, two hundred or more of them, as if before a stiff breeze.

The genius of the management plan in Galápagos—its success in preserving a feeling of wilderness warrants the word—rests on three principles. The park, first, exercises a high degree of control over where visitors go, with whom they go, and what they do. No one may travel in the park without a licensed guide and guides can—and sometimes do—send visitors too cavalier about the environment back to the boat; trails are marked and bounds have been established at each visitor site; and touching or feeding the animals, wandering off on one's own, or pocketing so much as a broken seashell are all prohibited. Second, because the boat itself incorporates the services of a hotel, a restaurant, and a souvenir shop, there is no onshore development aside from the villages. Last, the park works concertedly with the Charles Darwin Research Station, a nonprofit, international scientific program, to manage the islands and monitor their well-being.

As a result of these precautions, few sites appear overused. Occasionally you even have the illusion, because the animals don't flee at your approach, of being among the first to visit.

Galápagos gently, gradually, overpowers. As our small yacht made its long passage between islands at night (to put us at a new island at dawn), I would lie awake trying to remember some moment of the day just past. The very process of calling upon the details of color and sound was a reminder of how provocative the landscape is, to both the senses and the intellect. The sensual images I recalled in vivid bursts: the yellow-white incandescence of an iguana's head; a thick perfume, like the odor of frankincense, suspended through a grove of bursera trees. At the sheer headland on South Plaza, I watched swallow-tailed gulls rappel a violent draft of air, stall, quivering in the wind, then float slowly backward in the stream of it to land light as a sigh on their cliff nests. One afternoon while we drifted on a turquoise lagoon, Pacific green turtles rose continually to the calm surface to glance at us, the stillness broken only by water tinkling from their carapaces. They drew surprised, audible breath and sank. Behind them a long hillside of leafless palo santo trees shot up, a cinder wall of Chinese calligraphy leaning into an azure sky.

The most enduring image in Galápagos for me, however, was filled with terror rather than beauty. I stood an hour in a storm petrel colony, under heavy gray skies on the east coast of Tower Island. Galápagos and Madeiran petrels, adroit seabirds about the size of a robin but with thin, delicate legs, nested here in cracks and hollows on a flat expanse of barren lava. They were hunted down, even as I watched, by intense, compact lethal predators— short-eared owls. Wind had scattered the torn fragments of bone and feather like rubbish over the dark plain. Farther back from the sea, boobies and frigate birds had made nests in the first ranks of low *muyuyo* shrubs. The risk to these lives was apparent. Young birds dead of starvation, or victims of what ornithologists call sibling murder, lay crumpled on the bare ground like abandoned clothing. Detached wings hung like faded pennants in wickets of *Cordia lutea* bushes, the wreckage of fatal bad landings.

These deaths, one realizes, are all in the flow of natural selection; but the stark terror of it, like the sight of a sea lion's shark-torn flipper, makes the thought fresh and startling. Images of innocent repose and violence are never far apart in Galápagos and the visitor is nowhere spared the contrast. He or she scans the seascape and landscape at the storm petrel colony acutely aware of the light hold the biological has on the slow, brutal upheaval of the geological.

THE FIRST HUMANS to visit Galápagos may have been Indians from the South American mainland, who arrived on oceangoing balsa rafts in the eleventh century and probably used the islands only as a base for fishing operations. In 1535 Fray Tomás de Berlanga, bishop of Panama, sailing far off course, came on the islands by accident and gave them the name that later appeared in Abraham Ortelius's atlas of 1570—Insulae de los Galapagos. (The cleft fore-edge of a lowland tortoise's carapace resembles the sharply rising pommel of a sixteenth-century Spanish saddle, the old Spanish for which was *galopego*.) English buccaneers began using the islands as a raiding base late in the seventeenth century. Struck by the contrariness of local winds, they referred to the place as *las encantadas,* the enchanted ones.

Early in the nineteenth century whalers began visiting Galápagos regularly. They came to hunt sperm whales west of Isabela but found they were also able to careen their boats easily on the beaches for repairs and to provision them quickly with live tortoises, a source of fresh meat. The whalers turned pigs and goats loose on most of the islands, food for anyone who came up shipwrecked, but, too, animals easy to hunt down on a return visit. They barreled fresh water in the odd year when it was readily available. They idly beat thousands of marine iguanas and Galápagos doves to death with clubs, marveling at how the animals "do not get out of our way." And they buried their dead among the stones.

The legacy of those frontier days of whaling (and later of sealing) is still evident in Galápagos. Only 15,000 of an original population of perhaps 200,000 tortoises remain; four of fifteen subspecies are extinct and another is on the verge of extinction. The fur seal population, almost hunted out, is making a slow recovery; and black rats (from the ships) long ago eliminated at least one species of rice rat, the lone native mammals on the islands, aside from bats. Foraging goats have radically altered the structure of some of the islands' plant communities.

In addition to the whalers and sealers, three other groups, historically, had an impact on the biology of Galápagos. During World War II, American soldiers stationed on Baltra shot virtually all the larger animals there, and scientists, during the late nineteenth and early twentieth centuries, collected extensively for zoos and museums. The most deleterious effects, however, were caused by colonists.

The history of colonization in Galápagos is marked to an unusual degree by violence and periods of wretched, bare subsistence. The early settlements, founded on the hope of trading agricultural products to the mainland, all failed. In due course, each was turned into a penal colony by the Ecuadorian government. Attempts to raise sugarcane, coffee, citrus fruits, melons, and sweet potatoes, and small-scale efforts to export sulphur, seal hides, and tortoise oil, or to make stock-ranching profitable, were all schemes that didn't take sufficiently into account the thinness of the volcanic soils, the undependable climate, or the vicissitudes of a trade-based economy.

Along with the farmers came resident fishermen, who fared somewhat better. Utopian daydreamers, adventurers, and eccentrics followed, many of them poorly informed about the islands' climate, the extent of arable land, even their sovereign status. This pattern, in fact, carried far into the twentieth century.

The first scientific collectors in the islands, an expedition under the French, arrived in 1790. The next, under Captain Robert FitzRoy in HMS *Beagle* in 1835, fixed the archipelago indelibly in the minds of all who read the subsequent reports of the ship's naturalist, Charles Darwin. In 1905–1906 the California Academy of Sciences conducted the last major effort to collect in the islands, with an apparent excess of zeal—its leader killed the only tortoise ever recorded on Isla Fernandina.

The days when scientists trapped for zoos and collected indiscriminately are gone; settlers, however, still turn domestic animals loose to prey upon, and compete with, native animals, and residents still shoot Galápagos hawks as predators and occasionally poach tortoise meat. Colonists have also introduced nearly 250 exotic plants to the islands, some of which, in combination with the grazing of feral horses, goats, cattle, and donkeys, threaten several endemic plants with extinction. Scientists, too, sometimes contribute to alterations in the islands' plant communities by bringing ashore food and equipment that harbor seeds or insects from the mainland, or from one of the other islands.

Anxiety about the islands' natural communities stems from scientific knowledge that each island's flora and fauna are unique. Remarkably, this remains essentially true today, despite plant introductions, damage by feral animals, and the loss of some native plant and animal populations. Researchers, in other words, can still find in Galápagos an evolutionary puzzle with relatively few pieces missing.

A DESIRE TO PRESERVE a virtually undisturbed environment in the islands seems obsessive and unrealistic to some local villagers and farmers. Their pressing concerns are for food, a stable source of fresh water, and such things as raw building materials and supplementary income. (One encounters this basic difference in point of view, of course, with growing frequency in many countries—around the game parks of East Africa, for example, or in the rain forests of Guatemala.) In Galápagos, as elsewhere, things of the mind, including intellectual ramifications from evolutionary theory, and things of the spirit, like the feeling one gets from a Queen Anne's lace of stars in the moonless Galapagean sky, struggle toward accommodation with an elementary desire for material comfort. In Galápagos, however, the measure of accommodation is slightly different. Things of the mind and spirit exert more influence here because so many regard this archipelago as preeminently a terrain of the mind and spirit, a locus of biological thought and psychological rejuvenation. It represents the legacy of Charles Darwin, and the heritage of devotion to his thought.

The sheer strength alone of Darwin's insight into the development of biological life gently urges a visitor to be more than usually observant here—to notice, say, that while the thirteen Galapagean finches are all roughly the same hue, it is possible to separate them according to marked differences in the shapes of their bills and feeding habits. The eye catches similar nuances elsewhere—minor differences also separate eleven species of tortoise and fourteen species of scalesia tree. This close variety is tantalizing. Invariably, one begins to wonder why these related species look so much alike—and an encounter with adaptive radiation, with what Darwin called "descent with modification," becomes inevitable.

A vague intellectual current meanders continually through Galápagos, an ever present musing one senses among a certain steady stream of visitors, if but faintly. Evolution, an elegantly simple perception, is clarified by exceedingly complex speculation; Darwin's heroic attempt to understand evolutionary change forms part of the atmospheric pressure in Galápagos. The idea that an elucidation of natural selection or genetic drift, mechanisms by which evolution might operate, could contribute to more than just a clearer understanding of the universe, that it might make humanity's place in it plainer, is never far off.

One has no need, of course, to know how natural selection might have directed their destinies to appreciate unadorned variety among Darwin's finches. The Galápagos penguin is no less startling, the turquoise eyes of the Galápagos cormorant no less riveting, for not knowing precisely how each might have evolved since it arrived. Nor is a visitor required to brood over the economic fate of farmers and villagers in Galápagos, while staring down into the wondrous blowhole of a dolphin riding the bow wave of a tour boat. But at the close of the twentieth century, not to turn to the complexities of evolution in a real place, to the metaphorical richness and utility of Darwin's thought, or to turn away from the economic aspirations of a local people, seems to risk much. Our knowledge of life is slim. The undisturbed landscapes are rapidly dwindling. And no plan has yet emerged for a kind of wealth that will satisfy all people.

AS I SAILED between the islands—at dawn from the sea they look like heads of crows emerging from the ocean—I dwelled on the anomalies. Subsistence hunters pursue feral cattle high on the Sierra Negra with dogs and snares, the same cattle that are pursued by packs of resident feral dogs. What meat they get they sell in Puerto Villamil for ninety cents a pound. From their mountain redoubt they watch the tour boats far below, streaming east along the coastal margin. The park's wardens work 350 days a year for $8,000, part of the time on twenty-day patrols in the arid, rugged interior, hunting down feral dogs and goats to purify the park. A young farmer, proud of his shrewdness, says he will grow a diversity of condiment crops on his small holding and so be in a strong and exclusive position to supply new restaurants which are sure to come to Puerto Ayora. I remember an afternoon sitting at the Darwin Research Station, reading formal descriptions of nearly a hundred scientific projects under way in the islands. What a concise presentation of the inexhaustible range of human inquiry, I thought, what invigorating evidence of the desire to understand.

The evening before I departed I stood on the rim of a lagoon on Isla Rabida. Flamingos rode on its dark surface like pink swans, apparently asleep. Small, curved feathers, shed from their breasts, drifted away from them over the water on a light breeze. I did not move for an hour. It was a moment of such peace, every troubled thread in a human spirit might have uncoiled and sorted itself into graceful order. Other flamingos stood in the shallows with diffident elegance in the falling light, not feeding but only staring off toward the ocean. They seemed a kind of animal I had never quite seen before.

II

I LEFT FOR Quito with regrets. I had eaten the flesh of blue lobster and bacalao from Galápagos's waters and enjoyed prolonged moments of intimacy with the place; but I had not, as I had hoped, had the days to climb Volcán Alcedo, nor had I seen a shark or a violent thunderstorm. But I knew that I would be back. It was not the ethereal beauty of the flamingos, solely, or the dazzling appearance underwater of a school of blue-eyed damselfish that now pulled at me. It was the fastness of the archipelago, the fullness of its life; and the juxtaposition of violent death that signaled that more than scenery was here.

On the way to the Hotel Colón in Quito, the cabdriver spoke about Galápagos with resignation and yearning. A number of Ecuadorians think of Galápagos the way Americans once dreamed of the West—a place where one might start life over, fresh. I told him about a young couple who had just opened a small restaurant on the hill above Puerto Ayora. I had had coffee there after a long hike. I sat by myself on the veranda, watching sunlight filter through the forest. Far in the distance I could see the pale ocean. I could hear birdsong, which sharpened an irrational feeling of allegiance, of fierce camaraderie, with the trees, the wild tortoises I had seen that afternoon, the vermilion flycatchers that had followed me.

As we threaded our way through heavy traffic and billowing diesel exhaust from the municipal buses, the driver asked what sorts of birds I had seen. I told him. The litany made him gesture at the traffic, the different makes of vehicle pinning us in, and led him to smile ruefully.

¿Por qué quieres ir a las Galápagos? I asked. Why do you wish to go to Galápagos? For work? To buy a farm?

La paz, he said, turning to look at me, his thin, sharp face full of fervent belief. The peace.

Ah, Galápagos is not peaceful, I thought. It is full of the wild conflict that defines life. The groaning of the earth beneath fumaroles on Fermandina. Owl-dashed petrels. But what I reflected on wasn't what he meant at all. He meant a reprieve. Retreat. I thought to tell him, as I put the fare in his hand, of the flamingos at sunset on Rabida. People in Frankfurt and San Francisco, here in Quito, in Puerto Ayora, in Geneva, I wanted to assure him, are working to preserve such a retreat, a place out there in the ocean where men and women might gather themselves again. It would take wisdom and courtesy to effect a certain understanding between those who wish fewer people would come and those who want to see more. An understanding that what is beautiful and mysterious belongs to no one, is in fact a gift.

But these were my own feelings, too presuming. What came out of me, as I nodded gratitude for a desultory conversation in an unfamiliar city, was *Hallar la paz, eso es sabio. . . .* To go there to find peace, that is very wise.

4

INFORMED BY INDIFFERENCE

THE LONGEST FLIGHT I ever made—the meta-physical distance between points, not the hours aloft—was from Christchurch, New Zealand, to McMurdo Station, Antarctica. It was aboard a four-engine, propeller-driven cargo plane called a C-130, flown by the Royal New Zealand Air Force. It took eight hours to broach the Pacific with two dozen passengers and a full load of freight.

Once airborne, most of us found a niche among the cargo pallets. With earplugs firmly in place to moderate the engine noise, and cushioned by our heavy clothing and parkas, we all dozed and read. Some stared into space. It was too noisy to talk. Every hour or so I moved to a small porthole window and gazed at the vast ocean. In those moments above the cloudless sea, my body vibrating with the plane, I began to feel how remote Antarctica is.

We landed on the sea ice at McMurdo, and then the group of us—scientists, technicians, several official visitors—were driven across the ice to Ross Island, to our respective billets at the American station at McMurdo and at nearby Scott Base, the New Zealand station. I checked in with my host, the National Science Foundation, which runs the American scientific program on the continent; introduced myself to several scientists; and joined a small group for dinner.

It was hard to get the laconic, heavy-shouldered rhythm of McMurdo, the contradictory air of scientific earnestness and military lassitude. When we disembarked the plane I stood for a few moments, bags in hand, staring into the Royal Society Range on the far side of frozen McMurdo Sound. Sunlight pooled there in the glaciers like molten manganese. I did not want the pressure of time to build again; one goes through so much to leave the hammering and hawking of civilization behind. But then the jitney was there, insistent.

The next day I flew with several other visitors in a Navy helicopter to a place called Lake Vanda, about forty-five miles northwest of McMurdo, in the Wright Valley in Victoria Land. The New Zealanders have an advance base there, a cluster of five or six small buildings chained to the ground against the wind. The New Zealanders were gracious but demure. It took only a few minutes to show us around their station—spartan, solar-powered, snugly arranged. Our hosts then served us fresh scones and potato soup. Their hospitality, the cordial welcome that New Zealanders customarily extend to visitors in this peregrine region, is an Antarctic tradition. The richness of those moments is in vivid contrast to the wildness of the land. The pale green buildings are like a pod of dories alone on the North Atlantic.

I asked the station manager if I might return, if there was room. Marvelous, he said. A week later, after visiting with a score of scientists at research bases and field camps, after a tour of Ernest Shackleton's historic base camp at Cape Royds and Robert Scott's base at Cape Evans, both in a state of eerie, near perfect preservation, mesmerizing inside in their heroic gloom, I returned to Vanda.

THE WRIGHT and half a dozen other valleys in the Central Transantarctic Mountains are collectively referred to as the dry valleys. It has not rained here in two million years. No animal abides, no plant grows. A persistent, sometimes ferocious wind has stripped the country to stone and gravel, to streamers of sand. The huge valleys stand stark as empty fjords. You look in vain for any conventional sign of human history—the vestige of a protective wall, a bit of charcoal, a discarded arrowhead. Nothing. There is no history, until you bore into the layers of rock or until the balls of your fingertips run the rim of a partially exposed fossil. At the height of the austral summer, in December, you smell nothing but the sun-beaten stone. In a silence dense as water, your eye picks up no movement but the sloughing of sand, seeking its angle of repose.

On the flight in from New Zealand it had occurred to me, from what I had read and heard, that Antarctica retained Earth's primitive link, however tenuous, with space, with the void that stretched out to Jupiter and Uranus. At the seabird rookeries of the Canadian Arctic or on the grasslands of the Serengeti, you can feel the vitality of the original creation; in the dry valleys you sense sharply what came before. The Archeozoic is like fresh spoor here.

I took several long walks in the Wright and adjacent Taylor Valleys. I did not feel insignificant on these journeys, dwarfed or shrugged off by the land, but superfluous. It is a difficult landscape to enter, to develop a rapport with. It is not inimical or hostile, but indifferent, utterly remote, even as you stand in it. The light itself is aloof.

The dry valleys are breathtakingly beautiful. The air is so clear the eye can fasten effortlessly on the details, the sharp break of shadow creases, in distant mountains, making binoculars curiously redundant. The hues of yellow and brown, the tints of orange and red that elevate the sedimentary rocks above the igneous layers of granite, take the starkness out of the land but do not alter its line, which is bold, balanced, serene. Classic.

The stillness that permeates the valleys is visual as well as acoustical. On foot, traversing a landscape that is immense but simple, your point of view, looking right and left at the mountain walls or up the valley, changes only very slowly. I had sought this stillness; but unlike the stillness I'd found in similarly austere and deserted regions of the Earth—on the tundra of Ellesmere Island, in the Namib Desert—this stillness had an edge to it. I felt no security with the Earth here, no convincing epiphany of belief in the prevailing goodwill of human beings, which always seems in the offing in these irenic places. However the Earth consoles us in the troubling matter of civilization's acquisitiveness, its brutal disregard, this was not the landscape for it.

To say that nothing at all lives here is not true. Algae and other minute marine organisms have evolved in a handful of permanently frozen lakes (the ice of which insulates them from the cold and passes light for photosynthesis). And some yeasts, bacteria, blue-green algae, fungi, and lichens—a group of microorganisms collectively called crypto-endoliths—live inside the rocks, beneath the first few crystalline layers. A skua occasionally flies this far inland. But the long months of twilight and darkness, the intense cold, the failure of any but the most primordial forms of life to gain purchase here (and so serve as food for others)—these conditions and the wind militate against biology.

During the brief summer, it is warm enough for a few days or weeks to create meltwater; a few, inconsequential streams tumble down from the glaciers above the valleys. The sparkling surface of the water is aberrant, a false promise, the land's irony. The only really animate force here is the wind. It blows, always, from the interior, from the west—often, in the spring, at well over sixty knots. It wallops and scours the mountains, eroding and fracturing, sweeping clear the debris. It is this beast that has, too, made these huge, empty valleys the driest ground on Earth.

Uplifting in the Transantarctic Mountains took place so quickly here, apparently, that the mountains formed in this place alone a rampart against the East Antarctic ice sheet (which is the size of the United States). Cut off, the ice cannot flow down these valleys to the sea. Since then, each year's scant snowfall has been shattered and evaporated by the dry, incessant wind before it can accumulate. Only here (and at two other less spectacular sites on the Antarctic mainland, in the Bunger and Vestfold Hills in East Antarctica) is the land open to the sky, not buried under ice and snow.

The wind, a katabatic or gravity-driven wind, enters the valleys after falling vertically nearly two miles from the summit of the East Antarctic ice sheet; it comes into the valleys with a discernible hunger, and its effect on the land, which it abrades and lacerates with bits of sand and ice, is often peculiar.

In the Olympus Range on the north side of the Wright Valley, high up on the slope near a place called Bull Pass, I found a thin vein of dolerite, a drab, coarse, gray-black igneous rock similar to basalt. At this outcrop it had broken into pieces, and each piece, sitting on a sand base like a stone on a jeweler's dop, had been polished by the wind to the smoothness and luster, if not the density, of marble. Yet it was not this, really, that gave them their character; it was how the wind had cut them. They had the faceting, the angularity and curve, the impervious façades, of modern buildings. Even at this scale—hand-size—what lay before me was an imposing field of dark monoliths.

They are called, after the wind, ventifacts.

Insofar as the dry valleys of Victoria Land are known to the outer world, they are known for four things: for these rocks, the essence, in their form, of modern sculpture; for a mineral, antarcticite (calcium chloride hexahydrate), discovered in local ponds so heavily laden with salt they do not freeze in winter, when the temperature rests at -60 degrees and -70 degrees Fahrenheit; for their similarity, it is widely believed, to the rainless deserts of Mars (the Viking lander would have found no life on this ground either); and for a scattering of mummified creatures on the valley floors, mostly young crabeater seals and, rarely, a penguin or skua.

No one is certain why the seals come up here. A good guess is that they are inexperienced. They wander up from the coast, sometimes traveling as far as forty miles inland, hunching their way over the gravel fields with—to judge from the few, fresh trails that have been found—intractable determination. But it is travel utterly in the wrong direction.

They succumb eventually to starvation on these errant journeys; but an animal dead for a decade may be so well preserved that it looks, as one approaches, as if it might move off. A seal more exposed to the wind might over several years arch up in a curve like half an automobile tire, head and rear flippers high in the air, its eye sockets bored out, its mouth agape, a goblin.

The taut skin of these desiccated animals feels smooth under the hand and hard, like water-polished stone. The wind freeze-dries their flesh. No predator bothers them. The faces, if they can be said to have an expression, are distraught, catatonic with a sudden, horrible misunderstanding of geography. (It seems reckless to insist that only endocrine secretions and neural structures are here, that naught else abides.) The peculiar cheek teeth, ornate with tiny, interlocking cusps, stand out boldly in their highly evolved but useless efficiency.

Whenever I encountered these animals I found it difficult to leave them. And when I left, often as not, I turned back. They were inconsolable. They had made an error. Their lips parted in some final, incoherent noise. They had, most of them, died alone. Some lay with the clouded eyes of the blind, preserved for years in abject disbelief.

In a week of ambling, of looking among mountain boulders hoodooed by the wind, of sitting in windless bights amid glacial debris, of lining out like a Dinka on the heels of my hands and one knee to taste the salt ponds, I found the dry valleys unfetchable. Whatever one might impute to this landscape, of beauty or horror, seemed hardly to take hold; my entreaties for conversation met almost always with monumental indifference. I have never felt so strongly that unsettling aloofness of the adult that a small child knows, and fears. It is hard to locate the reassurance of affection in these circumstances. And yet this land informs, some would say teaches, for all its indifference. I can easily imagine some anchorite here, meditating in his room of stone, or pausing before a seal shipwrecked in this polar desert.

Over the years, one comes to measure a place, too, not just for the beauty it may give, the balminess of its breezes, the insouciance and relaxation it encourages, the sublime pleasures it offers, but for what it teaches. The way in which it alters our perception of the human. It is not so much that you want to return to indifferent or difficult places, but that you want not to forget.

If you returned it would be to pay your respects, for not being welcomed.

5

FLIGHT

ONE FOGGY January morning in 1977, a few hours before dawn, a DC-8 freighter crashed on takeoff at Anchorage International Airport, killing all five people aboard and fifty-six head of cattle bound for Tokyo. Rescuers found the white-faced Herefords flung in heaps through the thick, snowy woods, their bone-punctured bodies, dimly lit by kerosene fires, steaming in the chill air.

A few days after the accident I happened to land in Anchorage on a flight from Seattle, en route to Fairbanks. The grisly sight of the wreck and the long scar ripped through birch trees off the end of the runway made me philosophical about flying. Beyond the violent loss of human life, it was some element of innocence in the cattle I kept coming back to. Were they just standing there calmly in large metal pens when the plane crashed? And why were they needed in Tokyo? At 35,000 feet over the winter Pacific, cruising that frigid altitude at 400 knots, did their lowing and jostle seem as bucolic?

Like many people who fly often, I have watched dozens of windowless air freighters lumbering by on taxiways and wondered at their cargos. In the years after that accident I puzzled over them everywhere—in Quito, in Beijing, in Nairobi, in Frankfurt, in Edmonton. What could warrant a fleet of machines so sophisticated and expensive to operate? It must be more than plasma and vaccines they haul, materials desperately needed; more than cut flowers, gold, and fruit, things highly valued or perishable. Would it be simply the objects people most desire? A fresh strawberry on a winter morning in Toronto?

Watching pallets go aboard on monotonously similar tarmacs around the world, I became more and more curious. I wanted to know what the world craved. I wanted a clarifying annotation for the rag-doll scatter of cattle.

At two a.m. one December night I climbed aboard a 747 freighter in Chicago to begin a series of flights around the world with freight.* I would fly in and out of cities like Taipei, Rotterdam, and Los Angeles with drill pipe, pistol targets, frozen ostrich meat, lace teddies, dog food, digital tape machines, pythons, and ball caps; with tangerines from Johannesburg, gold bullion from Argentina, and orchid clusters from Bangkok. During the hourless penetration of space between continents, I would sidle among the eighty or more tons of airborne freight on the main deck, examining disparate labels like an inquiring bird. Out cockpit windows on the flight deck, I would become absorbed in the strange untapering stillness of the Earth seen from that altitude.

Before I boarded the first flight, however, I wanted to learn about the plane.

---

* The forty flights, covering about 110,000 nautical miles, were made aboard 747 freighters and on 747 passenger planes hauling substantial amounts of cargo in their lower-deck compartments or, with some aircraft configurations, on the aft portion of the main deck, separated from the passengers by a bulkhead.

II

THE ASSEMBLY BUILDING at Boeing's aircraft plant at Everett, Washington, is so large—ninety-eight acres under a single roof more than a hundred feet off the ground—that it has its own weather. Sometimes low clouds form in steelwork near the ceiling, where gantry cranes carrying subassembled sections of 747s, 767s, and 777s maneuver toward sites of final assembly. Over a single November night I watched swing-shift and third-shift crews at the plant complete the assembly of a 747-400 freighter, nearly the largest plane ever to fly. I studied it, and listened and touched, as its 68,000-pound wings were joined to a fuselage section, the six fuselage sections slid together and landing gear attached beneath, leaving it to tower above workers, empty as a cathedral, aloof as the moon.

As a boy I raised tumbler pigeons, a breed that at some height above the ground will destroy its aerodynamic lift and come plummeting down like a feathered stone, only to pull out at the very last moment, a terrifying demonstration of power and grace. Model airplanes—P-47, P-38, F-86, B-29—hung from the ceiling of my bedroom on black thread; I was mesmerized by the wind seething in eucalyptus trees around the house. Once I leaped hopefully from our roof with an open umbrella.

At seventeen I entered college as an aeronautical engineer, only to discover it was the metaphors of flight, not its mechanics, that moved me. I was less interested in engineering than in the imagination of an Antoine de Saint-Exupéry, who wrote of the "tender muslin of the meadows, the rich tweed of the woods," who climbed into the open cockpit of his Sahara-bound mail plane with heavy clothes and a tool bag, like a deep-sea diver, and who died in a crash in the Mediterranean in a P-38, a plane my mother's first husband helped design.

I switched to liberal arts, but the marvel of airborne flight never diminished for me. And the exotic allure of the Earth continued to tug. I saw the sky as an airscape of winds—West Africa's *harmattan*, Greece's damp *Apeloites*, California's Santa Ana, Japan's *daiboufu* ("the wind that knocks horses down").

I admired what I saw come tangibly together that night in the Boeing assembly building: a staggering achievement in engineering, in metallurgy, in economy of design. The assembly of a 747-400 freighter—232 feet long, 165 tons poised over eighteen tires like a barefoot gymnast on a balance beam, a six-story drop from the apex of its tail to the ground—suggests the assembly of a chronometer by tweezer, a sculptor's meaning with a jeweler's fastidiousness. Standing on a scaffold inside a wheel well, I marveled at a set of brass-colored steel screws securing six hydraulic lines in a pattern neat as a musical staff. Not a tool mark, not a misstep was to be seen. (Elsewhere, workers were buffing the airplane's aluminum skin to remove scratches I couldn't find with the pads of my fingers.) Fuselage sections came together smooth as a cap sliding onto a French fountain pen.

For twelve or thirteen hours that night I watched, wandering off to sift through a box of button-head rivets (three million of the plane's six million parts were rivets); or to observe agile men disappearing into the labyrinthine recesses of another 747's unfinished wing; or to heft "nuclear hardened" cable—flexible, shielded conduit that carries thick bundles of color-coded wire from controls on the flight deck to each engine. Then I circled back to the freighter—this particular one being built for Singapore Airlines—with another bit of understanding, a new appreciation of its elegance. People who saw the 747's first flight, in 1969, were impressed that something so huge could fly. What surprised the pilots were its nimbleness, its fluid response to their foot and hand pressures, the easy way the aircraft absorbed turbulence. Designing a plane to fly this well is exceedingly difficult. The engineering task, the working out of that single genetic code, proves to be beyond the reach of formulas. It's as intuitive and mysterious a process—and as prone to catastrophe—as developing and holding on to the financial market for such things.

The Boeing 747 is the one airplane every national airline strives to include in its fleet, to confirm its place in modern commerce, and it's tempting to see it as the ultimate embodiment of what our age stands for. Superficially, it represents an apotheosis in structural engineering and in the applied use of exotic metals and plastics. Its avionics and electronics systems incorporate all the speed and design efficiency of modern communications, and in terms both of manufacturing and of large-scale corporate organization, the swift assembly of its millions of parts is a model of streamlining and integration. In the air, the object itself is a virtuoso solution to flight, to Icarus's dream of escape and freedom. It operates with as little regard for geography, weather, political boundaries, intimidating physical distance, and time as anything humans have ever devised.

If subtleties in the plane's engineering were beyond my understanding, the spare grace of its long lines was not, nor its utilitarian perfection. The only thing that disturbed it, I was told, were rogue winds, the inevitable riptides and flash floods of the troposphere.

When I measured off the freighter's nearly completed main deck that night—sixty-eight paces down the bare interior—I was thinking of the quintessential symbol of another era, the Gothic cathedral of twelfth-century Europe, and of its emptiness, which we once filled with religious belief. Standing on the main deck, above the boxlike stub that joins the wing roots, standing where "nave" meets "transept" and looking up toward the pilots' "chancel," I recalled the intention behind Lúcio Costa's Brasília, a fresh city, aligned east and west like a cathedral but laid out in the shape of an airplane. But there on the assembly line the issue of spirituality, as serious a consideration as blood in the veins of a people, remained vague. The machine was magnificent, beautiful as staggered light on water, complex as an insoluble murmur of quadratic equations. But what placed within it could compare with religious faith?

In the assembly building that night, the 747 came together so quickly that to be away even for half an hour meant missing lines in a sketch that soon became a painting. I would stand in one place, then another amid the cocoon of jigs, cradles, floor jacks, elevated walkways, and web slings surrounding the plane, watching while teams of men, some in sleeveless shirts with ponytails and tattoos, polished off a task neat as a snap of dry fingers in slow motion. They were glad for the work. They knew it could disappear in a trice, depending on the banks, the market, a securities trader in Singapore.*

AN AIRCRAFT WILL give away some of its character to a slow walk-around. If you stare nose-on at a 747, you can tell whether the plane is fueled or not by the angle at which the wings sag. Empty, they assume an upward dihedral, making the plane appear to rest even more lightly on its wheel trucks. This vertical flexibility in the wings partly explains the sensation of unperturbed agility one feels as a passenger. If you let your eye run to the tip of either wing, you can see another key: a slight horizontal twist apparent in the last thirty feet or so, an engineer's quick, intuitive solution to damping a troublesome oscillation. A similar intuition once compelled Wilbur Wright to warp the leading edge of the wings of an experimental glider, lending it critical lateral stability. The glider metamorphosed into *Flyer,* in which, on December 17, 1903, at Kill Devil Hills on the North Carolina coast, Orville Wright achieved powered, sustained, controllable flight for the first time.

During the evening that I studied the buildup of the Singapore Airlines freighter, I was prompted, often, to reflect on early aviation. The vast interior of the Boeing plant and the peculiar absence of industrial noise combined to make the distant movement of messengers riding vintage bicycles seem almost timeless. The sight of these parts couriers gliding across the smooth concrete floors on fifties-era Schwinns triggered thoughts about the

---

* As a singular icon the 747 also symbolizes huge economic risk, brutal financial efficiency, and despotic corporate ego. Boeing president William Allen and Pan American's Juan Trippe dared each other to take the then mind-boggling steps of building and contracting for the 747. Who would go first? In 1969, when Boeing's total debt after developing the plane was thought to be larger than its net worth, it eliminated sixty thousand jobs to save the company, pushing Seattle's unemployment to 17 percent.

bicycle-building Wright brothers. The written history of all that led up to that December morning in 1903 reveals two young men who, beyond anything else, wanted to fly, at a time when most others were keen simply on winning the prize that feat would earn. While other people threw contraptions at the air, the Wright brothers worked out in painstaking detail the first practicable formulas for flight, challenging the previously revered mathematics of a German glider pilot named Otto Lilienthal, the author of *Birdflight as the Basis of Aviation* (1889). When *Flyer* flew, with its cambered wing and controllable elevator, its rudder and the world's first rudimentary ailerons, the Wright brothers knew exactly what they were doing. The achievement at Kill Devil Hills was not the fact that the plane sustained itself at about seven miles per hour over 120 feet, or the addition of a motor and props to a glider, but that Orville controlled it. He *flew* the plane.

The Wrights' entrepreneurial success embodies for many a vanquished innocence in America: this was an unprecedented thing, done for love, with little thought of personal gain, and financed largely out-of-pocket.

Orville's initial flight carried him about half the length of a 747 freighter's main deck. He was airborne for twelve seconds in a craft stripped of every bit of excess weight. The plane I was standing beside that night can carry 122 tons 5,000 nautical miles in about ten hours. The Wright brothers had little inkling of commercial advantage; without the support of government subsidies and the promise of private profit, without corporations competing fiercely for shares in a marketplace, without continuous turnover in what's considered fashionable in consumer goods, the 747 freighter might easily have gotten no further than a draftsman's table.

My last impression of the plane, the rainy morning I drove away, was of accomplishment. Whatever people might do with it, however they might fill this empty vessel, it gleamed to my way of thinking like an ideal. It was an exquisite reification of the desire for beauty.

Sometime later, I returned to Everett to inspect the finished cockpit. I wanted to crawl into every space that would admit me:

low, tight bays on either side of the nosewheel doghouse that hold tiers of maintenance computers; the transverse avionics bay aft of them, where the plane's triple-redundant inertial navigation system and flight deck computers are located (and from where, via hatches above and below, one can either drop to the tarmac or emerge on the main deck). I wanted to orient myself among banks of Halon bottles (the fire-fighting system) and emergency oxygen tanks on the lower cargo deck. I wanted to enter the compartment aft of the rear pressure bulkhead and see the massive jackscrew that tilts the horizontal stabilizer (the fins that protrude like a rear wing from the plane's tail).

Once the plane was fitted with four Pratt & Whitney engines— each developing up to 56,000 pounds of thrust (about 21,000 horsepower)—Singapore Airlines would take it away. At something like $155 million, it was an enormous capital investment; but with an international airfreight market currently expanding at about three times the rate of the passenger market, Boeing's plane number RR835 would soon pay for itself. After that, grossing upward of $750,000 per load against an operating cost of roughly $15,000 per hour, it would begin to earn its owners a substantial and unencumbered profit.

III

AFTER FRANKFURT'S Rheim/Main Airport and London's Heathrow, Amsterdam's Schiphol International Airport is Europe's largest airfreight depot site. KLM's operation here is efficient and organized—dangerous goods here, live animals there, valuables (jewelry, currency, silver bars, uncut gemstones) over here, drugs in yet another place. In this world "perishable," I learned right away, refers to more than flowers, food, and newspapers; it includes everything in tenuous fashion: watches, video games, shades of lipstick, a cut of trouser—objects for which a few days' head start on store shelves is crucial.

On an upper half-floor of the cavernous outbound-freight building—the main floor includes an open space perhaps 600 by 200 feet, and 40 feet high—there is no one, only automated equipment, enslaved by a computerized sorting program that is updated continually in response to aircraft schedule changes and new delivery priorities. The loaders, moving on floor tracks, pull standard-size pallets and cargo containers from steel shelves at just the right moment to launch them on a path terminating promptly at the cargo doors of their intended airplane. It is stark, bloodless work. On the main floor the mechanical tedium is relieved in three ways: in the buildup of single pallets, with workers arranging dozens of small packages trimly in an eight-by-ten-foot-square load, at heights to fit either the upper or lower deck of a particular aircraft, and with one top edge rounded slightly to conform to the curve of the plane's sidewall; by the loading of oddly shaped or remarkable objects—a matched set of four, dark blue Porsche 911s, a complete prefabricated California ranch-style house; and by the sheer variety of goods—bins of chilled horse-meat, Persian carpets, diplomatic mail bound in sisal twine and sealed with red wax, bear testicles, museum art exhibits, cases of explosives.

The impression one gets amid tiers of briefly stored cargo and whizzing forklifts is of mirthless haste. A polite but impatient rectitude about the importance of commerce prevails, and it forestalls simple questions: Have they run out of mechanical pencils in Houston? Is the need for eelpout in Osaka now excruciating? Are there no more shirtmakers in Rangoon?

THE FOLLOWING DAY I departed the freezing rain and spitting snow of Amsterdam for Cape Town, six thousand miles and an opposing season to the south, where one of KLM's smallest facilities operates on a decidedly different scale. We came in by way of Johannesburg and brought, among other things, two Goeldi's marmosets and eight white ear-tufted marmosets, both endangered, inbound from South America for a local attraction called Monkey Den.

When my escort completed our tour—a semienclosed metal shed, no automation—he very kindly suggested we go for a drive. He felt harried by shippers' phone calls, cajoling for more space than he could provide on the outbound flight. I, too, wanted to get away from the clamor.

For the past six days I had been flying a heavy schedule, mostly in and out of the Far East. I was bewildered by the speed with which everything moved, by how quickly I came and went through the countries. In a few hours I would turn around and fly back to Johannesburg, there to pick up fresh flowers, hunting trophies, and raw diamonds before returning to wintry Amsterdam.

We drove east through windblown sand scrub on the Cape Flats, rather quickly through Cape Town itself, and around to Clifton Bay on the west side of Table Mountain. The weather had been hot, but it was cooler now, seventy-two, with a brisk southeast wind, the one they call the Doctor.

For a long while I stood there on the bluff in the summer sunshine, staring into the transparent blue water of the Atlantic. I was acutely aware of history here at Bartolomeu Dias's Cabo Tormentoso (the Portuguese navigator's Cape of Storms, a foreboding appellation his king would later change to Cabo da Bõa Esperança, Cape of Good Hope). Cook and Darwin anchored here as did, in 1522, a remnant of that part of Magellan's crew under Sebastián del Cano. In those days it had taken as many months as it now takes hours to come this far south from Europe, and an indifferent sea swamped and crushed the Dutch *jachts* and Iberian caravels like a child's paper sailers. Robben Island, where Nelson Mandela spent so many years, was just to the north. A few miles to the southeast was Skildergat Cave, a 35,000-year-old early human site. All this was once the landscape of the Khoikhoi people, now long since gone to Namibia and Botswana, where they are called San people and among whom are the much studied !Kung.

My companion was speaking English with a friend. When he lapsed into Afrikaans I recalled how, over the past few days, I had been scrambling to get the simplest grasp of Malay, Thai, then Hindi. I was moving carelessly around the planet. Beneath the familiar jet lag I began to sense something else: physical geography was not only spatial, it was temporal. I looked up past my shoulder at the serene oak and pine forests of Table Mountain, da Gama's defining pivot. It had a peculiar time to it, as indigenous as its rock. I could not take that time with me, nor bring my own time here and drape it possessively over the mountain. In that moment I glimpsed the impunity with which I was traveling, as well as the inseparability of time and space in geography. The dispensation I enjoyed from the historical restraints of immense distance had created an illusion about time: the Earth's spaces might vary terrifically—the moonlight reflecting for me last night on Shatt Al-Meghir, a saline lake in barren eastern Algeria, was not the same moonlight shining back from the icy reaches of Cook Inlet in Anchorage—but time, until this moment, had seemed a seamless thing, never qualitatively different. Everywhere I went time continued the same, an imperial present. At most, in these new depots and their environs, I was resetting my watch.

As I stood there gazing at Table Mountain, then back at the transparent Atlantic, I knew the mountain's time was not my time. And that I would not, now, give in to its time. I was on this other, no-Sunday, no-night, on-time, international commercial time. I sought out my friend and asked, "Shouldn't we be getting back?" I was starting to behave as if the present were only a preparation for the future. When I phoned my wife from some point along the way to confide that I was deeply bewildered, that it was as though all the rests in a symphony score had become threats, she said, "It's because you're not going anywhere, you're just going."

TWO CHANGES IN the late eighties boosted the growth of international airfreight. Up until then shipping by air meant being assured your goods would arrive at such-and-such an airport within forty-eight hours of a promised time. Today, for an average of one to four dollars a pound, a customer expects guaranteed, on-time delivery; and increasingly that service is door-to-door, not airport-to-airport. The largest airfreight operation in the world (though the bulk of what they haul is small packets) is Federal Express. Next, in descending order of tonnage carried, are Lufthansa, UPS, and Air France, then Korean Air and Singapore. (At present, profitability in the industry remains marginal while airlines continue to maneuver for market share.)

Most air cargo, according to an industry forecaster, now consists of "high-value, time-perishable, consumer items." The business is driven by three things: the growing expectation, worldwide, of having whatever one wants tomorrow, not next week or next month; by frequent changes in fashion and in the design of basic products; and by a great disparity in labor costs from one country to the next. Much of what one sees aboard a freighter is placeless merchandise; except for the cost of employing a person, it might have been manufactured almost anywhere, including the country of destination. A museum director in Los Angeles found it less expensive, for example, to have the museum's entire red sandstone façade quarried in India, airfreighted to Japan to be dressed, and then flown to Los Angeles than to have it quarried, dressed, and trucked in from Minnesota.

Companies ship city phone books from the United States to China to have the names inexpensively keyed in on mailing lists. Automobile insurance claims travel by the boxful from Miami to Manila to be processed by people who are not only cheaper to employ but who make fewer mistakes than the clerks for hire in Miami. And air shippers, exploiting the same small margins currency traders use, find it less costly to have, say, nine tons of rayon blouses machine-cut in Hong Kong and flown to Beijing to be finished by hand than to have all the work done in Hong Kong—before the blouses are flown on to customers in Berlin or Chicago.

On long eight- and ten-hour trips on the freighters, I regularly left the flight deck, though it seemed always to be offering me some spectacular view of the Earth—Mt. Pinatubo smoldering in the depopulated Zambales Mountains on Luzon, or L'Anse aux Meadows, a bleak site on the northern tip of Newfoundland where Norse people established a community about A.D. 1000. Leaving these, I'd climb down the narrow, folding aluminum stairs and stroll the aisles at the perimeter of the cargo load. Containerized or shrink-wrapped in heavy plastic, tagged with routing labels in code, the shipments were frequently difficult to identify without the help of manifests or air waybills. One night out of Taipei: 17 cartons of basketballs for Boston; 5,898 pounds of sunglasses headed for Atlanta; 85 cartons of women's polyester pajamas for Columbus, Ohio; cameras, men's ties, battery-operated action-hero toys; 312 pounds of wristwatches for New York. What I saw very often seemed the fulfillment of mail-order-catalog dreams. The celerity in airfreight, in fact, and the freighter's ability to gather and distribute goods over huge distances in a matter of hours, have made the growth of 800-number stores like J. Crew, Lands' End, and Victoria's Secret possible. By promoting "just in time" delivery—neither a sweater, a comic book, nor a jet engine arrives until the moment it's needed—freight companies have also (1) changed the way businesses define inventory, (2) made it possible for stores to turn storage space into display space, and (3) forced governments to reconsider the notion of an inventory tax.

What planes fly, generally, is what people imagine they want. Right now.

BACK AT D. F. Malan International Airport in Cape Town, I watched a six-man crew load freight—Cape wines, salted snook headed for New York fish counters, 3,056 pounds of ostrich meat bound for Brussels, one Wheaton terrier named Diggs for Toronto.

Standing there on the ramp, I asked my companion if he knew about the first shipment of airfreight, in 1910. No, he didn't. It was 542 square yards of silk, I said, carried sixty miles from Dayton to Columbus, Ohio. It cost Morehouse-Martens of Columbus $5,000, but they made a profit of more than $1,000 by cutting the fabric up into small pieces and selling them as souvenirs to customers at their dry-goods store.

He told me the fellow shipping ostrich meat, frustrated by a lack of cargo space out of Cape Town, had a restaurant in California interested, but without the space he couldn't close the deal. We were looking, at that moment, at the aircraft I had come in on, a 747-400 passenger plane with about 5,900 cubic feet of lower-hold cargo space (passenger baggage might take up only 20 percent of this). Depending on the demand for seating, KLM might occasionally fly a 747-400 Combi into Cape Town. In this aircraft, the aft section of the main deck is given over to seven pallets of freight, while passengers are seated in the forward section—an efficient way for airlines to take advantage of fluctuations in both passenger and freight markets.

Tons of fish, he said, let alone more ostrich meat, could be shipped from Cape Town, if only he could guarantee his customers the room. Today he'd be happy to squeeze a surfboard into the bulk-cargo hold, the space farthest aft on the lower deck, a last-on, first-off, loose-loaded compartment, where mail, air waybills, crew baggage, and, today, the Wheaton terrier went. We continued to exchange stories about peculiar things one sees on board—a yacht headed for an America's Cup race; a tropical-hardwood bowling alley from Bangkok; in San Francisco enough boxed Bing cherries, tied three to a bunch and packed neat as flashlight batteries, to fill one 747 freighter after another (27,000 cubic feet). They're not supposed to, I said, but one of the pilots told me he liked to sit in the Ferraris and Lamborghinis he flew. "I've driven them many miles," the pilot mused, "and very fast."

Business was good, I told my guide, but strange. Two days before, on what pilots call the Tashkent Route between Europe and the cities of Karachi, Delhi, Bangkok, Singapore, and Jakarta (via Russia, Kazakhstan, Uzbekistan, and Afghanistan, because the Himalayas are too high and Iranian air space too dangerous), I had seen rocket fire and streams of tracer ammunition in Kabul, Taliban "extremists" and their entrenched opponents. People were being shot dead below, but to the east a full moon was rising rapidly, orange and huge as the sun. It silhouetted sharply the sawtooth peaks of southern ranges in the Hindu Kush. And farther to the southeast, beyond the Khyber Pass and high above the Indus River, a hundred miles of lightning bolts flared and jangled along a storm front. With one glance I took it all in: rockets flaming across the streets below, the silent moon, rain falling in the Indus Valley from a ceiling of cloud, above which the black vault of the sky glittered with stars.

On the Tashkent Route, I continued, air-traffic controllers in Dushanbe, Tajikistan, pass you on to Lahore, skipping chaotic Kabul altogether. Their voices crackle on the high-frequency radio like explosions of glass, trilling aviation English in the high-pitched intonation of a muezzin. At Lahore, you can see the Pakistani border stretching away north into the Punjab, a beaded snake of security lighting. From here west all the way to Libya (whose air-traffic controllers reprimand careless pilots that it is not "Libya" but "Libyan Arab Jamahiriyah Territory"), religious and political tension is pointedly apparent from the sky. Coming up from Dubai, we would swing far out to the west, over Saudi Arabia, to fly wide of Iraq, then dogleg north across Jordan, staying to the east of Israel. Leaving Lebanon's skies, we'd enter disputed air space over eastern Cyprus. Greek Cypriot and Turkish Cypriot air-traffic controllers do not play dangerous games with commercial aircraft, but, together with the Syrians, they contest the right among themselves to assign you flight levels and headings. Once across Turkey we'd bear north to stay wide of Bosnia-Herzegovina.

Every pilot I spoke with, I said to the young KLM freight manager, had a story of the white-orange flash of lethal fighting seen from above, the named and unnamed wars of the modern era, fought in Timor, in the Punjab, in what were once called the lawless hinterlands, but which are now as accessible as Detroit or Alice Springs.

ON THE RETURN FLIGHT from Cape Town to Johannesburg, I glanced through data comparing this 747-400 with others in KLM's fleet.* Each 747, despite being built to the same specifica-

---

* Virtually all wide-body passenger aircraft carry a diverse and often substantial belly cargo of manufactured goods, flowers, fresh food, and live animals. With so many people now living and working abroad, they also commonly carry large containers of personal effects and the coffins of returning nationals.

tions and being fitted with the same engines, consistently burns slightly more or less fuel, or "performs differently against the book." Northwest Airlines flies eight 747-200 freighters into the Far East; I flew on four of them, trying to gain a feeling for their personalities. (With so much history, distance, and weather, I reasoned—so many minor accidents, replaced engines, and strange cargos—there had to be personality.) Once I stayed with a single aircraft through five crew changes, from Hong Kong to Tokyo, then on to Anchorage, Chicago, and New York before turning back for Seattle—in all about 12,000 nautical miles in 56 hours. Reading the plane's operating certificates (posted on a lavatory bulkhead in the cockpit) and its logbooks, and poking into all its accessible spaces, what I found was distinctiveness, not personality.

It was 2:30 in the morning and raining when we landed in Seattle. After the dehydrating hours aloft, mildly hypoxic, my tissues swollen from undissolved nitrogen, I was glad for the wet, oxygen-rich air at sea level. With a security escort shifting idly from one foot to the other at my side, I drew the night air in deeply and brushed rain across my face. I'd been with the plane for so many hours—I periodically rolled a pad and sleeping bag out on the floor of the flight deck to sleep—that an uncomplicated affection had built up for all it had accomplished while the crews came and went. Its engines were silent now, still. I walked beneath it in the dim illumination from warehouse lights.

The freighter's belly—this was plane 6729F—was glazed with a thin oil film. In it, and in exhaust grime on the engines' housings, mechanics had finger-traced graffiti. (Inside, on cargo compartment walls, ground crews often scrawl insults—some of a sexual nature—aimed at ground crews in other cities. On inaccessible surfaces within the wings, I was told by riveters at the Boeing plant, some paint declarations of love.) I made a mental note to check 6729F's technical log, a sort of running medical history of the aircraft, to see when it had last been "A-B-C-Ded," a forty-day swarming by mechanics during which every structural part, every rivet, every wire, is examined or X-rayed.

The fifteen-year-old plane's thin (.063 inches) tempered aluminum skin was scraped and dented and it bore a half dozen aluminum patches. (In an effort to keep a plane on schedule, some of these minor tears are first repaired provisionally with "speed tape.") Its windows were micropitted, its 32-ply tires slightly worn, its livery paint chipped. Looking aft from a point near the turn of its flat, streaked belly, I realized the plane had the curved flanks of a baleen whale, in an identical scale, exact to the extended flukes of its horizonal stabilizer.

Overall the freighter had a lean, polished, muscular patina. It flew in the working world.

IV

I FIRST FLEW with horses on another Northwest flight, out of Chicago's O'Hare on a bitterly cold February night.* These sixteen were headed for lives on Hokkaido ranches among the well-to-do: a Percheron stallion, twelve Appaloosas, and three quarter horses, accompanied by two handlers.

We were delayed three hours getting out. The driver of one of the loaders, a steerable platform used to raise cargo fifteen feet to the rear cargo door, accidentally rammed the plane, punching a hole in a canoe fairing (a cover protecting the jackscrew that extends and retracts the plane's flaps, and which "fairs" or tapers this protrusion into the wing). We also had to replace an exhaust-gas temperature gauge on the number-three engine, the sort of maintenance that goes on regularly.

The pilot made a shallow climb out of Chicago to lessen the strain on the horses' back legs. He headed out over Wisconsin and Minnesota on a slight zigzag that would take us from one way point to another en route to Anchorage. Planes rarely fly a direct route between airports unless the skies are relatively empty, usually late at night, the time when most freight moves. Freighter

---

* Thoroughbred horses fly back and forth between the continents constantly during the respective national racing seasons. Slaughter horses, mostly young draft horses, are carried to the Far East from the United States and Canada, 116 head at a time in 29 pens on a 747. With a reduction in import duties on fresh meat in the Far East, smaller animals like the slaughter cattle killed in the Anchorage crash, have become less economical to fly live.

pilots, some of whom wear bat wings on their tunics instead of eagle wings and refer to themselves as "freight dogs," call it "flying the backside of the clock."

Soon after we're airborne I go down to look at the horses. The main deck temperature has been set at 55 degrees so I take a jacket. The animals are lined up in six stalls on the right side of the aircraft, the 2,100-pound black Percheron in the first stall with a bred quarter horse; behind them a leopard Appaloosa stallion with a bred Appaloosa; and behind them, downwind in the flow of air, four stalls of bred and "open" mares, with four fillies and colts. They aren't sedated, most are dozing. They've been left unshod to give them a better hold on the stall floor, and won't be watered or fed for twenty-four hours in transit. Hemmed in by the usual farrago—aortic valves, poultry-processing equipment, mainframe computers, golf clubs, men's knit underwear—the horses seem strangely peaceful. I can't hear their breathing or stomach noises over the sound of the engines. I turn the lights out and leave them be.

On the flight deck, a narrow space like a railway-car living room, the horse handlers are slumped with novels in a single row of three tourist-class seats toward the rear, the only three passenger seats available besides the jump seat. The flight engineer has just brewed a fresh pot of coffee. I settle in behind the captain to peruse the flight manifests. I gaze out the window. Every few minutes I look at the instrument panel in front of the copilot and at the hydraulic, fuel, and electrical panels in front of the flight engineer, sitting a few inches to my right.

The 747 is not the biggest freighter in the world, but in every other way—making long hauls economically on a scheduled basis—it is unrivaled. The biggest plane in regular service is the Russian Antonov 124, a fuel-guzzling, hulking beast of an aircraft that works at the fringes of the world of airfreight, hauling unusual loads on a charter basis. The only way to move emergency equipment (oil-skimming boats, fire-fighting trucks) or large quantities of emergency supplies (medicine, food, gas masks, cots) quickly around the world is on airfreighters, and the Antonov 124 ferries such material routinely, and many more unusual things: French fighter planes to Venezuela; 132 tons of stage equipment for a Michael Jackson concert in Bucharest; a Pepsi-Cola bottling plant, complete, to Buenos Aires; a 38-ton bull gear to repair an oil tanker stranded in the Persian Gulf; 36,000 cubic feet of cigarettes per flight on repeated trips between Amsterdam and Moscow during the breakup of the Soviet Union.

When we pass through 18,000 feet, the flight engineer sets our altimeters to read against an atmospheric pressure of 29.92 inches of mercury. We'll calibrate altitude against this pressure until we descend on approach into Anchorage, an agreed-upon standard that ensures planes all over the world will be figuring their altitudes on the same basis once they leave the air space around an airport. We've also left local time behind. Now all our communications are based on Coordinated Universal Time (UTC), formerly Greenwich Mean Time or Zulu time, as it is still sometimes called (the Earth's time zones having once been divided among the letters of the alphabet). Another universal grid we are fixed in is degrees and minutes of latitude and longitude. And altitude, of course. (The altimeter always shows altitude above mean sea level; if the altimeter reads 7,500 feet over Mexico City, you are 100 feet off the ground.)

These grids provide a common reference, and their uniformity makes flying safer; but there are dissenters around the globe, especially where time zones are concerned. Tonga, along with Russia's Chukotski Peninsula, insists on occupying a twenty-fifth time zone. When it's 12:15 Sunday morning in Tonga, it's 11:15 Friday night in Western Samoa, a few hundred miles to the northeast. And against UTC whole hours, central Australia stays on the half hour, Nepal keeps to a three-quarter hour, and Suriname adheres to ten minutes before the hour.*

---

* It is largely forgotten today that the notion of "standard time" in the United States, as opposed to local time, was one promulgated by railroad commissions to coordinate the needs of railroads and other businesses engaged in long-distance commerce. A nationwide system, enforced by railroads and then by factories, was entrenched by 1883. Congress eventually gave its official approval, though several states—Utah, Minnesota, California—fought the inconvenience until 1917. The principal objection was that standard time distorted the natural rhythms of human life for the sake of greater efficiency in business and commerce. Today Cincinnati lives, more or less complacently, by Boston's sunrise.

Virtually everyone communicates over the radio in English, but it is often heavily accented English, and outside customary requests and responses, English is of limited use in areas like China or in what pilots call Sea Asia. Russian pilots, for their part, are unique in insisting on the use of meters per second instead of knots for air speed, and on meters instead of feet for altitude. In addition, Russian commercial planes don't use the Traffic Collision Avoidance System, which warns of approaching aircraft; nor do they send out a signal so planes with that system will know they're there. To politely register their disapproval of these tenuous arrangements, European pilots flash their landing lights at approaching Russian planes (which air-traffic controllers have alerted them are there) and wait for a response.

The wide acceptance of such standardized measurements and procedures can lead to the impression that a generally convivial agreement obtains throughout the world. And when, in one week, you transport the same sorts of freight to Cairo, Melbourne, and Rio de Janeiro, it is also easy to draw the conclusion that people everywhere want more or less the same things. However pervasive, the view is illusory. The airplane's speed and geographic reach benefit the spread of a European and North American consumer ethic, but not all the world's cultures can be folded into this shape. One need only leave the airport in Lima or Calcutta or Harare to see how true this is. It is not merely poverty and starvation you see, the ringing of another music you hear, or inversions of Western intuition you observe. It is starkly different renderings of the valuable.

Again and again, stalled in boulevard traffic in hot, choking air, feeling the taxi bumped by a languid crosscurrent of beggars, I thought of the speed of the plane, how much it could leave behind. If we fled quickly enough, I thought, nothing would catch up.

One morning at KLM's corporate headquarters in Amsterdam, I spoke with a vice president in his corner office. Beyond us, planes were taking off every couple of minutes like salvos. "When I was a boy," he said, "I was given my father's watch. I thought that would be my watch for the rest of my life. But I have five watches now. I choose one in the morning to match my suit, a tie. You just buy them." He spread his hands, a gesture of lament and consternation. In an adjacent office, another vice president told me, "Speed is the word. Air cargo is the answer to speed, it makes speed happen." I could not tell from his piercing look whether he meant it as a summary or an indictment.

AN OCEANIC EXPANSE of pre-dawn gray white below obscures a checkered grid of Saskatchewan, a snow plain nicked by the dark, unruly lines of woody swales. One might imagine that little is to be seen from a plane at night, but above the clouds the Milky Way is a dense, blazing arch. A full moon often lights the planet freshly, and patterns of human culture, artificially lit, are striking in ways not visible in daylight. One evening I saw the distinctive glows of Bhiwani, Rohtak, Ghaziabad, and a dozen other cities around Delhi diffused like spiral galaxies in a continuous deck of stratus clouds far below us. In Algeria and on the Asian steppes, wind-whipped pennants of gas flared. The jungle burned in incandescent spots on peninsular Malaysia and in southern Brazil. One clear evening at 20,000 feet over Manhattan, I could see, it seemed, every streetlight halfway to the end of Long Island, as far east as Port Jefferson. A summer lightning bolt once unexpectedly revealed thousands of bright dots on the ink-black veld of the northern Transvaal: sheep. Another night, off the eastern coast of Korea, I arose from a nap to see a tight throw of the brightest lights I'd ever observed. I thought we were low over a city until I glanced at the horizon and saw the pallid glow of coastal towns between Yŏngdŏk and Samch'ŏk. The lights directly below, brilliant as magnesium flares, were those of a South Korean fishing fleet.

Over Anchorage we slam into severe turbulence at 34,000 feet. The plane seems suddenly to shrink, and we are pitched through the sky like a wood chip for ten minutes before we get clear of it and divert to Fairbanks. When I go below with a handler, the horses appear to have come through the violence unfazed. The handler knows each of the animals and speaks soothingly to them. As we proceed down the line, he recalls their breeding histories. Draft horses like the Percheron, he says, are the calmest breeds, and working quarter horses are bred for calmness. He isn't surprised they're all right, or that they settle down quickly.

If you ask pilots which loads they most remember, they mention either costly objects—a $319,000 Bentley, flying 70,000 pounds of gold into Riyadh—or animals, the things that are animated in a freight shipment. Most say Vietnamese potbelly pigs are the worst creatures to haul, their stench so permeating that pilots have to strip off their uniforms, seal them in plastic bags, and fly in clothes that they later throw away. As bad, they say, is a planeload of durians, a pulpy, melon-size fruit whose scent reminds most Western people of vomit. A problem that occurs on some cattle flights turns on their rank perspiration. Rising as a vapor, it penetrates the ceiling insulation and freezes to the plane's interior skin surfaces. Melted by warmer outside temperatures at lower altitudes on descent, the fluid funnels forward and begins dripping on the pilots.

When large animals—draft horses and bulls—kick their stalls in midflight, you can feel the plane shudder. Goats and ostriches will chew at whatever cargo they can reach. One pilot told me about going down one night to look at a white tiger. Believing she'd been sedated, he drew close to the bars to peer in. She charged as ferociously as the cage permitted, sending the pilot reeling onto his back. The animal's roar, he said, drowned out the sound of the engines and nearly stopped his heart.

Pilots remember animals in some detail—wolf puppies turned loose in the cockpit, a killer whale in a tank—because they are alive and making these formidable journeys. Like the pilots.

WE WAIT IN Fairbanks until the Anchorage weather quiets and then fly back, landing in light turbulence. A 747 freighter taking off just after we land hits a wind shear and in less than two seconds accelerates from 210 to 260 knots. An hour later, on takeoff, we abruptly lose 20 knots of airspeed when a headwind collapses. We're barely airborne when the departure threshold on the runway passes under our wheels. Two hours later our automatic pilot malfunctions. The nose plunges violently and we are in a rapid descent. In one of the most assured and swiftest moves I've ever seen a human being make, the pilot recovers the plane and brings it back level before we fall 500 feet.

When I again accompany the handlers below, we find the horses awakened by the fall and spooked by our soundless approach. They glare a while, then doze off. The rich odors in their corrals don't drift up to the flight deck. I thought they might, and take the edge of indifference off the electronic atmosphere up there.

In those same minutes the sun had just risen (at 30,000 feet it clears the horizon about twenty-two minutes earlier than it does when seen from a spot on the Earth directly below), but the moon had not yet set, and for a while I held both in the same gaze, in a sky that goes from azure to milk blue between horizons. We are pushing against a 120-knot headwind, common this time of year over the North Pacific. When I ask whether the pilots have names for these winds aloft around the world, the captain says, "No, we haven't been flying long enough." I ask whether the jet stream—"the jets," they call these winds—blows strongest here. Yes, he answers, here and over the North Atlantic. By then the copilot has located something he's been searching for in his personal logbook. On this same route last year, he shows me, headed the other way with a tailwind, he made the fastest ground speed he's experienced in a 747—702 knots.

Far beneath us the winds are calmer. The burnished surface of the ocean seven miles below appears still as a slab of stone, and crinkled like an elephant's skin. I see only one ship headed southwest against the Okhotsk Current, far off the coast of Kamchatka, its wake flared at the characteristic 39-degree angle.

When Japan looms I feel suddenly very tired. I haven't slept for thirty hours—traveling to Chicago, then caught up in events surrounding the horses, anticipating en route to Anchorage an appearance of the aurora borealis, listening to the pilots tell stories, looking out the window at the remoteness of Alaska, at the spectacle of clouds. Beneath us, every day, I'd seen buttermilk, mare's tail, and mackerel skies, and then looked in vain through phrase books and small dictionaries for what they are called in Korean, in Spanish.

We touch down at Narita International Airport at 12:42 p.m. local standard time. At 12:45 we set the plane's parking brake at Gate 211.* At 12:54 Japanese officials open the door and a quarantine officer boards to inspect the horses. Once he is assured of their good health, he leads us down the air stairs where, one by one, we step gingerly through a plastic basin of disinfectant. The horse handlers, wearing fine-looking Western boots, hesitate a moment.

The wood stalls are to be burned. The horses will be in quarantine here for three weeks before being flown to Hokkaido. I remember the snorts of steam and billowing breath on the frigid ramp at O'Hare and wish I could see them now, standing, like us, in the sunshine and balmy breezes outside the plane.

V

FROM MY ACCUSTOMED SEAT, just behind and slightly to the left of the pilot, I have a clear view to the southeast over the South China Sea. Though it is slightly awkward to manage, I often lean into this window. Just those few inches closer and my view widens appreciably. I look back at the port wing, the sleek gape of the winking engines, at a pinpoint of nuclear light wink-

---

* Pilots use different methods to compute their actual (as distinct from scheduled) flying time. One is "block to block," from the pulling of the nosewheel chocks at one end to their being set at the other end. Another is doors closed to doors open. Northwest pilots are limited, on this latter basis, to 82.5 hours of flying per month and to no more than 30 hours in any seven-day period.

ing on a windshield ten miles away. At night, if I rotate my head 180 degrees and hold the upper edge of this canted window against the stars, the world is utterly still. We do not appear to move at all.

Far to the south, just now, a ribbon of sunlit cumulus towers, fumaroles and haystacks, great pompadour waves of this cloud. I never tire of seeing them, the most dominating evanescent form on the planet. We have seen a great range of them since leaving Tokyo some hours ago. East of Honshu, over the Pacific, the ocean was occluded by a vast sheet of wool-nap cumulus. When that flat plain opened into a lattice hundreds of miles later, the formation appeared serried in three dimensions, away from me and down. These puffs eventually thinned and I thought the sky cloudless until I looked up to see a rice-paper layer of cirrostratus. Then it, too, thinned to blue space, and for a while there was nothing but an occasional fair-weather cumulus, built up over a distant Pacific atoll, until we came to the rampart of heaped clouds—*cumulus congestus*. For all their beauty, the impossibly slow tai chi of their movement, clouds are of almost no help, claim the pilots, in anchoring a sense of depth or distance in the troposphere. They accentuate, however, the peculiar and insistent, ethereal nature of the sky.

I need to stretch. None of the three pilots wants anything from the galley,* so I raise the smoke door (which would give us some protection in case of a main-deck fire) and descend the stairs to take a turn around the cargo. Unlike the pilots, I cannot resist a look each time the plane's contents change. I am drawn by the promise of revelation in the main hold. "Used clothing" might

---

* The heritage of oceangoing vessels is preserved in the language and some of the design of modern airplanes. Pilots frequently call the plane a ship, its fuselage a hull. Its interior space is divided into decks that extend fore and aft. The captain might refer to starting an engine as turning a wheel. He steers the plane on the ground with a tiller and speaks of docking the ship, after which, on a freighter, cargo is always taken off the main deck on the port side (originally, the side of a ship designed for use in port). A rudder in the plane's vertical stabilizer changes its course. Waterline-like numbers stenciled on the interior of the fuselage indicate height above the ground. Sailboat fairings taper engine mounts into wings that bear green running lights to starboard, red lights to port.

mean a boutique-consignment of East German military uniforms. A persistent rumor of fabled cargo might be confirmed.* The pilots, who speak animatedly about circus tigers, Lamborghini Diablos, and small wooden pallets of gold bars, each in its own burlap bag, seem uninterested or vaguely embarrassed by the bulk of what fills the space behind their heads.†

The specter of a fire down here is, of course, terrifying, as is the thought of a printing press or a stack of steel pipe breaking loose in turbulence. For this reason the contents of air shipments are carefully reviewed and documented; pilots receive written notification of even the smallest quantities of corrosives, explosives, and radioactive materials on board—anything that could start a fire. Cargo loads are tightly secured and neatly arranged so as to be accessible in flight. The flight engineer's last responsibility on walk-around before departure is to check each piece of fire-fighting equipment and make sure that each pallet and container is secure; the ones I watched were thorough about it.

On flights to North America from the Far East's "new tigers"—Jakarta, Singapore, Bangkok, Hong Kong, Taipei—the planes ferried (in descending order, by weight) personal computers, sound-recording equipment, athletic shoes, photocopying equipment, and clothes. Traveling from North America to the Far East are comparable loads of motors and engines, personal computers, telecommunications equipment, and tractor parts. Such commodities formed the bulk of most shipments I accompanied, but it was the condiments, so to speak, that made a load memorable:

---

* One story I heard many times but couldn't confirm concerned shipments of large bluefin tuna to Japan from Newport, Rhode Island. A Newport buyer with a small plane on standby reportedly offers returning sport fishermen a premium price for any bluefin over 500 pounds. The fish is iced, flown immediately to JFK, and put aboard the first available commercial flight to Tokyo.

† About four a.m. one December night in Hong Kong, I stood at the top of our air stairs scanning close-by office buildings with my binoculars. Decorated Christmas trees twinkled on a dozen floors. I'd seen Christmas trees banked with brightly wrapped gift boxes in Muslim Dubai and in the Buddhist city of Bangkok, as well as in Amsterdam and Houston. The displays, of course, had nothing to do with the Christianity of, say, Joseph of Arimathea. "This time of year," one pilot told me while we waited for cargo in Hong Kong, "we're flying freighters out of here wingtip to wingtip."

two hundred Styrofoam cases of live tropical fish (labeled LTF), swimming in bags of oxygenated water, bound for Los Angeles from Manila; two Cadillac Eldorados—right-hand drive—for Osaka; canvas bags of homebound paper bills (the accumulation from currency exchanges); munitions of war (MUW) for Khartoum; bundles of mesquite wood, for restaurant cooking fires, out of Houston; and noisome industrial chemicals (OBX).

In a fully loaded 747-200, cargo is palletized on thin aluminum "cookie sheets," wrapped tightly in clear plastic weatherproofing (or opaque plastic, to discourage thieves), and secured against shifting on the pallet by webs or rope nets. Twenty-two rectangular sealed containers and pallets, dogged down to a floor of steel caster bearings and roller-track with red latches, stand in pairs down the middle of the freighter, leaving narrow outboard aisles. Two additional units, canted to the taper of the plane, hug the starboard wall into the nose. In the tail, aft of a ten-foot-wide cross aisle directly opposite a cargo door, stand another four units. A twenty-ninth unit, the last, stands behind them, near the open wall rack that holds the plane's flight data recorder and cockpit voice recorder (the "black boxes").

I sideslip past the containers and pallets on the port side and look back from the cross aisle at the mass of our freight for Singapore and Bangkok. It shimmies in the cobblestone turbulence of what Wilbur Wright called "the infinite highway of the air," a rickety but firm, continuous vibration. (From a viewport on the flight deck, with the area lit dimly by only a few safety lights, the plastic-wrapped cargo looks like a double row of huge jellyfish strung up in a freezer.) I turn and clamber over the rearmost loads, reaching a white concave hemisphere marking the aft edge of the main deck. Here, as far as possible from the plane's compasses, is where any magnetized cargo is palletized.

Moving forward up the starboard aisle, I finally stand in an eerie place, at the forward edge of the main deck, looking at the backside of the fiberglass radar dome that fills the plane's nose. I look down into an open bay framed on either side by large jackscrews which push the nose out and up for loading through the front. The lip of this precipice, which I grip with my toes, is as close as one can get to standing on the bow of a ship. I spread my arms wide for balance, shut my eyes, and lean into the velocity of the plane. The sound of the engines is behind me, inaudible over the scream of air.

CHIEF PILOTS, or captains, men in their early fifties "in the left-hand seat," tend to gaze to some purpose out the windows of the cockpit, while copilots, men (and, rarely, women), in their midthirties, remain focused within the plane.

In the evolution of modern jet flight, there has been a dramatic shift away from the use of navigation references outside the plane, such as rivers, to the use of electronically displayed information within the plane. Some of the copilots I spoke with, in fact, had only hazy notions of the geography they flew over. They were inclined to fly "heads down," studying a route map, reviewing the flight plan (a sequence of way points, an expected fuel burn, the speed and direction of winds aloft), and watching their instruments and display screens. On the most advanced commercial aircraft, it is the copilots who are frequently caught up in the protracted task of programming the plane's computers. ("I don't fly anymore," they joke, "but I can type sixty words a minute.")*

The chief pilots, many of them, possess a notable, unique knowledge of how the Earth has changed over the past thirty years; how much farther south the Sahara Desert has crept, how much the Aral Sea has shrunk, how far center-pivot irrigation has spread in Saudi Arabia. It's knowledge that predates satellite imagery and often is more historically integrated. Many of these pilots learned the Earth's surfaces when older planes held them to lower altitudes, when ground marks like pipelines and lakes were more important to navigation. Today, in advanced aircraft,

---

* Pilots refer to newer planes like the Boeing 777 and the Airbus 320 synecdochically as "glass cockpits," planes in which the information most frequently reviewed is displayed in color overlays on videolike screens. The instrument cluster in older jet aircraft is referred to collectively as "steam gauges."

they routinely fly high above the weather, on automatic pilot, and descend less often for fuel. A dispatcher in a windowless international office half a world away may organize a sense of geography for them and radio in, even telephone with any changes in the flight plan, due, say, to increased storm activity. There's little need to watch the weather, or anything else.

Pilots say they "fly by wire" now, no longer sensing the plane's response in their hands and feet. They refer to "cockpit management skills" more often than their "stick-and-rudder ability." In the 747-400, they monitor six separate cathode-ray screens, mesmerizing as small televisions. In this kind of self-absorbed travel, built on a dashboard knowledge of one's surroundings, a sense of both geographic scale and particularity is ruptured. Flights cover huge distances in a few hours; matriculation at a chain hotel, often reached on a crew bus driven down an advertising corridor like the airport's passenger corridors, is brief. English is spoken everywhere. Anacin, 7-Up, *Rambo,* CNN, Ray-Ban, and *Time* are omnipresent. Reality outside the plane slowly merges with a comforting, authoritative, and self-referential world found within it.

JET LAG IS popularly construed as an affliction of the unseasoned traveler, a preventable distraction. No pilot I talked to regarded it as such but rather as a sort of spatial and temporal abuse which, by the time you reach your fifties, can overwhelm you on a single trip.

Over many days of flying, I fought my own idiosyncratic battle with jet lag, following the common advice of pilots to sleep when you're tired and eat when you're hungry. When I got home, after traveling 30,000 or 40,000 miles in ten days, I would fall into bed like an iron ingot dropped in the dust. On the road, like the pilots, I endured the symptoms of a jagged, asynchronous life. No matter how exhilarating a trip might have been, I sensed upon leaving the plane that a thrashing like the agitation of a washing machine had ended, and that, slightly dazed, I was now drifting off my path, a yawing ship. My tissues felt leaden.

Memory seemed a pea suspended in the empty hulk of my body. I had the impression my mind was searching for the matching ends of myriad broken connections and that it was vaguely panicked by the effort. The fabric of awareness felt discontinuous. Time shoaled, losing its familiar depth and resonance. I craved darkness and stillness. I believed that without darkness and stillness no dreams would come and that without dreams there would be no recovery. Once, in a hotel, I slept on solely to dream.

If you drink copious amounts of water, breathe oxygen occasionally while you're aloft, eat very sparingly during the flight, and decline coffee and other diuretics, you can diminish the effects of jet lag. But the pilots and aeromedical officers I spoke with said the symptoms are so inevitable and intractable, you have to learn to accommodate them.

Pilots get regular checkups, many of them exercise, and most appear and feel fit. The physical hazards of long-term flying are relatively minor—an increased incidence of cataracts, high-frequency hearing loss (beginning in the right ear for copilots and becoming more severe in the left ear with pilots)—or are unknown—the effect, for example, of regular exposure to high doses of cosmic radiation. Pilots more than copilots will tell you that whatever health hazards they may face, they love flying too much to give it up. Many think that jet lag is the principal cause of chronic moodiness, a prime source of tension in their domestic relationships. But they view separation and divorce as grim contemporary realities, and say resignedly that they are very well paid for what they do.

I liked the pilots I flew with. They have a remarkable ability to relax for hours in a state of alertness (pilots describe the job as "hours of boredom punctuated by minutes of terror"). They seem able to monitor an instrument's unwavering reading and run technical checklists repeatedly without mentally wandering or reimagining the information. Their hand movements in the cockpit are slow, smooth, direct; they concentrate on precision and routine, on thoroughness. The virtues they admire—

dedication to a job, loyalty, allegiance to a code—are more military than corporate. Some, like generals, carry with them a peculiar, haggard isolation.

STANDING BETWEEN the pilots on the Singapore flight, my neck bowed beneath the overhead instrument panel, I could take the most commanding view possible of space outside the plane. From here, still over the South China Sea, I could see outlying islands in the Spratly Archipelago to the southeast. To the northwest were the distant mouths of the Mekong: Cua Tranh De, Cua Dinh An, Cua Ham Luong. A while later, Indonesia's Bunguran Selatan Archipelago loomed off the port side, the translucent sea turquoise over its reefs. Afternoon light from the bare orb of the sun filled the clear air at 37,000 feet with a tangible effulgence that made the island of Subi and the water seem closer. We looked down from the keep of our own wind, through layers of wind, to wind on the water; below that, the surface current ran at an angle to currents still deeper. Toward Karimata Strait, between Borneo and Belitung Island to the south, a single layer of thin stratus cloud cast its shadow over a hundred square miles of water. Beyond, the sea was brightly lit once more. Because detail on the water resumed there again with the same brilliance after fading in the foreground, the huge shadow's interruption created the illusion that the distant water was lit by light from another kingdom.

Ending a long silence in the cockpit, the captain said, "The Earth is beautiful."

On our approach to Singapore smoke began pouring out of the window vents—warm, humid air from outside condensing in our dry interior. The pilots enjoyed my alarm.

On the ground, while the plane was unloaded, and then reloaded for Bangkok and Tokyo, I strolled through mown grasses in an adjacent field. Two common mynah birds landed on the plane's port wing.

VI

THE HOTEL IN Seoul was just west of Mt. Namsan Park in Yongsan-Ku, in the city's southwest quarter. The crew bus would not leave for the airport for four hours, and I had risen before sunrise to take a long walk. I wanted to see things that couldn't be purchased.

I walked north from the hotel through a cramped residential district. Seoul is a city of granite hills, of crags and pinnacles. On this winter morning it filled gradually with a diffuse gray light under heavy, overcast skies. As I wandered the narrow streets, I endeavored not to seem too curious about what was displayed on the shelves of small stores attached to small two-story houses. Instead I observed what sort of bicycles people rode, what kind of clothing they wore against the cold—indigenous solutions to common problems. I studied the spines of books displayed in a window, the Chinese, Japanese, and Korean titles mixed, their ideograms so clearly different in comparison. I could not see past a street reflection in the window glass whether a companion volume was in Arabic.

Some Westerners traveling today in the Middle East may experience what they take for irritation over religious differences; in Seoul—or Bangkok or Wuhan—the look a Westerner may get walking through residential streets seems more often one of resentment or bewilderment at the imposition of economic change. You are the one responsible, the looks imply, for swift, large-scale painful alterations to my culture; you see them as improvements, but they are designed really only to make business—your sort of business—flow more smoothly. It is you, they seem to say, who define, often and titanically, what is of value.

What I felt—the discomforting gospel of world-encircling consumerism of which I was an inadvertent symbol—I could have felt as an indictment in a dozen other cities. It needn't have been here, where I only wanted relief from the impact of culture I felt every time the plane landed.

Early in the morning in a city like this, you may see several hundred years of history unfold in just a few hours. The earliest people out are those packing fish up from boats on the Han River, people selling charcoal to shopkeepers or transporting food in handcarts, a manner of life relatively unchanged from 1750. Appearing later are factory workers, headed for parts of Seoul where the smoke and grit ash of nineteenth-century Pittsburgh still cling. Then come department store clerks and employees of large firms, the lower and middle levels of white-collar work. Last out on the sidewalks are expensively dressed men, headed for the Samsung Building or for other corporate offices.

Some in the West see in such rearrangements net gains, others net losses. I do not lean strongly either way, though I'm saddened, as a traveler, by the erosion of languages, the diminishment of other systems of aesthetics, and the loss of what might be called a philosophy of hand tools. It is easy to rue the lack of restraint in promoting consumption as a way of life, but we daily accept myriad commercial solutions to our own discontent—the assuagement of new clothing, new investments, new therapies to ease our disaffections. Some who endure such accelerated living (our advertising presumes) find it a relief periodically to sweep everything into the past, making room for less obligating, more promising products or situations.

It is not difficult to disparage the capitulation in such manic living; what is hard is avoiding the impulse to blame, or the instinct to exempt oneself. Getting dressed at the hotel, I had to smile at the labels in my clothing: J. Crew, Gap, Territory Ahead, Patagonia. My shoes, dark brown suede wingtips, had been made in Korea.

Once, suspended over the North Pacific, I held the image of a loom in my mind. If these flights back and forth across the Pacific are the weft, I wondered, what is the warp, the world already strung, through which my shuttle cuts back and forth? And what pattern will the weave produce?

I picked my way around rain-pocked mounds of snow back to the hotel, down tight alleys backed with fishmongers' crates.

THE PLANE I boarded out of Seoul was a passenger flight with lower-deck cargo for Narita. There I boarded a freighter bound for New York via Anchorage. In the Jeppesen Manual that most United States pilots carry—a two-inch-thick ring binder of tissue-thin pages containing detailed information about airports—Anchorage is described as a consistently dangerous place to get in and out of. The nearby area experiences a lot of wind shear and turbulence; icing is common in winter.*

Pilots recall with little prompting the details of commercial airplane crashes going back many years. Each one is a warning. Their interest is almost entirely technical and legal, not macabre. While I was flying in the Middle East a freighter crashed in Kansas City, killing the three pilots aboard. Although the crew I was with read the story in the *International Herald Tribune,* no one commented. The pilots presume such reports are always confused and therefore misleading. They wait instead for the National Transportation Safety Board findings to appear in *Aviation Week and Space Technology.*

We had no trouble getting into or out of Anchorage, and we enjoyed an unperturbed flight to New York, with spectacular views of the Canadian Rockies. On the next leg, from JFK to San Francisco, I fell into conversation with the pilot about the history of aerodynamic design that produced the 747. Like many pilots, he had an intuitive sense of the volume of abstract space, and he was a gazer-out-of-windows. It was about one in the morning. Air-traffic control in New York had given us a direct path to San Francisco. Our flight plan showed no areas of turbulence ahead, and no one in front of us was reporting any. The moonless sky was glimmering, deep. I asked the pilot if he had ever heard of James Turrell. He hadn't.

---

* The turbulence we encountered over Anchorage on the flight with the horses was the worst one pilot had ever experienced. On another flight outbound from Anchorage, the freighter built up the heaviest loads of ice the chief pilot had ever had to contend with.

I'd hoped for weeks to speak with someone who had. Turrell is best known for an enormous project called Roden Crater near Flagstaff in northern Arizona. He reconformed the crater with bulldozers and road graders, believing celestial space actually had shape, that one could perceive the "celestial vault" above the Earth, and that a view from within the crater could reveal that architecture by so disposing the viewer. Turrell, a pilot, once said, "For me, flying really dealt with these spaces delineated by air conditions, by visual penetration, by sky conditions; some were visual, some were only felt. These are the kinds of space I wanted to work with."

People who have traveled to Roden Crater—heavy-equipment operators as well as museum curators—say, yes, you do see that the sky has shape from the crater. I'd like to go, I told the pilot.

After a while the pilot turned around in his seat and said, "He's right. I know what he's talking about. The space you fly the plane through has shape." I asked if he thought time had boundary or dimension, and told him what I had felt at Cape Town, that time pooled in every part of the world as if in a basin. The dimension, the transparency, and the agitation were everywhere different. He nodded, as if together we were working out an equation.

A while later he said, "Being 'on time' is like being on fire."

ONE OF MY LAST FLIGHTS takes me to Buenos Aires, seat of the old viceroyalty on the Río de la Plata, the river of silver. Here, as in other places I visited, people in the freight depot are friendly and open, and sometimes quite sophisticated about ironies in the airfreight business. I go to lunch with four men who treat me to a meal of Argentine beef and a good Argentine red wine. Affecting philosophical detachment, they explain the non-European way to conduct business in Buenos Aires, the paths money might take here. We laugh. Three of us then go to a strong room to inspect a shipment of gold bullion.

I walk out to the tarmac afterward with the KLM freight manager. He is directing the loading of Flight 798 from Buenos Aires to Amsterdam, a thirteen-hour run. In the crackle blast of combusting kerosene, swept by hot winds, I watch the pallets go aboard. These, I have come to understand, are the goods. This lovely, shrieking behemoth, the apotheosis of modern imagination and invention, is being filled yet again with what we believe in. I watch, as agnostics must once have watched at Chartres, for a sign, a confirmation of faith. I see frozen trout; fresh strawberries; eighty cases of live worms; seventy-three pounds of gold for Geneva, packed in light green metal boxes sealed with embossed aluminum bands, wrapped in clear plastic, banded again with steel strapping. An armed security officer stands by until the bulk-cargo door is closed, then stands at a distance, watching.

The last load in the aft compartment is four tons of horsemeat. The temperature is set at 53 degrees and the door is closed. The last load in the forward compartment will be 175 penguins. They have come in on the plane from Santiago and are headed for Tokyo. They wait in the noise and heat around the airplane while freight in the forward compartment is rearranged, the weight more evenly distributed.

The penguins stand erect in narrow cells, five cells forming a wooden crate. A wire mesh panel on the front, beginning at chest level, slants up and back, reaching the top of the crate just above their head height. So constructed, air can reach those on the inside of the load, thirty-five crates stacked in tiers on a single pallet. The gangs of five face in four directions; some see us, some see one another, some see the plane, some the back of another box. I recognize magellanic and rockhopper penguins. If they're making any noise I cannot hear it over the jet engines. A few strike at the wire mesh with their bills. Some of the rockhoppers rise on their toes, cramping their heads, and flap their flippers repeatedly against the dividers.

After they are loaded, the temperature of their compartment is set at 43 degrees and the door is closed.

KL 798, a passenger flight, takes us up the southern coast of Brazil, above the Serra do Mar and Serra do Espinhaço and out over the Atlantic near Natal. There is a lightning storm near Recife, on the coast. I send my worn letter of introduction to the cockpit to see if it would be possible to watch and talk for a while. The purser comes back with a smile. Yes.

I take my place in the jump seat, assure the chief pilot I am familiar with how to operate the oxygen mask and with my responsibilities in case of an emergency. This is a 747-400. With this new design, the flight engineer's job has been eliminated; a relief crew of two is now asleep in bunks along the port side, just aft of the cockpit.

We watch cobra strikes of yellow-and-blue light on the starboard horizon. Against the display of lightning I hesitate to speak. I take in the instruments to learn our heading, the speed and direction of the wind, our altitude, the outside temperature. I'm aware of my faith in the integrity of the aircraft. I recognize the familiar, impetuous hurtling toward the void, a space to be filled only briefly, then to yawn again, hopeful and acquisitive.

Out over the Atlantic I lean forward and ask the captain how long he's been flying, which routes he knows best. Twenty-eight years, he says. He speaks of the South American and Caribbean routes. I think of the penguins two decks below, whose wings have become flippers, slamming them against the walls of their pens.

PART TWO

Indwelling

6

APOLOGIA

A FEW MILES EAST of home in the Cascades I slow down and pull over for two raccoons, sprawled still as stones in the road. I carry them to the side and lay them in sunshot, windblown grass in the barrow pit. In eastern Oregon, along U.S. 20, black-tailed jackrabbits lie like welts of sod—three, four, then a fifth. By the bridge over Jordan Creek, just shy of the Idaho border in the drainage of the Owyhee River, a crumpled adolescent porcupine leers up almost maniacally over its blood-flecked teeth. I carry each one away from the pavement into a cover of grass or brush out of decency, I think. And worry. Who are these animals, their lights gone out? What journeys have fallen apart here?

I do not stop to remove each dark blister from the road. I wince before the recently dead, feel my lips tighten, see something else, a fence post, in the spontaneous aversion of my eyes, and pull over. I imagine white silk threads of life still vibrating inside them, even if the body's husk is stretched out for yards, stuck like oiled muslin to the road. The energy that once held them erect leaves like a bullet, but the memory of that energy fades slowly from the wrinkled cornea, the bloodless fur.

The raccoons and, later, a red fox carry like sacks of wet gravel and sand. Each animal is like a solitary child's shoe in the road.

Once a man asked, Why do you bother? You never know, I said. The ones you give some semblance of burial, to whom you offer an apology, may have been like seers in a parallel culture. It is an act of respect, a technique of awareness.

In Idaho I hit a young sage sparrow—*thwack* against the right fender in the very split second I see it. Its companion rises from the same spot but a foot higher, slow as smoke, and sails off clean into the desert. I rest the walloped bird in my left hand, my right thumb pressed to its chest. I feel for the wail of the heart. Its eyes glisten like rain on crystal. Nothing but warmth. I shut the tiny eyelids and lay it beside a clump of bunchgrass. Beyond a barbed-wire fence the overgrazed range is littered with cow flops. The road curves away to the south. I nod before I go, a ridiculous gesture, out of simple grief.

I pass four spotted skunks. The swirling air is acrid with the rupture of each life.

DARKNESS RISES in the valleys of Idaho. East of Grand View, south of the Snake River, nighthawks swoop the roads for gnats, silent on the wing as owls. On a descending curve I see two of them lying soft as clouds in the road. I turn around and come back. The sudden slowing down and my K-turn at the bottom of the hill draw the attention of a man who steps away from a tractor, a dozen yards from where the birds lie. I can tell by his step, the suspicious tilt of his head, that he is wary, vaguely proprietary. Offended, or irritated, he may throw the birds back into the road when I leave. So I wait, subdued like a penitent, a body in each hand.

He speaks first, a low voice, a deep murmur weighted with awe. He has been watching these flocks feeding just above the road for several evenings. He calls them whippoorwills. He gestures for a carcass. How odd, yes, the way they concentrate their hunting right on the road, I say. He runs a finger down the smooth arc of the belly and remarks on the small whiskered bill. He pulls one long wing out straight, but not roughly. He marvels. He glances at my car, baffled by this out-of-state courtesy. Two dozen nighthawks careen past, back and forth at arm's length, feeding at our height and lower. He asks if I would mind—as though I owned it—if he took the bird up to the house to show his wife. "She's never seen anything like this." He's fascinated. "Not close."

I trust, later, he will put it in the fields, not throw the body in the trash, a whirligig.

NORTH OF PINEDALE in western Wyoming on U.S. 189, below the Gros Ventre Range, I see a big doe from a great distance, the low rays of first light gleaming in her tawny reddish hair. She rests askew, like a crushed tree. I drag her to the shoulder, then down a long slope by the petals of her ears. A gunnysack of plaster mud, ears cold as rain gutters. All of her doesn't come. I climb back up for the missing leg. The stain of her is darker than the black asphalt. The stains go north and off to the south as far as I can see.

On an afternoon trafficless, quiet as a cloister, headed across South Pass in the Wind River Range, I swerve violently but hit a bird, and then try to wrestle the gravel-spewing skid in a straight line along the lip of an embankment. I know even as I struggle for control the irony of this: I could easily pitch off here to my own death. The bird is dead somewhere in the road behind me. Only a few seconds and I am safely back on the road, nauseated, light-headed.

It is hard to distinguish among younger gulls. I turn this one around slowly in my hands. It could be a western gull, a mew gull, a California gull. I do not remember well enough the bill markings, the color of the legs. I have no doubt about the vertebrae shattered beneath the seamless white of its ropy neck.

East of Lusk, Wyoming, in Nebraska, I stop for a badger. I squat on the macadam to admire the long claws, the perfect set of its teeth in the broken jaw, the ramulose shading of its fur—how it differs slightly, as does every badger's, from the drawings and pictures in the field guides. A car drifts toward us over the prairie, coming on in the other lane, a white 1962 Chevrolet station wagon. The driver slows to pass. In the bright sunlight I can't see his face, only an arm and the gesture of his thick left hand. It opens in a kind of shrug, hangs briefly in limp sadness, then extends itself in supplication. Gone past, it curls into itself against the car door and is still.

Farther on in western Nebraska I pick up the small bodies of mice and birds. While I wait to retrieve these creatures I do not meet the eyes of passing drivers. Whoever they are, I feel anger toward them, in spite of the sparrow and the gull I myself have killed. We treat the attrition of lives on the road like the attrition of lives in war: horrifying, unavoidable, justified. Accepting the slaughter leaves people momentarily fractious, embarrassed. South of Broken Bow, at dawn, I cannot avoid an immature barn swallow. It hangs by its head, motionless in the slats of the grille.

I stop for a rabbit on Nebraska 806 and find, only a few feet away, a garter snake. What else have I missed, too small, too narrow? What has gone under or past me while I stared at mountains, hay meadows, fencerows, the beryl surface of rivers? In Wyoming I could not help but see pronghorn antelope swollen big as barrels by the side of the road, their legs splayed rigidly aloft. For animals so large, people will stop. But how many have this habit of clearing the road of smaller creatures, people who would remove the ones I miss? I do not imagine I am alone. As much sorrow as the man's hand conveyed in Nebraska, it meant gratitude too for burying the dead.

Still, I do not wish to meet anyone's eyes.

IN SOUTHWESTERN IOWA, outside Clarinda, I haul a deer into high grass out of sight of the road and begin to examine it. It is still whole, but the destruction is breathtaking. The skull, I soon discover, is fractured in four places; the jaw, hanging by shreds of mandibular muscle, is broken at the symphysis, beneath the incisors. The pelvis is crushed, the left hind leg unsocketed. All but two ribs are dislocated along the vertebral column, which is complexly fractured. The intestines have been driven forward into the chest. The heart and lungs have ruptured the chest wall at the base of the neck. The signature of a tractor-trailer truck: 80,000 pounds at 65 mph.

In front of a motel room in Ottumwa I finger-scrape the dry, stiff carcasses of bumblebees, wasps, and butterflies from the grille and headlight mountings, and I scrub with a wet cloth to soften and wipe away the nap of crumbles, the insects, the aerial plankton of spiders and mites. I am uneasy carrying so many of the dead. The carnage is so obvious.

In Illinois, west of Kankakee, two raccoons as young as the ones in Oregon. In Indiana another raccoon, a gray squirrel. When I make the left turn into the driveway at the house of a friend outside South Bend, it is evening, hot and muggy. I can hear cicadas in a lone elm. I'm glad to be here.

From the driveway entrance I look back down Indiana 23, toward Indiana 8, remembering the farm roads of Illinois and Iowa. I remember how beautiful it was in the limpid air to drive Nebraska 2 through the sand hills, to see how far at dusk the land was etched east and west of Wyoming 28. I remember the imposition of the Wind River Range in a hard, blue sky beneath white ranks of buttonhook clouds, windy hay fields on the Snake River plain, the welcome of Russian olive trees and willows in western creek bottoms. The transformation of the heart such beauty engenders is not enough tonight to let me shed the heavier memory, a catalog too morbid to write out, too vivid to ignore.

I stand in the driveway now, listening to the cicadas whirring in the dark tree. My hands grip the sill of the open window at the driver's side, and I lean down as if to speak to someone still sitting there. The weight I wish to fall I cannot fathom, a sorrow over the world's dark hunger.

A light comes on over the porch. I hear a dead bolt thrown, the shiver of a door pulled free. The words of atonement I pronounce are too inept to offer me release. Or forgiveness. My friend is floating across the tree-shadowed lawn. What is to be done with the desire for exculpation?

"Later than we thought you'd be," he says.

I do not want the lavabo. I wish to make amends.

"I made more stops than I thought I would," I answer.

"Well, bring in your things. And whatever I can take," he offers.

I anticipate, in the powerful antidote of our conversation, the reassurance of a human enterprise, the forgiving embrace of the rational. It waits within, beyond the slow tail-wagging of two dogs standing at the screen door.

7

IN A COUNTRY OF LIGHT,
AMONG ANIMALS

THE UTUKOK RIVER FLOWS north out of Alaska's
De Long Mountains in the western Brooks Range, east
along the base of a treeless spine called Archimedes
Ridge, then north again across the tundra and into the Arctic
Ocean at Kasegaluk Lagoon. No one lives along its two hundred
miles of braided channels or in the hills nearby. Inupiat people
occasionally set up fishing camps at the river's mouth, but they
do not venture far inland. The country, several thousand square
miles of it draining into the Utukok, belongs to the resident
animals.

The benign and seemingly endless light of an arctic summer
here and the abrupt musical notes of nesting birds in the great
silence impart a gentleness to this landscape; a profusion of arctic

lupine and other flowers vaguely familiar to a temperate-zone eye make the gentle hills seem knowable and hospitable, but this northern edge of the continent must be viewed as foreign territory. Human beings are infrequent summer visitors. Most of them are biologists who stay a few weeks and then are gone. Or geologists, whose prospecting for oil makes the fieldwork of the biologists exploring this ecosystem seem more compelling—and meeting the gaze of resident caribou somewhat unsettling.

It seems presumptuous in a country so far-flung to be inquiring into the lives of animals—wolverine and the wolves and grizzlies that hunt the caribou—but the best biologists know you have to come to places like this to understand animals. A few will go further and tell you that, really, you must spend a lifetime at it, your own and the animal's. But few are able to. Like the rest of us they run out of money or management transfers them, or they simply go back to thinking about human beings.

So, even though a few field biologists have the wherewithal to get to places as untrammeled as the drainage of the Utukok River, rarely do they approach the heart of our difficulty in assessing animal lives. In addition, under the press of orthodoxy in Western science, they tend to overlook mystery. They dismiss, for fear of the complexity they introduce, many factors that set an individual animal apart from the standard description of the species. Fearful of being thought anthropomorphic, they shy away from any evidence of reason or emotion in animals. In formal reports they imply that such incidents never occur or are rare. But working up your field notes in the earth's wildest places—up here on the Utukok—you feel vaguely uncomfortable. You are very far from home. Your language is spoken by no one in the region.

IN JUNE 1978 I joined Bob Stephenson, a wolf biologist with Alaska Fish and Game, at a native village in the central Brooks Range called Anaktuvuk Pass. Stephenson owns a home here and for years he has been traveling back and forth from Fairbanks to interview resident Nunamiut (inland Eskimo or Inupiat) about their experiences with animals and to study, with their help, the lives of creatures in the surrounding steep mountains and valleys.

The belief that hunting cultures like the Nunamiut can offer wildlife biologists invaluable information is not new, but it is now an idea in its ascendancy. And it is not just the daily observations of such hunting peoples that contain a wealth of information about wild animals; in their clothing, dance, and artifacts are metaphorical clues about animal behavior. Generally speaking, native people examine intuitive and personal feelings about wild animals with no fear of anthropomorphism or "pathetic fallacy." And no incident a person witnesses need conform to prior knowledge. This view is based, of course, on assumptions different from Western views, which presume a species' behavior remains relatively unchanged and that with the right tools it's possible to figure out what animals are doing, even to predict their behavior.

In a place like Anaktuvuk Pass, a still more-or-less intact hunting culture of 110 people, where the senior men have thirty or forty years of experience with wild animals to call on, and the experience of their fathers and grandfathers, one's prejudices in favor of a superior Western system of knowledge are so obvious, so racist, they bring conversation to a halt.

During the week we spent in this mountain village, Bob transferred the locations of several new wolf dens to his field maps and made notes every night on a variety of encounters hunters had had with animals during the previous winter. We shared in the Nunamiut's caribou stew and *muktuk* (squares of bowhead whale skin and fat, traded up from Eskimos on the coast 200 miles away), and they eagerly partook of our canned fish and cheddar cheese. Late one afternoon a plane took us 230 miles west to a field camp on the Utukok River, where Bob's current field project with wolves was based and where five other biologists working with grizzly bear, wolverine, and caribou were encamped. I'd just finished writing a book about wolves and was keenly interested in them still, but on this trip I had no greater intention than to pay my respects and to sojourn in their country.

I DON'T KNOW, of course, whether you've ever been in the high Arctic in the summer, but I would begin by telling you how striking the light is. For two months or more the sun doesn't dip below the horizon. In a treeless, winter-hammered landscape like Alaska's north slope, the light creates a feeling of compassion that is almost palpable. Each minute of light experienced feels like one stolen from a crushing winter. You walk gently about, respectful of flowering plants, with a sense of how your body breaks the sunshine, creating shadow. You converse in soft tones. The light is—perhaps there is no other word—precious. You are careful around it.

The wind always feels close here, a gentle breeze, a heavy blow, the breathing of an unfathomable welter of clouds which passes continually overhead, an ocean in which weather is being conceived. It's figuring out what it wants to do before moving south and east across North America: now altostratus, now cirrus, now cumulonimbus, like exercises. After lunch a mare's tail sky; at one in the morning a rainbow appears to the south, half as broad as my fist, driven into the tundra like a sheet of iridescent steel.

But for the wind against your ear and the keening of fifty species of birds, it is as quiet as the moon. The wind surrounds the bark of a fox and it evaporates. In sun-warmed, goose-down clothing, you turn your cheek to the source of light and feel sheltered; you see amid the dwarf birch and dwarf willow at your feet speckled eggs cradled in birds' nests. The grace so apparent in first life seems nowhere else so tender, because night never comes here.

From the slope of a hill above this river, you can look out across two hundred square miles of tundra through air transparent as a polished windowpane. If the Earth were flat you could see all the way to Iowa. It was into this expansive country, this place of interminable light and clear, rolling air, that Bob and I had come. In it we would watch wolves.

BOB SPENT our first morning in base camp transferring data from his field notebooks to a pile of topographic maps. I heated three gallons of river water, stripped my clothes, and bathed. We were sharing this wall-tent camp with other biologists from Alaska and Montana living in varying degrees of general excitement and anxiety about, respectively, the calving close by of a herd of thirty thousand caribou and the proximity of tundra grizzlies.

Fourteen miles to the west of us was an active wolf den, set just below the rim of a high cutbank above a twenty-foot-wide stream called Iligluruk Creek. Two miles south of the den, across an open valley, was an elongated barren rise where Bob and I planned to camp. From this ridge, running roughly parallel to the cutbank, Bob and I could watch the seven Iligluruk adult wolves in this pack and the four pups born to them earlier that June.

One evening Craig Lofstedt, a pilot Bob and I had flown with on other wolf research trips in Nelchina Basin in the Alaska Range, six hundred miles to the southeast, helicoptered us out to our campsite on Ilingnorak Ridge. On the way we landed to inspect a caribou kill made just the day before by a yearling Iligluruk wolf. Bob retrieved the lower jaw, from which the caribou's age could be determined, and a femur. From its bone marrow the animal's general state of health could be deduced. The carcass had been picked clean. One kill had fed many of *amaguk*'s neighbors, likely *tulugak,* raven, and *kaiyukuk,* red fox.

As Craig flew us in a wide arc high above the den, we watched a light-colored yearling female stand up and stretch—she was "baby-sitting" while the other wolves were off to the west, hunting into a good wind.

Craig put us and our gear down on the ridge. We agreed on a rendezvous hour three days hence and he slipped away, lifting the Bell 206 off quietly to the south before heading back east, a courtesy to the wolf at the den.

Bob and I set up our spotting scopes immediately. Straight across the tundra plain in front of us the light-colored female had lain back down. To the east and west were a scatter of caribou, sixty or seventy of them. The wind was strong from the northwest, gusting to twenty-five miles per hour, and the air was chilly. An hour after we began our watch, two adult wolves loped into view from the west, headed for home. We studied them while they followed the cutbank above Iligluruk Creek for three miles. When they arrived the pups bounded up out of the den. Amid much tail wagging and face licking, the returning adults regurgitated meat for the pups, which they ravenously consumed. A few minutes later the scene was still. All seven animals were resting on the shallow slope above the den entrance.

Bob and I felt initiated into the country.

BECAUSE OF the perpetual light and our unobstructed view, we were able to observe animals at any hour over almost forty square miles of tundra. During the odd hours we chose to sleep, we set up a spotting scope in the tent entrance. If you woke up, you'd take a quick look around. Something new—a ground squirrel hiding behind a rock from something, a wolverine preparing to lie down—was always going on.

The suffusion of sunlight, seeming to empty the landscape of any threat, could make you forget how very remote the country was. When I lay down to sleep I was aware the soil only a few feet below my head was frozen solid, that in the hills around us grizzly bears were tearing up the earth in pursuit of ground squirrels, that somewhere a willow ptarmigan had become an explosion of feathers in a gyrfalcon's fists.

At 2:30 one morning Bob rose to look through his scope and spotted a grizzly bear at the wolf den. A yearling male, the lone sentinel with the pups, charged immediately and drove it back down the cutbank. Even at this distance we could see the puffs of dust at their feet as they raced down the incline. Suddenly the bear spun around and chased the wolf, but only about twenty-five feet before they faced off. Motionless, they stared at each other for a few seconds; then the wolf turned his back and walked away. The bear, now some four hundred feet from the den entrance, his curiosity piqued, walked around to the north and stood up on his hind legs, looking around, sniffing. The young wolf eyed him. The bear quartered back slowly toward the den and then charged. The wolf ran to meet him. Both stopped short, staring. In a few moments the wolf turned around and walked calmly back to the den. The bear ambled down to the creek and disappeared in the willows. The wolf weighed perhaps eighty pounds; the bear weighed three to four hundred pounds and appeared to Bob to be a young boar.

The wolf spent the next fifteen minutes with his nose to the ground, retracing all the bear's movements before finally lying down to sleep.

Baby-sitting. And learning about *aklak*.

I left my spotting scope occasionally to stretch and walk around Ilingnorak Ridge, inspecting frost-shattered rocks, bending close to see tiny Persian blue forget-me-nots, five blooms of which did not cover my thumbnail, and craning my neck at the phantasms of cloud. I picked up fox dung and short-tailed weasel dung to discover what they had been eating.

Within a few yards of the tent a golden plover, a horned lark, and a whimbrel had built nests—without trees everyone must nest on the ground, relying for protection on camouflage and distraction ploys when predators show up. With patience you can locate the epicenter of a bird's distraction displays and find the nest—four or five speckled or spotted or brindled eggs in a grass-lined cup. But the feeling that you've invaded the bird's privacy is too sharp, the *skree, skree, skree* of the alarmed plover somehow humiliating. I would back away carefully.

Four and a half hours after the yearling wolf drove the bear off, about seven in the morning, we saw an adult female wolf traveling toward the den at a steady trot, a laminar flow over the contours of the land. The slight discoloration of hair around her mammae, her round-as-a-melon belly, and her overall bearing revealed—to the Nunamiut, who taught Bob, who showed me—who she was (mother), where she'd been (successfully hunting), and where she was going (home). She stopped briefly a quarter mile west of her current den at a new den site the wolves had been excavating, and then continued on. She came to a sudden dead halt at a spot where the bear's still fresh trail crossed hers. She investigated it for a few moments before going on quickly to the den. The pups charged up out of the ground to greet her, jumping and pawing and bowling one another over in their efforts, seemingly, to embrace. She regurgitated meat for them and the yearling. After nursing the pups, she sniffed all around the den area and curled up to sleep.

An hour and a half later she roused her pups and headed west with all of them trailing clumsily after her. She led them to the new den, a move, we speculated, precipitated by the bear.

ONE EVENING I sat on the tundra near the tent watching *nagrulik*, horned lark, on her nest. It was cold. The lark, her feathers ruffled to insulate herself, sat resolutely on four eggs, staring back at me. I recalled a story. Bob and several Nunamiut were out looking for animals one summer night when a chilling fog settled over them. The men began gathering willows for a fire to heat tea. Suddenly one man made a beckoning gesture with a willow stick. At first no one could see what was up—he was waving at a porcupine, telling him to come over and join them.

When I looked up (it was as though I had been telling *nagrulik* this story), a caribou cow was looking at me, a hundred feet away. When finally she caught my scent she snorted violently and trotted off. Whatever I was to her, she'd grasped it and dispensed with me. A good feeling, I thought, for an interloper like myself to imagine here.

At midnight each night, when the sun was low in the northern sky, the clouds seemed to glow in greatest spectacle. We'd fix dinner and sit with our tin cups of tea, bundled in parkas and wind pants, and watch solar iridescence, a faint, translucent lime green and soft pink marbling in the clouds. Our rudimentary meals, under such auspices, seemed exquisite. We would glance at each other and cock our heads, speechless before the expanse of pleasure.

At 3:30 one morning a light-gray female wolf appeared at our camp. She came up over a rise, watched us for fifteen or twenty seconds, then moved away obliquely downhill. Every hundred yards or so she stopped and looked back at us, until she was about six hundred yards away. We watched her for a half hour as she continued north toward the den, investigating a clump of dwarf birch, flushing a ptarmigan, rolling on her back in the lichens, leaping in the air repeatedly to snap at long-tailed jaegers dive-bombing her.

She might have stumbled onto us while returning from a hunt, or come over on purpose to see who we were, in her country.

Late one afternoon we started out across the stretch of tundra that separated us from the den, to see if we could get any closer to the wolves. There is no walking on level, open ground as arduous as walking across wet tundra in summer. It's like walking across a field of bedsprings covered with a layer of basketballs. In an hour we'd gotten no more than three quarters of a mile. By then we'd lost sight of the den behind a rise of land and a storm had begun piling up clouds in the west. We turned back. *Nipailuktak*, short-eared owl, watched us from his hunting perch on a tussock. We passed *avinnak*'s house. *Avinnak*, tundra vole, was poised right there in his entrance. Hey, *nipailuktak*! Look at this! On the vast plain, Bob and I were like two small birds, sparrows or warblers, against the sky.

The wind changed around to the east that evening. When the wolves left to hunt they headed east for the first time since we'd arrived. We followed a single wolf with our scopes. He was sneaking up a willow-lined ravine, drawing close to several grazing caribou. The caribou got wind of him and exploded away. A second wolf appeared and both wolves gave chase. The gap between the caribou and the first wolf remained at two hundred yards or so for four or five hundred yards before the second wolf broke away to disappear over a rise, followed soon by the first wolf. A mile later the caribou slowed back to a walk.

The storm came up while we slept, holding us tent-bound for twelve hours. When I stepped outside once to re-anchor the tent against the savage punch of the wind, I suddenly saw golden plover in my mind and horned lark, the birds I'd been visiting, sitting there on their nests in the wind and rain.

After the storm passed, the evening warmed and a few mosquitoes came out, the first we'd seen. Nunamiut distinguish between juvenile mosquitoes, *migulaitchiak* (literally, "white socks"), and larger mosquitoes, *kiktugiak.* These were *kiktugiak,* big as horseflies. But the wind picked up and they were swept away.

About eight that night Bob stood away from his scope, stretched, and wandered off. I continued to study the country in slow, methodical sweeps, along Iligluruk Creek, along the ridges, down each crease in the land, the likeliest places to pick up something. Caribou were moving west, several hundred of them in enclaves small and large, drifting over some twenty square miles. One group of fourteen would pass, I saw, within three or four hundred yards of the den if they grazed on in a straight line. Four of the adult wolves were off hunting and two more were asleep in willows at the foot of the cutbank, where they wouldn't see the caribou. The seventh adult was sleeping at the crest of the bank. If for some reason she woke and stood up, she might see them.

The caribou came on unawares. I called to Bob to return to his scope, though it seemed unlikely anything dramatic would happen. The caribou were now almost in line with the den, just to the north of it. The three wolves remained asleep. Then the one at the crest rose to stretch. She saw the caribou and took off quickly to the east, downwind of them. One of the two wolves at the foot of the cutbank, responding to some signal, bounded out of the willows and ran up the cutbank. He, too, looked at the caribou before taking off after the first wolf.

Several minutes later, fourteen placidly grazing caribou jerked their heads upright and bolted west in a stiff-legged trot. The wolves might have let themselves be seen, to set up an ambush by the third wolf, or the caribou might have caught the scent of the den. We didn't see them following in the caribou's wake. Like most caribou-wolf encounters, this one came to nothing.

While we were watching this event unfold, Craig Lofstedt flew up and landed on Ilingnorak Ridge. He shut down the helicopter's turbine. The ridge fell back into its deep quiet. The three of us stood there with our hands in our parkas. I wondered if I would be able to remember the *skree* of the plovers, if I could make that sound in my head again; or remember the resistance to my arms and shoulders of rocks the size of oil barrels a grizzly bear had shoved aside in its search for a ground squirrel; or recall an image of caribou crossing the gray-green Utukok late at night, shaking off water in twos and threes against the sun, the explosion of diamond fragments.

After we loaded the helicopter I walked away in a wide circle to say good-bye to the birds.

The following day I flew out of our base camp, south up the Utukok, over the De Long Mountains, and down the Noatak River into Kotzebue. A single seat was available on a commercial flight headed south to Nome, then on to Anchorage. I took it, and phoned a friend in Anchorage to arrange for a shower during the layover necessary before I could get a flight south to Oregon, a straight-line descent from Iligluruk Creek of 2,300 miles.

The evening of the day I arrived at my home in the western Cascades, I walked down to the riverbank below the house and stood in the Douglas fir and ash trees. The sky above was newly dark to me, blue-black with thousands of stars shining. A visible moon. It was warm enough to stand there barefoot. I heard salmon slapping the water. *Ikalugruak,* the Nunamiut might have hazarded, male migrating salmon, their bellies red as the edge of a rainbow. Swimming right here, in this place, on this night.

8

THE AMERICAN GEOGRAPHIES

*I*T HAS BECOME COMMONPLACE to observe that Americans know little of the geography of their country, that they are innocent of it as a landscape of rivers, mountains, and towns. They do not know, supposedly, the location of the Delaware Water Gap, the Olympic Mountains, or the Piedmont Plateau; and, the indictment continues, they have little conception of the way the individual components of this landscape are imperiled, from a human perspective, by modern farming practices or industrial pollution.

I do not know how true this is, but it is easy to believe that it is truer than most of us would wish. A recent Gallup Organization and National Geographic Society survey found Americans woefully ignorant of world geography. Three out of four couldn't locate the Persian Gulf. The implication was that we knew no

more about our own homeland, and that this ignorance undermined the integrity of our political processes and the efficiency of
our business enterprises.

As Americans, we profess a sincere and fierce love for the
American landscape, for our rolling prairies, free-flowing rivers,
and "purple mountains' majesty"; but it is hard to imagine, actually, where this particular landscape is. It is not just that a nostalgic landscape has passed away—Mark Twain's Mississippi is now
dammed from Illinois to Louisiana and the prairies have all been
sold and fenced. It is that it's always been a romantic's landscape.
In the attenuated form in which it is presented on television
today, in magazine articles and in calendar photographs, the
essential wildness of the American landscape is reduced to attractive scenery. We look out on a familiar, memorized landscape
that portends adventure and promises enrichment. There are no
distracting people in it and few artifacts of human life. The animals are all beautiful, diligent, one might even say well behaved.
Nature's unruliness, the power of rivers and skies to intimidate,
and any evidence of disastrous human land management practices are all but invisible. It is, in short, a magnificent garden, a
colonial vision of paradise imposed on a real place that is, at best,
only selectively known.

THE REAL AMERICAN LANDSCAPE is a face of almost incomprehensible depth and complexity. If one were to sit for a few
days, for example, among the ponderosa pine forests and black
lava fields of the Cascade Mountains in western Oregon, inhaling
the pines' sweet balm on an evening breeze from some point on
the barren rock, and then were to step off to the Olympic Peninsula in Washington, to those rain forests with sphagnum moss
floors soft as fleece underfoot and Douglas firs too big around for
five people to hug, and then head south to walk the ephemeral
creeks and sun-blistered playas of the Mojave Desert in southern
California, one would be reeling under the sensations. The contrast is not only one of plants and soils, a different array, say, of

brilliantly colored beetles. The shock to the senses comes from a different shape to the silence, a difference in the very quality of light, in the weight of the air. And this relatively short journey down the West Coast would still leave the traveler with all that lay to the east to explore—the anomalous sand hills of Nebraska, the heat and frog voices of Okefenokee Swamp, the fetch of Chesapeake Bay, the hardwood copses and black bears of the Ozark Mountains.

No one of these places, of course, can be entirely fathomed, biologically or aesthetically. They are mysteries upon which we impose names. Enchantments. We tick the names off glibly but lovingly. We mean no disrespect. Our genuine desire, though we may be skeptical about the time it would take and uncertain of its practical value to us, is to actually know these places. As deeply ingrained in the American psyche as the desire to conquer and control the land is the desire to sojourn in it, to sail up and down Pamlico Sound, to paddle a canoe through Minnesota's boundary waters, to walk on the desert of the Great Salt Lake, to camp in the stony hardwood valleys of Vermont.

To do this well, to really come to an understanding of a specific American geography, requires not only time but a kind of local expertise, an intimacy with place few of us ever develop. There is no way around the former requirement: if you want to know you must take the time. It is not in books. A specific geographical understanding, however, can be sought out and borrowed. It resides with men and women more or less sworn to a place, who abide there, who have a feel for the soil and history, for the turn of leaves and night sounds. Often they are glad to take the outlander in tow.

These local geniuses of American landscape, in my experience, are people in whom geography thrives. They are the antithesis of geographical ignorance. Rarely known outside their own communities, they often seem, at the first encounter, unremarkable and anonymous. They may not be able to recall the name of a particular wildflower—or they may have given it a name known only to them. They might have forgotten the precise circumstances of a local historical event. Or they can't say for certain when the last of the Canada geese passed through in the fall, or can't differentiate between two kinds of trout in the same creek. Like all of us, they have fallen prey to the fallacies of memory and are burdened with ignorance; but they are nearly flawless in the respect they bear these places they love. Their knowledge is intimate rather than encyclopedic, human but not necessarily scholarly. It rings with the concrete details of experience.

America, I believe, teems with such people. The paradox here, between a faulty grasp of geographical knowledge for which Americans are indicted and the intimate, apparently contradictory familiarity of a group of largely anonymous people, is not solely a matter of confused scale. (The local landscape is easier to know than a national landscape—and many local geographers, of course, are relatively ignorant of a national geography.)

And it is not simply ironic. The paradox is dark. To be succinct: the politics and advertising that seek a national audience must project a national geography; to be broadly useful that geography must, inevitably, be generalized and it is often romantic. It is therefore frequently misleading and imprecise. The same holds true with the entertainment industry, but here the problem might be clearer. The same films, magazines, and television features that honor an imaginary American landscape also tout the worth of the anonymous men and women who interpret it. Their affinity for the land is lauded, their local allegiance admired. But the rigor of their local geographies, taken as a whole, contradicts a patriotic, national vision of unspoiled, untroubled land. These men and women are ultimately forgotten, along with the details of the landscapes they speak for, in the face of more pressing national matters. It is the chilling nature of modern society to find an ignorance of geography, local or national, as excusable as an ignorance of hand tools; and to find the commitment of people to their home places only momentarily entertaining. And finally naïve.

———

IF ONE WERE TO PASS time among Basawara people in the Kalahari Desert, or with Tikuna on the upper Amazon, or with Pitjantjatjara Aborigines in Australia, the most salient impression they might leave is of an absolutely stunning knowledge of their local geography—geology, hydrology, biology, and weather. In short, the extensive particulars of their intercourse with it.

In forty thousand years of human history, it has only been in the last few hundred years or so that a people could afford to ignore their local geographies as completely as we do and still survive. Technological innovations from refrigerated trucks to artificial fertilizers, from sophisticated cost accounting to mass air transportation, have utterly changed concepts of season, distance, soil productivity, and the real cost of drawing sustenance from the land. It is now possible for a resident of Kansas City to bite into a fresh mango in the dead of winter; for someone in San Francisco to travel to Atlanta in a few hours with no worry of how formidable might be crossings of the Great Basin Desert or the Mississippi River; for an absentee farmer to gain a tax advantage from a farm that leaches poisons into its water table and on which crops are left to rot. The Pitjantjatjara might shake their heads in bewilderment and bemusement, not because they are primitive or ignorant people, not because they have no sense of irony or are incapable of marveling, but because they have not (many would say not yet) realized a world in which such manipulation of the land—surmounting the imperatives of distance it imposes, for example, or turning the large-scale destruction of forests and arable land into wealth—is desirable or plausible.

In the years I have traveled through America, in cars and on horseback, on foot and by raft, I have repeatedly been brought to a sudden state of awe by some gracile or savage movement of animal, some odd wrapping of a tree's foliage by the wind, an unimpeded run of dew-laden prairie stretching to a horizon flat as a coin where a pin-dot sun pales the dawn sky pink. I know these things are beyond intellection, that they are the vivid edges of a world that includes but also transcends the human world. In memory, when I dwell on these things, I know that in a truly national literature there should be odes to the Triassic reds of the Colorado Plateau, to the sharp and ghostly light of the Florida Keys, to the aeolian soils of southern Minnesota and the Palouse in Washington, though the modern mind abjures the literary potential of such subjects. (If the sand and floodwater farmers of Arizona and New Mexico were to take the black loams of Louisiana in their hands they would be flabbergasted, and that is the beginning of literature.) I know there should be eloquent evocations of the cobbled beaches of Maine, the plutonic walls of the Sierra Nevada, the orange canyons of the Kaibab Plateau. I have no doubt, in fact, that there are. They are as numerous and diverse as the eyes and fingers that ponder the country—it is that only a handful of them are known. The great majority are to be found in drawers and boxes, in the letters and private journals of millions of workaday people who have regarded their encounters with the land as an engagement bordering on the spiritual, as being fundamentally linked to their state of health.

One cannot acknowledge the extent and the history of this kind of testimony without being forced to the realization that something strange, if not dangerous, is afoot. Year by year, the number of people with firsthand experience in the land dwindles. Rural populations continue to shift to the cities. The family farm is in a state of demise, and government and industry continue to apply pressure on the native peoples of North America to sever their ties with the land. In the wake of this loss of personal and local knowledge, the knowledge from which a real geography is derived, the knowledge on which a country must ultimately stand, has come something hard to define but I think sinister and unsettling—the packaging and marketing of land as a form of entertainment. An incipient industry, capitalizing on the nostalgia Americans feel for the imagined virgin landscapes of their ancestors, and on a desire for adventure, now offers people a convenient though sometimes incomplete or even spurious geography as an inducement to purchase a unique experience. But the line between authentic experience and a superficial exposure to the elements of experience is blurred. And the real landscape, in all its complexity, is distorted even further in the public imagination. No longer innately mysterious and dignified, a ground from which experience grows, it becomes a curiously generic backdrop on which experience is imposed.

In theme parks the profound, subtle, and protracted experience of running a river is reduced to a loud, quick, safe equivalence, a pleasant distraction. People only able to venture into the countryside on annual vacations are, increasingly, schooled in the belief that wild land will, and should, provide thrills and exceptional scenery on a timely basis. If it does not, something is wrong, either with the land itself or possibly with the company outfitting the trip.

People in America, then, face a convoluted situation. The land itself, vast and differentiated, defies the notion of a national geography. If applied at all it must be applied lightly, and it must grow out of the concrete detail of local geographies. Yet Americans are daily presented with, and have become accustomed to talking about, a homogenized national geography, one that seems to operate independently of the land, a collection of objects rather than a continuous bolt of fabric. It appears in advertisements, as a background in movies, and in patriotic calendars. The suggestion is that there *can* be a national geography because the constituent parts are interchangeable and can be treated as commodities. In day-to-day affairs, in other words, one place serves as well as another to convey one's point. On reflection, this is an appalling condescension and a terrible imprecision, the very antithesis of knowledge. The idea that either the Green River in Utah or the Salmon River in Idaho will do, or that the valleys of Kentucky and West Virginia are virtually interchangeable, is not just misleading. For people still dependent on the soil for their sustenance, or for people whose memories tie them to those places, it betrays a numbing casualness, a utilitarian, expedient, and commercial frame of mind. It heralds a society in which it is no longer necessary for human beings to know where they live, except as those places are described and fixed by numbers. The truly difficult and lifelong task of discovering where one lives is finally disdained.

If a society forgets or no longer cares where it lives, then anyone with the political power and the will to do so can manipulate the landscape to conform to certain social ideals or nostalgic visions. People may hardly notice that anything has happened, or assume that whatever happens—a mountain stripped of timber and eroding into its creeks—is for the common good. The more superficial a society's knowledge of the real dimensions of the land it occupies becomes, the more vulnerable the land is to exploitation, to manipulation for short-term gain. The land, virtually powerless before political and commercial entities, finds itself finally with no defenders. It finds itself bereft of intimates with indispensable, concrete knowledge. (Oddly, or perhaps not oddly, while American society continues to value local knowledge as a quaint part of its heritage, it continues to cut such people off from any real political power. This is as true for small farmers and illiterate cowboys as it is for American Indians, native Hawaiians, and Eskimos.)

The intense pressure of imagery in America, and the manipulation of images necessary to a society with specific goals, means the land will inevitably be treated like a commodity; and voices that tend to contradict the proffered image will, one way or another, be silenced or discredited by those in power. This is not new to America; the promulgation in America of a false or imposed geography has been the case from the beginning. All local geographies, as they were defined by hundreds of separate, independent native traditions, were denied in the beginning in favor of an imported and unifying vision of America's natural history. The country, the landscape itself, was eventually defined according to dictates of Progress like Manifest Destiny, and laws like the Homestead Act which reflected a poor understanding of the physical lay of the land.

WHEN I WAS growing up in southern California, I formed the rudiments of a local geography—eucalyptus trees, February rains, desert cottontails. I lost much of it when my family moved to New York City, a move typical of the modern, peripatetic style of American life, responding to the exigencies of divorce and employment. As a boy I felt a hunger to know the American landscape that was extreme; when I was finally able to travel on my own, I did so. Eventually I visited most of the United States, living for brief periods of time in Arizona, Indiana, Alabama, Georgia, Wyoming, New Jersey, and Montana before settling years ago in western Oregon.

The astonishing level of my ignorance confronted me everywhere I went. I knew early on that the country could not be held together in a few phrases, that its geography was magnificent and incomprehensible, that a man or woman could devote a lifetime to its elucidation and still feel in the end that he or she had but sailed many thousands of miles over the surface of the ocean. So I came into the habit of traversing landscapes I wanted to know with local tutors and reading what had previously been written about, and in, those places. I came to value exceedingly novels and essays and works of nonfiction that connected human enterprise to real and specific places, and I grew to be mildly distrustful of work that occurred in no particular place, work so cerebral and detached as to be refutable only in an argument of ideas.

These sojourns in various corners of the country infused me, somewhat to my surprise on thinking about it, with a great sense of hope. Whatever despair I had come to feel at a waning sense of the real land and the emergence of false geographies—elements of the land being manipulated, for example, to create erroneous but useful patterns in advertising—was dispelled by the depth of a single person's local knowledge, by the serenity that seemed to come with that intelligence. Any harm that might be done by people who cared nothing for the land, to whom it was not innately worthy but only something ultimately for sale, I thought, would one day have to meet this kind of integrity, people with the same dignity and transcendence as the land they occupied. So when I traveled, when I rolled my sleeping bag out on the shores of the Beaufort Sea or in the high pastures of the Absaroka Range in Wyoming, or at the bottom of the Grand Canyon, I absorbed those particular testaments to life, the indigenous color and songbird song, the smell of sun-bleached rock, damp earth, and wild honey, with some crude appreciation of the singular magnificence of each of those places. And the reassurance I felt expanded in the knowledge that there were, and would likely always be, people speaking out whenever they felt the dignity of the earth imperiled in these places.

The promulgation of false geographies, which threaten the fundamental notion of what it means to live somewhere, is a current with a stable and perhaps growing countercurrent. People living in New York City are familiar with the stone basements, the cratonic geology, of that island and have a feeling for birds migrating through in the fall, their sequence and number. They do not find the city alien but human, its attenuated natural history merely different from that of rural Georgia or Wisconsin. I find the countermeasure, too, among Eskimos who cannot read but who might engage you for days on the subtleties of sea-ice topography. And among men and women who, though they have followed in the footsteps of their parents, have come to the conclusion that they cannot farm or fish or log in the way their ancestors did; the finite boundaries to this sort of wealth have appeared in their lifetime. Or among young men and women who have taken several decades of book-learned agronomy, zoology, silviculture and horticulture, ecology, ethnobotany, and fluvial geomorphology and turned it into a new kind of local knowledge, who have taken up residence in a place and sought, both because of and in spite of their education, to develop a deep intimacy with it. Or they have gone to work, idealistically, for the National Park Service or the fish and wildlife services or for a private institution like the Nature Conservancy. They are people to whom the land is more than politics or economics. These are people for whom the land is alive. It feeds them, directly, and that is how and why they learn its geography.

IN THE END, then, if you begin among the blue crabs of Chesapeake Bay and wander for several years, down through the Smoky Mountains and back to the bluegrass hills, along the drainages of the Ohio and into the hill country of Missouri, where in summer a chorus of cicadas might drown out human conversation, then up the Missouri itself, reading on the way the entries of Meriwether Lewis and William Clark and musing on the demise of the plains grizzly and the sturgeon, cross west into the drainage of the Platte and spend the evenings with Gene Weltfish's *The Lost Universe,* her book about the Pawnee who once thrived there, then drop south to Palo Duro Canyon and the irrigated farms of the Llano Estacado in Texas, turn west across the Sangre de Cristo, southernmost of the Rocky Mountain ranges, and move north and west up onto the slickrock mesas of Utah, those browns and oranges, the ocherous hues reverberating in the deep canyons, then go north, swinging west to the insular ranges that sit like battleships in the pelagic space of Nevada, camp at the steaming edge of sulphur springs in the Black Rock Desert, where alkaline pans are glazed with a ferocious light, a heat to melt iron, then cross the northern Sierra Nevada, waist-deep in summer snow in the passes, to descend to the valley of the Sacramento, and rise through groves of elephantine redwoods in the Coast Range, to arrive at Cape Mendocino, before Balboa's Pacific, cormorants and gulls, gray whales headed north for Unimak Pass in the Aleutians, the winds crashing down on you, facing the ocean over the blue ocean that gives the scene its true vastness, making this crossing, having been so often astonished at the line and the color of the land, the ingenious lives of its plants and animals, the varieties of its darknesses, the intensity of the stars overhead, you would be ashamed to discover, then, in yourself, any capacity to focus on ravages in the land that left you unsettled. You would have seen so much, breathtaking, startling, and outsize, that you might not be able for a long time to break the spell, the sense, especially finishing your journey in the West, that the land had not been as rearranged or quite as compromised as you had first imagined.

After you had slept some nights on the beach, however, with that finite line of the ocean before you and the land stretching out behind you, the wind first battering then cradling you, you would be compelled by memory, obligated by your own involvement, to speak of what left you troubled. To find the rivers dammed and shrunken, the soil washed away, the land fenced, a tracery of pipes and wires and roads laid down everywhere, blocking and channeling the movement of water and animals, cutting the eye off repeatedly and confining it—you had expected this. It troubles you no more than your despair over the ruthlessness, the insensitivity, the impetuousness of modern life. What underlies this obvious change, however, is a less noticeable pattern of disruption: acidic lakes, skies empty of birds, fouled beaches, the poisonous slags of industry, the sun burning like a molten coin in ruined air.

It is a tenet of certain ideologies that man is responsible for all that is ugly, that everything nature creates is beautiful. Nature's darkness goes partly unreported, of course, and human brilliance is often perversely ignored. What is true is that man has a power, literally beyond his comprehension, to destroy. The lethality of some of what he manufactures, the incompetence with which he stores it or seeks to dispose of it, the cavalier way in which he employs in his daily living substances that threaten his health, the leniency of the courts in these matters (as though products as well as people enjoyed the protection of the Fifth Amendment), and the treatment of open land, rivers, and the atmosphere as if, in some medieval way, they could still be regarded as disposal sinks of infinite capacity, would make you wonder, standing face to in the wind at Cape Mendocino, if we weren't bent on an errand of madness.

The geographies of North America, the myriad small landscapes that make up the national fabric, are threatened—by ignorance of what makes them unique, by utilitarian attitudes, by failure to include them in the moral universe, and by brutal disregard. A testament of minor voices can clear away an ignorance of any place, can inform us of its special qualities; but no voice, by merely telling a story, can cause the poisonous wastes that saturate some parts of the land to decompose, to evaporate. This responsibility falls ultimately to the national community, a vague and fragile entity to be sure, but one that, in America, can be ferocious in exerting its will.

Geography, the formal way in which we grapple with this areal mystery, is finally knowledge that calls up something in the land we recognize and respond to. It gives us a sense of place and a sense of community. Both are indispensable to a state of well-being, an individual's and a country's.

ONE AFTERNOON on the Siuslaw River in the Coast Range of Oregon, in January, I hooked a steelhead, a sea-run trout, that told me, through the muscles of my hands and arms and shoulders, something of the nature of the thing I was calling "the Siuslaw River." Years ago I had stood under a pecan tree in Upson County, Georgia, idly eating the nuts, when slowly it occurred to me that these nuts would taste different from pecans growing somewhere up in South Carolina. I didn't need a sharp sense of taste to know this, only to pay attention at a level no one had ever told me was necessary. One November dawn, long before the sun rose, I began a vigil at the Dumont Dunes in the Mojave Desert in California, which I kept until a few minutes after the sun broke the horizon. During that time I named to myself the colors by which the sky changed and by which the sand itself flowed like a rising tide through grays and silvers and blues into yellows, pinks, washed duns, and fallow beiges.

It is through the power of observation, the gifts of eye and ear, of tongue and nose and finger, that a place first rises up in our mind; afterward it is memory that carries the place, that allows it to grow in depth and complexity. For as long as our records go back, we have held these two things dear, landscape and memory. Each infuses us with a different kind of life. The one feeds us, figuratively and literally. The other protects us from lies and tyranny. To keep landscapes intact and the memory of them, our history in them, alive, seems as imperative a task in modern time as finding the extent to which individual expression can be accommodated before it threatens to destroy the fabric of society.

If I were to now visit another country, I would ask my local companion, before I saw any museum or library, any factory or fabled town, to walk me in the country of his or her youth, to tell me the names of things and how, traditionally, they have been fitted together in a community. I would ask for the stories, the voice of memory over the land. I would ask to taste the wild nuts and fruits, to see their fishing lures, their bouquets, their fences. I would ask about the history of storms there, the age of the trees, the winter color of the hills. Only then would I ask to see the museums. I would want first the sense of a real place, to know that I was not inhabiting an idea. I would want to know the lay of the land first, the real geography, and take some measure of the love of it in my companion before I stood before the paintings or read works of scholarship. I would want to have something real and remembered against which I might hope to measure their truth.

9

EFFLEURAGE:
THE STROKE OF FIRE

L ET ME BEGIN by confessing some prevarication. The man called here Jack is not named Jack. He does not live near Chinook, which town doesn't exist in the Coast Range of Oregon. But this story is truthfully set in that country, and what I am about to write down—people's emotions, a natural history of the region, the description of a wood-fired kiln, an aesthetic of anagama ceramics—is as true to what I witnessed as I can make it. If the story that follows is flawed by my tactic, I can't help it. I know no other way to protect the people and the place in their privacy, without which there would be no story for me to tell.

I'VE WALKED IN the Quartz Creek drainage near my home in the Cascade Mountains for almost thirty years, and recently have begun to feel I've reached a kind of agreement with the beaver living on its lower stretch, despite obvious manifold gaps in my understanding of their lives. For these years and longer, until he was incapacitated by a stroke, my downriver neighbor has trapped and killed them and sold their pelts, a tactic of life that never arrived for me, though I, too, have sought something from them. I wanted permission to remove, from the back eddies and banks of their reserve, twigs of alder, willow, and cottonwood which they'd stripped of edible bark. I regarded the abandoned cobs as lumber needed neither for dams nor for shelter. That permission could come in only one way, as I saw it: I would need to make restitution. I would have to establish reciprocity with them.

Managing an arrangement like this is like starting life over in the woods with no help, though I've been at the practice awhile. I've met men of my own culture—middle-class, educated, white—engaged in a similar way, exploring moral relations with what we still differentiate as "the natural world." Mostly, in my understanding, equity here comes down to listening. With the beaver, I stand where they've been felling timber or sit somewhere on creek cobbles by willows they've been cutting into. I remain a few hours, not trying to achieve anything, just trying to listen. I then gather a few beaver sticks, depending, and go home. Each one I pick up I heft. I try to get its measure. Are you finished with this one? I think. May I take this one?

I put the sticks in my truck and add them to a pile at home. Most are small, a few feet long, maybe an inch through. In this tenuous exchange with the Quartz Creek beaver, however, a few stout logs—eight or ten inches through, ten or twelve feet long after I buck them—have also come my way. It's taken more than a year to assemble a half cord of beaver wood. I need four cords. It doesn't bother me that this is going to take a while. The slowness of it is another lesson.

The beaver wood is for a particular fire, to be stoked in the maw of a large pottery kiln in the central Coast Range. Fed splits, it will mount and intensify until in the sixtieth hour, devouring Douglas fir, maple, hemlock, and alder chunks the size of a man's leg, it will be as nuclear in aspect as anything seen on Earth. The wood heat will surge through the kiln at 2400 degrees Fahrenheit, rippling like a river through decks of pottery, clay stabilized just shy of a threshold beyond which it would buckle and ooze like volcanic magma.

The kiln I keep in mind stands in a copse of red alder a few miles from the crossroads village of Chinook. It's misleading to say that someone owns the kiln, in the sense of possessing it like an automobile or a painting, but the man we shall call Jack is its chief interpreter. I'm inclined to call him the kiln's human companion, though paragraphs from now you may choose some other appellation. Local people call it Jack's kiln; or they say the Dragon Kiln, because sometimes flame lashes Gorgon-like from its sideports, because the cavity of its mouth roars white-orange when it's being fed. And because, over a three-day firing, its brick spine arches.

Some among the group of potters who fire there speak of the kiln as though it were sentient. I've watched Jack run his hand over its heated flanks, a light stroke, the way a man might massage the swollen belly of a pregnant woman. Effleurage, it's called. The tender, encouraging motion of his hand is a sign that one is not within the realm of a technology here, but nearer cooperation with a mystery.

When the kiln is hibernating and I'm at Jack's to cut wood, I've still seen him reach for it, his inquiring touch lingering while he considers where, exactly, to stack new wood so that the splits will rotate in right, meld into a flow of firewood so they will wind up at the mouth of the kiln at the right moment, dry, and with the least human effort.

Once Jack and I were felling black locust in the town of Forest Grove near Pacific University, where in 1974 he took a degree in ceramics and comparative religion. I glanced across at him—the two of us quick-lopping limbs with axes—an affirmation without words. It seemed we were sprung on white threads, tethers that rose from our shoulders into the bright September sky and shuddered in the wind's carry across mountains to the Dragon Kiln on a far hillside, to cold decks of firewood there, to an adjacent studio in a converted barn where Jack fisted clay and worked antlers, freshwater mussel shells, bird wings, and a dozen other earthy cantles into his handforms. In that moment, breathing black locust perfume, we were the kiln's antennae, gathering histories human and natural embedded in the logs. The wood's stories would debouch in the kiln. What had happened to the trees would imbue the pots.

Years from now, when the beaver firing Jack and I plan is finished, I'll carry back a few bowls, a ceramic mask, maybe a stone whistle. I'll set them amid the cottonwood and alder growing along Quartz Creek, votives placed incongruous on the ground. If I don't, the beaver will intuit something missing, and I will ever after have to walk the creek through their country an exile.

ANAGAMA KILNS like Jack's, wood-burning tube chambers built on a gentle slope to promote draft, burn hot enough to fire porcelain. In 1980, perhaps a dozen of them were operating in the United States; by the late 1990s the number was passing a hundred. Part of the explanation for their popularity lies with the pottery itself. Licked and scorched by wood flame, glazed and encrusted with wood ash, anagama ware contrasts sharply with ware produced in tamer environments like that in an electric kiln. Anagama pots also have standout character because the effects of a wood firing are so much less predictable than those achieved in the carefully modulated heat of other kilns. Even an experienced anagama fire boss may be unable to explain the outcome of a particular firing, not know how to achieve such beauty again. Strikingly distinguished from the domesticated (some would say staid) appearance of much contemporary pottery, anagama ware impinges on the 1990s the way raku pottery impinged on the 1970s. Its popularity, however, has as much to do with the process as the look.

The physical effort required to prepare wood and feed the fire night and day for several days means a small human community has to coalesce. The communal aspect of this protracted firing, and the fact that the fire changes its nature with a change in stokers or the type of wood being burned, attract potters drawn to social cooperation, physical work, and subtle firings. Anagama is the antithesis of the rigid commercial kiln processes that produce the indifferent stoneware people most often buy to vase flowers, dish trinkets, and store their pasta in.

I knew none of this when I sought an invitation to one of two anagama kilns I knew were operating in the Coast Range near my home. I approached a woman I shall call Nora, an internationally known Wasco Indian ceramist, and asked if she'd consider introducing me to one of the anagama communities she fired with. Weeks later she called to say, "I think you and Jack should meet." I thought she meant I should learn the anagama process at Jack's kiln near Chinook, but she meant exactly what she said. Jack, half Hawaiian, had grown up in a logging family. He spent a lot of time in the woods and was caught up in the lives of wild animals. Nora believed we had much in common. Before I ever thought of it, she saw the beaver firing coming. And she knew just how Jack would respond.

THE LANDSCAPE CRADLING the Chinook Dragon Kiln is a patchwork of low-lying pasture and wooded hills, mostly second- and third-growth Douglas fir. (The surrounding area has been heavily and repeatedly logged.) Jack's home stands at the edge of a river valley cleaved by sloughs and wire-fenced into great, green paddocks where meat and dairy cattle graze and where wild birds strike and wheel and glean—herring gulls, ring-billed gulls, crows, cliff swallows, Brewer's blackbirds, red-winged blackbirds, red-tailed hawks, and great blue herons. His few-acre landhold on a southeast-facing slope of alder and Douglas fir sits a few miles inland from the Pacific and includes a beaver-dammed creek.

The kiln shed, roofed with sheet tin and fiberglass panels and corniced with a jerry-built section of clerestory windows, stands on a wooded bench at the back of his property. It closes out most inclement weather—light winter snows and about eighty inches of annual rain—but admits the wind. The shed's wide entrance is bunked with ricks of wood and fronted on one side by two long, shallow sheds jammed with kiln fuel: old-growth hemlock, bundles of trim from planing mills, dimension lumber salvaged from house demolitions and dumps, alder, locust, and cherry logs, Douglas fir limbs, shipping pallets, and furniture stiles.

On each of a dozen visits to Jack's to assist at firings and to deliver wood, I've regarded the kiln as a site of repose. It has the feel of a structure built for semireligious purposes or periodic social gatherings, an Eskimo *kargi* or Hopi kiva. (An unspoken agreement keeps radios, recorded-music players, and cameras out.) Artificial lights are used at night as needed, but only briefly, as though darkness itself were a fuel necessary to the firing. No materials but firewood are stored inside and no other human activity occurs within. After an unloading the kiln is swept clean.

Stepping into this oblong shed on the day before a firing, one enters a trenchlike corridor formed by two six-foot-high walls of dry wood, neatly squared and divided according to species. Passing between these ricks, one arrives at the mouth of the kiln. A semisubterranean tunnel about three feet high, it slopes upward into a hillside at an angle of 12 degrees and is abutted on each flank by a flagstone walkway. These walks, beginning as steps on either side of the main fire door, start at a point about halfway up the catenary arch that describes the kiln's cross section. They rise at a slightly steeper angle than the kiln and run out into the same hillside.

Outside these stone paths are long decks of short lumberwood, kindling-size pieces that will be fed through the kiln's sideports. About twenty-five feet from the front fire door, the kiln narrows to form a smoke trace or underground smoke trail, which carries exhaust gases to a yellow-tan firebrick chimney. The flame path from fire door to chimney cap is about fifty-two feet.

Jack once showed me the original drawing for the design, a stub-pencil sketch on ruled paper torn from a notebook. It is characteristic of Jack that he would take a traditional design idea—the layout for an anagama kiln—and adapt it to a task he envisioned but had not performed, using whatever materials he had to hand. Traditional anagamas have no fixed length, but they typically consist of a main firebox separated from a ware chamber by an open lattice of stacked brick called a bagwall. The kiln tapers at both ends; its floor ascends in a staircase of long, shallow steps to provide level surfaces on what is customarily a 15-degree slope. The vaulted roof is also arched front to back, forming an interior frequently likened to the shape of a candle flame or the inside of an inverted canoe.

Jack's kiln differs in two ways. Its rise is slightly shallower (the consequent reduction in draft, Jack imagined, would promote a reducing or oxygen-poor atmosphere in the ware chamber). And it's got a loading port about halfway back on the right side. Traditional anagamas are loaded through the front fire door.

Although the Japanese are generally credited with perfecting the anagama kiln, the design is Korean, brought over to Japan perhaps as early as the fifth century. All anagamas are cross-draft kilns; air enters at one end, passes through a ware chamber, and exits through a flue. Because of the length of the chamber—the one at Jack's is about nineteen feet—it can take many hours to build uniformly high temperatures throughout. Anagama firings, therefore, tend to be long, from a few days to a month or more. (Longer firings are deliberately designed to retard the rate at which the chamber gains temperature, an approach some prefer for curing the pots.)

The variables in the anagama process, especially with regard to types of wood burned and the way in which it's fired, range toward the incalculable. It is largely for this reason that no other pottery currently produced in the United States departs so dramatically in its conception and execution from traditional European ideas of what constitutes art, beauty, and refinement.

Jack built the Dragon Kiln with a friend in 1985, after first experimenting with a salt kiln, a cave kiln, and other firing methods in pursuit of a particular look, an aesthetic grounded in the forms and colors of the Pacific tidal zone and mountains he'd lived in all his life. He built the refractory (heat-reflecting) interior of the kiln with brick salvaged from the lining of a cannery boiler dumped in the Columbia River near Astoria. In place of a second layer of insulating firebrick, which he couldn't afford, Jack chose a nontraditional route. He cased a second layer of hard brick in several layers of insulating and heat-resistant material— mixtures of fireclay, portland cement, and alumina hydrate reinforced with chicken wire. The outermost skin is a pale gray layer of smooth clay mud checked with sooty cracks. (The Japanese contend that in the best anagamas this last layer always cracks in a pattern like a turtle's shell.) Inset in it above the fire door are a black-tailed deer antler, seashells, and other natural objects on the verge of a handprint at the center.

The kiln walls are about 13 inches thick. The openings to its interior include the main fire door (9" × 10"), which surmounts a draft hole 11 inches high by 14 inches wide; four sideport fire holes (4" × 5") with bottom-hinged firebrick doors; and a side loading port, an open catenary arch 36 inches across on the floor and 35 inches high (this entry is bricked up and insulated before a firing begins). At the end of a firing, the draft hole and the doored ports are bricked and mudded over and the pots are left to cook. During a seven-day cooling period the temperature drops about 2300 degrees, to about 90 degrees Fahrenheit.

A trained eye, one that had taken in the functional architecture of the famed anagama kilns of medieval Japan in Aichi and Shiga Prefectures near Nagoya and studied firings at modern Japanese anagama kilns, would see the lines of Jack's kiln fighting the idea of institutionalized anagama. Indeed, that well-versed visitor, noting that neither the length nor the species of wood here is standardized, that stoking procedures are not regimented nor the stoking shifts formalized, would be inclined to call the Dragon Kiln process chaotic. In curé Jack, however, he would recognize an anagama master (a notion to make Jack smile, break into laughter at the absurd, and quickly change the subject.)

The idea that the individual ceramic artist possesses genius and that the kiln is a servant technology, long the prevailing European view, is replaced at the Dragon Kiln by the idea of a community of artists working alongside a powerful and enigmatic partner. The learned visitor from Aichi, studying the scene at Jack's on a winter night while rain pounds the tin roof, observing a sweat-drenched stoker shooting a thirty-four-inch split of clear fir through the fire door and hearing the flame careening through pots and sculpture would recognize anagama, however deinstitutionalized.

One evening, after Jack and I had unloaded three quarters of a cord of wood from my trailer (a firing typically consumes four cords of wood in seventy-two hours), we took seats in his living room and I asked about his history with the kiln. He recalled building at least six chimneys before getting the draft right. He burned up two or three steel damper plates in the smoke trace ("They couldn't take the energy") and experimented with various air delivery systems before finding one he felt worked. (Well designed, the latter system ensures the kiln will reach and hold temperatures within a certain time frame; it conveys heat evenly through the ware chamber; and it maintains a reducing or oxidizing atmosphere around the pots, as required.)

Jack's still not entirely happy with the design. And the kiln itself, he points out, changes with every firing. "It changes *during* a firing," he says. "It's always changing, growing older. Like you."

A COMMUNITY OF POTTERS—a core group of ten or twelve but sometimes more than twenty—fires regularly at Jack's every three or four months. They cut and haul wood together and they share chores and potluck food at the firings, around which rotate, like planets, a certain number of Jack's neighbors, curious visitors from outside the United States, assorted friends, dogs, and a few children. Though their aesthetics are divergent, the potters take obvious pleasure in examining one another's work before and after a firing. Some are seasoned clay artists, others determined amateurs, but no system of seniority prevails. Jack's is the only conspicuous presence.

Early on in the development of his art, Jack wrapped his pots in natural material—grass, feathers—to create surface effects. Seeing how high-temperature fire warped pots, he began melting species of rock—feldspar, obsidian, basalt—into and through his forms. This way, he said, he became "involved for a very short time in the geology of the rock." When we talked about wood that night in his living room he referred to bark as "the expressive and emotional face of the tree." (The distinctive character of an anagama pot comes largely from its contact with gases and ash from mineral-laden wood bark.)

Perhaps the most compelling aspects of Jack's art are the near recklessness with which he approaches the requirement for order, his constant experimentation with unpredictable materials, and the extent to which he includes the accidental. (A Japanese formal garden is considered more beautiful if a few fallen leaves lie scattered about. Jack's taste approximates this principle of *shibumi*.) His singular devotion to the refinement of his aesthetic, and the fact that he eschews notions of commerce and career, have made Jack, at the age of forty-eight, something of a hero to other Oregon artists. He's also criticized for favoring process over product; for his lack of interest in perfecting technique ("People focused in on technique," he told me once, "tend to want to make the same thing all over again"); and for his fascination with funk, with most any wamper-jawed object.

The evening we talked about his history with the Dragon Kiln, Jack discoursed about his neighbors at length, as if this group of people, none of them potters, had as much to do with what Jack was up to as clay or alder wood. He wasn't gossiping. He was clearly intrigued with their skills, their farming success, interested in their self-sufficiency and savvy. Jack grew up within a few miles of here. He joined the Navy after high school and went to Vietnam, but he's deeply rooted in this agrarian landscape. Until 1978, when he became a full-time potter, he supported his wife,

Carol, and himself working as a logger for Crown Zellerbach. His respect for several older men who farm nearby, and who drop in regularly during firings, is based on regard for their physical endurance, the depth of their experience with the surrounding country, and a knowledge of tools and techniques of which they are the last masters. I've seen Jack's cups and pots in their living rooms and kitchens, and I've seen their families' grave monuments curing in his kiln. Jack's heritage is theirs, his art merely another mystery, like the life of the wood duck.

In the years since he first started working with clay, Jack has come to focus exclusively on local materials; he serves as an anchor for a local community of potters; and he prefers to show his work in local galleries. I've never known an artist more insistently local. It took many conversations before Jack concurred there was little appreciation around Chinook for what he wants to do. He wants to redefine the relationship of a clay artist to natural materials in an era of manufactured materials; and he wants to redefine the artist's relationship to community in an era of gallery courting and self-promotion. The absence of local understanding only compels him to pursue his ideals more ardently. He doesn't want to embrace any artistic success that would take him out of daily contact with his neighbors.

"The kiln's very American," Jack said once. "Everyone is welcome, the accomplished artist with commissioned work, the beginner. We've had a Japanese anagama artist feeding wood alongside a twelve-year-old girl at her first firing. We're always tinkering, you know, looking for new ways to help the community, to make good pots, to involve the wood, the history of the trees. The residue of animals that once lived here is in the clay, my neighbor's cows walk around on it out there."

Jack wants to narrow the rift between human society and nature in a work of art. And he wants to insinuate that art in the lives of people who feel they do not have the education or the social standing to appreciate it. In *Wood-Fired Stoneware and Porcelain* (1995), author J. Troy underscores an often repeated maxim of modern anagama, explaining that it's a spirited rejection of an older English tradition of mastering the materials and exercising a high degree of control to produce an object stopped in time like a portrait. Fire potters, he says, are set apart by a desire to enter the mystery, not merely accommodate it. For them, he writes, quoting another historian, "the pot may be considered not so much a static object as a record of the play of various forces."

A striking difference between Troy, an international spokesman for wood-fire technique, and Jack is that for Jack these forces are more pervasive, unruly, and beautiful, and collaboration with them perhaps more salvific.

Walking me up to my truck that evening, Jack said, "When I started sketching the kiln out, talking to potters up in Portland and wherever, talking to my dad, you know, thinking where am I gonna get the materials for this, how am I gonna learn it, I saw this was a big, big, big idea." He shook his head, as if to say it is only by such naïveté, such miscalculation that he ever seems to find illumination. It's also, of course, the beginner's mind to which Buddhists aspire.

Jack asked me to wait at the truck while he ran back to the house. From the gravel drive on the hill I could see bufflehead and American wigeon at rest on a pond, the dark crowns of huge maple trees motionless in the night air, and cattle grazing slow as winter in a pasture where I'd heard coyotes howl. Jack returned with a small package, backstrap meat from an elk he'd taken that fall. In exchange for the wood I'd brought. When I took the package from him I held his hands briefly in mine, then slipped them like a released salmon.

A FIRST-TIME VISITOR to the Dragon Kiln spots the signs posted around the eaves of the kiln shed: QUIET PLEASE, DO NOT DISTURB THE STOKERS; CHECK-OUT TIME 2 A.M.; IF IN DOUBT, STOKE. Stenciled on the side of a wheelbarrow is HARDLY MINING CO. One catches the eclectic array of seats right away. A legless office chair is suspended on cords from the roof beams. Twisted wheelchairs, backless dining chairs, and chairs cobbled together from scrap lumber are clues to funk at the kiln. Taken together with the stokers' clothing ("singewear"), the soot and wood debris that smudges people's faces and clings to their hair, and the mud that forms around the shed entrances during a firing in the rain, the chairs offer a stark contrast to the raison d'être, the spectral eggs visible in a fundament of white heat when a fire door is opened for a stoke.

The first time I came to Jack's, arriving late on a fall evening and walking up the steep drive in a light mist to find him and a friend silhouetted against light projected from the draft hole, I marked the chairs. At night they convey an informal conviviality, suggest the comfort of a battered sofa in a well-used clubhouse. I held back in the mist for a while, watching the two men, the sideways incline of their heads, a gesture of the hand indicating an occasional remark. Later, I would understand that Jack's concentration was on the color of the flame, on listening to sonic amplitudes that signaled the fire's rhythm and intensity, and that he was second-guessing the load, his placement of some three hundred pieces of stemware, flatware, and hollowware. The reactions inside the kiln—quartz inversions in the clay, the melting of glazes in the Hyrcanian fire—belied the tranquility, the domesticity of the scene.

On first encounter Jack seems extremely polite and slightly scattered. Dark brown eyes, short black hair. His corded muscles lean not bulked. He walks quickly, with a slight forward cant as if compensating for a lumbar injury. His habit of lacing his boots in such a way as to bind in his lower pant legs, an assortment of odd ballcaps, and the way his belt bypasses belt loops contribute to an impression of absentmindedness. The idiosyncracies form an effective barrier, however, for someone exceedingly private. Behind the ready laugh, the urgency with which he seeks someone else's view on a problem, he's alert like a wild animal, as focused as a cutting torch.

In the months following our introduction, Jack and I drove about a good deal in his truck or mine, cutting firewood, culling used lumber from dump sites, collecting fresh mussels and clams for dinner. We stopped for anything that looked useful. Sometimes we dug clay.

Jack has a good grasp of local geology and of the soils within fifty miles of his home. I found it difficult at first to grasp "clay." Most clays derive from the disintegration of granitic and feldspathic rock and consist of silicates and aluminum oxides bound with water molecules. Stoneware clays, unlike earthenware clays, hold their shape at very high temperatures; all clays render color according to impurities they contain, mostly metallic oxides of iron and some manganese, copper, and chromium. Clay is further textured and colored by the action of glazes and slips and, in wood-firing, by the deposition of cinders and fly ash, by moisture and minerals in the wood, and by fluctuations in the intensity and quantity of energy in the fire.

Selecting or mixing clay for an anagama firing is like setting out the two-by-fours for a house. While the framing lumber is essential, there's slight hint of the architecture in it.

The chemistry and geology of clays (a staple component of the protracted conversation around a firing), like the throwing of pots, didn't draw me as did the kiln process, the central mystery in anagama. At Jack's an elementary dragon inhaled massive drafts of air from a grove of alders to feed a fire so hot it melted stone, and the earth within it was wrung of water. Around these primal elements, a group of men and women, some with Native American or Asian backgrounds, worked hard on the problematic themes of community life: loyalty, selflessness, respect, generosity. How, they would inquire, feeding wood, can such desirable attributes be maintained in a culture where consumption has replaced communion, where the consumer has replaced the neighbor? More than quartz inversions, more even than potters' gossip sometimes, these topics bearing on communality drove the anagama conversation.

Here is what Gaston Bachelard, the French scientist and philosopher, had to say about the animating element in this event:

Fire is the ultra-living element. It is intimate and universal. It lives in our heart. It lives in the sky. It rises from the depth of the substance and hides there, latent and pent-up, like hate and vengeance. Among all phenomena, it is really the only one to which there can be so definitely attributed the opposing values of good and evil. It shines in paradise. It burns in hell.

THAT NIGHT I CAME UP the hill and met Jack and the others for the first time, I knew I was at the edge of something right away, a kind of knowledge I didn't have but which I might intuit. Given the late hour, I was reluctant to stride up the grade. Someone's dogs might be loose in the bucolic dark. The firings were closed, the community close-knit. Why make room for a stranger? All I possessed, really, was the introduction from Nora, my enthusiasm, and, by a slight stretch, the credential of local residence.

Jack's curious about enthusiasm. His initial handshake was cordial and without preamble we fell into a conversation about wood, which is alchemical for him. We talked like two paleontologists passing an inscrutable bone back and forth. (The first time I brought Jack a load of black locust, a wood with which he was not familiar, he took a narrow split and sat with it, turning it over and examining it carefully, as if it were an expensive vase. He laid it to his cheek to get its moisture. After a while he suggested it compared with cascara by smell and color. He went back to the deck of logs we'd stacked and picked at them with his fingernail. He likened its texture to elderberry wood. A while later he pronounced the locust "imposing" as a kiln wood because of its thick bark. What you could get from an index to firewood—locust's specific gravity, its porosity—was not as interesting to him as the sound of his fingernail popping away from the runnels of its bark.)

The summer after I started firing with Jack I learned a house lot in a nearby town was being cleared of trees and I went to look it over. The owners had felled big-leaf maple, Douglas fir, Lombardy poplar, red cedar, that black locust, and a little cherry. I cut about three cords of locust, maple, and cherry, using my truck like a tractor to skid the big logs free of one other and swamping them out with a limbing ax and a bow saw. I bucked them into thirty-four-inch lengths with a chain saw, split the bolts, and loaded them.

I like working alone at a steady pace, using the mechanical advantage of a truck and employing good hand tools in combination with power tools. The days I was cutting were sweltering, and I gorged on water. I worked the day long damp with sweat. Canada geese and ducks flew by over the river, and when the saw wasn't running I could hear woodpeckers tappeting and osprey cries. Splitting the locust revealed pale green heartwood and creamy white sapwood. It split cleanly through the bole, but called for a wedge higher up in its stout limbs. The cherry split as cleanly, its heartwood golden in the sunlight and bound by a rind of pale tan sapwood. The organic smells were intoxicating. The textures in the saw kerfs drew my eye, drew my hand.

I was refreshed by the physical labor and surprised to find a set of river otter tracks etched sharply in a patch of silt. When I asked the owners, a couple, what decided them to cut the trees down, they shrugged. The man said a larger lawn would improve the property. The woodpeckers, I thought, the osprey, the otters tangent to the trees, were they just to move along now? I nodded politely to his logic.

When I told Jack the story of the man's disdain for the life around him, he asked me to describe the otter tracks. He told me about a time he found a Lincoln-head cent in a coyote scat.

You load the Dragon on hands and knees. You squat in its dank interior like someone preparing to trowel a flower bed. The refractory walls gleam chocolate, the color of impurities boiled out of the brick over time. The tang of a fresh coat of kiln wash rises off the cream-colored floor. The air is damp from a hosing out the day before and cool because of the heat sink of the earth underneath. The stark record of sixty-some firings is apparent where fireclay mortar has cracked or where wood ash has bonded to the walls.

Stacking (or "loading" or "setting") an anagama kiln is guided, as is all else in this process, by a mixture of the irrational and the intuitive, set within the ambit of the known. The same pot fired in a different place in the kiln—high or low, front or back—will come out looking different. It will take its look, too, from the pots it's placed beside. Pots toward the front will be more affected by ash deposits. They'll mature in this, the hottest part of the kiln, in a reducing (oxygen-lean) environment, in which dark black and deep purple wood-ash glazes commonly emerge. The floor at the back of the kiln, where the flame tongue is at its thinnest, is the coolest section, usually. An oxidizing (oxygen-rich) atmosphere here most often produces softer blushes of color. But every kiln has microenvironments; and the way the kiln is loaded sets up wind currents that affect the circulation of the flame and ash, sometimes creating strong back eddies that will accentuate the asymmetric glazing typical of anagama pottery.

The stacker is charged with building the rapids around which the river of fire will stream. The usual practice is to stack tightly near the top to force the flame down to the floor, but the loader must also stack firmly and securely so pieces won't fall over or get knocked down by a stick of side wood. He or she also has to select, in consultation with the artist, a "front" for each piece, the part of it that will face the flame. Some pieces are tumble-stacked together, leaning against each other or a wall; others are set on silicon-carbide shelves, which then are tiered up using posts of the same material or firebricks set on end. To keep melting glazes and slips from bonding pots to the shelves or the floor, the pieces are footed on hand-formed wads of kaolin (a porcelain clay) or similar material.

At Jack's, considering all the variables, a conscientious stacker will want two days to load, though he or she rarely gets it.

Potters bring three sorts of ware to the kiln: unfired pots, called greenware; bisque ware (short for biscuit ware), which has already been fired but at a lower temperature; and ware previously fired at high temperatures that is to be fired over again, anagama style. The majority is bisque ware. Its pale tan, pink, and white coloration gives no indication of the primary colors—ethereal, tortured, deep—that will emerge days hence.

The loader will also set out test bowls, draw tiles, and cone packs. Test bowls contain minerals in loose or powdered form. The way fire affects these bits of glass and rock gives the potters some idea of how they might behave used in glazes at high temperature. Draw tiles (or draw "trials") are pulled from the kiln during a firing. Their condition gives stokers a sense of how various glazes are fusing—though not what their colors might be, because the tiles are cooled too quickly, plunged hissing and spitting into a bucket of water.

Cone packs (or "plaques") are temperature indicators. They consist of four or five pastel-colored clay posts, each one with a different melting point, set up like a picket row of three-inch fangs in a base of high-temperature clay. Six or eight cone packs, placed atop the bagwall and within view of the side stokers, give the fire boss an idea of time and temperature relationships in the kiln and of differences in heat distribution. At Jack's the desired goal most often is to "get cone ten down" at the back of the kiln and to "get twelve down and fourteen leaning a little" at the bagwall. (If the kiln has been gaining temperature at about 108 degrees Fahrenheit per hour, cone twelve will go down at 2383° F, cone fourteen at 2530° F. Above these temperatures, very few things on Earth hold together. The most refractory materials known, carbides like tantalum carbide, borides, and sulfides, and a few elements like hafnium, have melting points approaching 4000° F. Outside these rare and often unstable exotics, common clay—$2SiO_2Al_2O_32H_2O$—is nearly the most heat-resistant earthly compound.)

It's commonly suggested by fire potters that commercial clays don't fare well in wood-fired kilns. Many Dragon Kiln potters mix their own clays. They're after a certain degree of plasticity in the clay body. They'll also blend in preferred fluxes like talc and bone ash that act like shortening in a cake mix. For color they'll wedge in mineral impurities, coarsely or finely ground. And they'll add a greater measure of refractory material like alumina (aluminum oxide) or kaolin to help the pot hold its shape in very high temperatures but still open its pores to the wood ash.

One evening, stoking at a sideport and taking a few extra moments—with the head stoker's permission—to stare into the fire with a pair of welder's glasses, I actually saw the current of white heat moving slowly through the kiln. It flowed visibly around sculpture, vases, and kimchi jars, stroking the larger pieces, as Jack had described. It moved through like a storm front unfolding over low hills and a wooded plain, a silent susurration. The head stoker signaled me to close the port. He didn't want to lose temperature.

I sat there in the darkness, listening to big winds coming in off the Pacific and seething in the alder grove without, to the clatter of rain spat and alder twigs on the corrugated roof. The weather, especially the wind, is one of the uncontrolled natural elements that help form anagama ware; in the stacking and in the stoking of the kiln, however, one can't miss the clear assertion of human will, a desire to exercise authority very much in keeping with human nature, East and West. The Dragon Kiln potters deliberately try to achieve some of the very effects their progenitors in Japan were trying to prevent, by not paying such scrupulous attention to heat and temperature fluctuation, and by not controlling so tightly the spacing and duration of cycles of reduction and oxidizing.

"We have this incredible tool," Jack mused one day. "The hard part is knowing what you want."

AT MIDPOINT IN a long firing, the kiln and its environs have come to feel as comfortable as old clothes to the participants. To an outsider, the scene may seem as intimidating as an unfamiliar urban neighborhood. Especially confusing is the temporal disarray. Three or four people may be upstairs in the loft above Jack's studio, sleeping off a night shift. Someone else might be grilling a whole salmon on a bed of coals taken from the kiln's firebox. Someone else is racking splits of wood in a rick closer to the head stoker's reach. Another person might be shaking off a nap with a cold breakfast, thrown together from an array of casseroles and fresh and fast food arranged on long tables in a covered area adjacent to Jack's studio.

It's hard to discern a clear pattern of work, but the fire is never without a head stoker, without a personality to engage with. Someone's always driving. It's the map that eludes an observer, and to a lesser degree the participants.

THE FIRE-BAKING of clay, the oldest and most widespread human art, begins with wood fire. Fred Olsen, in a review of the history of ceramics, calls wood "the most alluring of fuels," but its allure defies analysis. To a stoker it has two salient characteristics beyond its species and mineral content. First, how wet is it? What is its degree of greenness? While green wood may come into play at some point (to hold temperature but not increase it), it's dry wood the stoker wants. Each split of wood, secondly, has its own volume and surface area. The smaller and drier the pieces, the farther back in the kiln the flame will reach. Softwoods will produce fewer coals than hardwoods and release their energy more quickly, though hardwoods hold more potential energy in any given volume of wood. Barkwood will provide most of the ash and cinder for natural glazing, but the stoker, either as a variable in his or her own regime or in concert with other head stokers, might want to stay with lumberwood for a few hours in order to raise temperature in the kiln more quickly.

Ideally, the head stoker will examine every piece of wood he or she pitches in, watching especially for painted wood, plywood, wood with nails, and driftwood. Their salt, metal, glues, and enamels could mar the pots. (Such possibilities, again, might be attractive to potters at a particular firing. As a rule, however, stokers set aside any material likely to corrode the interior of the kiln, such as driftwood, because of its salt content.)

Whatever wood a stoker selects and with whatever rhythm it's fed, the combination will have three basic effects. It will raise or lower temperature (a measure of the intensity of the energy being released by combustion). It will increase or lower heat (a measure of the quantity of energy flooding the interior of the kiln). And it will change the atmosphere in the kiln. Understoking makes more oxygen available, producing an oxidizing atmosphere for the pots. It will also promote an increase in temperature and allow for fuller combustion of carbon in the wood, resulting in fewer coals. Overstoking removes oxygen from the kiln, creating a reducing atmosphere. It retards a rise in temperature, but permits more ash to circulate in the kiln wind. It also produces an excess of coals, which may crowd the firebox and have to be removed.

Depending on the stage of the firing, and what effect the stoker is after, he or she will favor either a reducing or an oxidizing fire. (The nature of Jack's kiln and the method of firing it are such that it's more often in an oxidizing state.) A stoker can quickly judge the condition of the kiln atmosphere with a glance at the chimney cap. A dunce hat of flame there indicates reduction, a cone of clear shimmering air, oxidation.

Troy writes that fire has five important characteristics: tempo, velocity, sound, color, and texture. By a regular visual inspection of the fire, by exchanging information with the side stokers, noting the gradual collapse of the cones, and paying attention to the roar, a good stoker can keep track of the behavior of the fire and convey that information to his or her successor at a shift change. (At Jack's much of this is written down in a kiln log for later review.)

Traditionally, anagama firings start out slowly. The fire at the Dragon Kiln is lit on bare ground in front of the draft hole. It's a small fire, meant to heat the interior of the kiln very gradually. Hours later, after the kiln has developed a good draft, the fire is pushed into the firebox. The sideport doors, left open to vent moisture from the kiln during the initial heating phase, are closed and the fire is slowly built up. Sixty or so hours later the temperature at the front of the kiln peaks at over 2400 degrees. The head stoker holds it there for another twelve hours or so, a final, high-temperature "soaking" of the sculpture and pots.

Firings at Jack's always seem to end about two in the morning. The last few sticks might be passed around and people present might hand-rub them along their length before sliding them through the fire door, sometimes with a generous soaking of sake. The fire door is then closed for the last time and mudded over along with the sideports and the main draft. The chimney is damped and capped, and the fire is left to burn itself out. At a temperature of about 1075 degrees, a few days after the kiln is shut down, its interior has cooled enough to no longer glow. For the first time since a fire was struck at its mouth, the inside of the Dragon is dark.

SOME FRONT STOKERS WORK in a relaxed manner but are highly focused. Others are fastidiously organized and intense. Some exude confidence, others are unsure, self-conscious. Over the years, Jack's seen many personalities come and go at the Dragon Kiln, and he has been through the trials of human community with them. In a group like this, where little money changes hands, no one who arrives without wood or food stays long. Jack and the others pose silent questions to any newcomer: Can you imagine the other fellow's needs? Can you recognize and take on the less glamorous, more onerous tasks? Can you put a young visitor at ease? Will you give as much as you take?

Since it requires an integrated human community to properly load, fuel, and operate an anagama kiln, keeping the community well integrated is a sine qua non of memorable anagama pots. As the linchpin of a leaderless group, Jack exerts a great influence on the direction a firing takes; and for as serious an artist as he is, he shows remarkable flexibility and patience. During several firings I watched him observe petulance, competition, and immaturity without a ripple. To him, such expressions of frustration are just another stick in that particular fire.

When I pressed him, about a year after we met, he confided that only three things really bothered him. People who didn't bring wood or ever join wood-gathering or wood-cutting expeditions. Loadings that went too quickly, because everyone waited until the last minute to bring their pots. And the way people scattered so soon after an unloading. There was no time, then, to savor what happened, to study it.

In the beginning, probably like any outsider, I perceived a relatively seamless group of fifteen or so people ebbing and flowing in their emotions through a firing, all of them clearly at ease with one another and enjoying one another's company. (Very few human events anymore, of course, bring people together this intensely for this long on a regular basis.) But over the two years I attended firings, I saw people who didn't have much to offer except their pots eased gently out of the group; and I watched others struggle with new responsibilities as a fire boss. One person's dog interrupted another person's sleep or ate someone's unguarded food and it was roundly denounced to its owner. People kvetched when someone else wouldn't relinquish his position as head stoker. What I saw was the prosaic stumbling in human endeavor. What always seemed praiseworthy about this polyglot group, what overrode any individual failing, was their willingness to work, to cooperate, to give in to one another. And Jack was the exemplar.

Toward the end of my time in their community, the Dragon Kiln potters were getting ready for their first group show. The artist's statements they prepared for it were revealing. Wrote one, "There is no switch to flip to turn the kiln on, and no computer to monitor its progress, so there is room for human ignorance, and therefore room for brilliance as well." A ceramics instructor wrote of the kiln sometimes speaking "a language hard to understand," and of the harmonious relationship he found between the "gestural qualities" of his pieces and the action of the wood fire. And he wrote that the ritual of firing helped him reestablish the connections he wanted to have with other people and with the landscape he lived in.

Nearly every potter used the same terms of wonder, curiosity, and respect in referring to the Dragon Kiln community and in describing ceramic sculpture and pots. They saw each as integral to the most important element of a firing—creation, making beautiful and useful objects within the frame of a working community.

A potter who'd attended firings at the kiln since the early nineties wrote of how Jack's neighbors—loggers, fishermen, farmers, store owners, high school teachers—and a small but steady stream of visitors had affected him. "It is the most unusual coming together of divergent personalities and occupations that I have ever seen," he wrote. "And each time I look at one of the pots that came from the kiln, I am reminded of these many different people who made a difference in the looks of that pot."

Jack remarked once that stoking the fire was like "groping in an energy field." He could as easily have said this of building relations with potters in his community. It annoys him when people don't attend to each other, or presume they know what someone else is going to say. In response to this tendency toward inattentiveness he once removed a pyrometer (a device that measures temperatures inside a kiln) which he'd reluctantly agreed to install. "People were watching the pyrometer," he told me. "They weren't listening to the kiln."

SAD MOMENTS COME at a firing—a pot is seen to break down inside or someone suffers a burn or an allergic reaction to the terrific heat. The saddest moments are at the end, when it's finished and there's nothing to do but wait out the week and see what's happened. People drift off to their cars and trucks, some omitting their good-byes. Others collapse in makeshift beds or on sleeping pads in the summer woods and sleep away the rest of the night.

One time I drove up to Jack's the evening before an unloading. I found him in the shed, his back to me, his hands to the kiln's blunt nose above the fire door. He brushed its surface like a man comforting a stranded whale. I went down to the house and waited for him.

In my memory unloadings often fall on sunny days. (Because

so many in the community have other jobs—nurse, set designer, computer technician, freelance photographer—firings usually begin on a Thursday and end on a Sunday, with the unloading a week later.) Robins, Swainson's thrushes, and fox sparrows call from the alders, and more children than attend a firing are running around, with more dogs. The mood is festive, but anxious. While most of the work in the kiln is personal or even experimental, some potters have expensive commissioned pieces inside and may be on tenterhooks. The chimney is uncapped and undamped and the stoking ports are opened to vent the last of the heat before the wall in the loading port is dismantled. The interior is always warm and, entering the kiln, it's easy to believe it's still breathing, still alive.

It takes only half as many hours to unload or "draw" the kiln. Each piece is examined first in the low-temperature light of an incandescent bulb, then handed to someone outside who looks at it quickly in the warmer but still shaded light of the kiln shed. Finally it's passed to someone in bright sunshine, where the pale ware of ten days ago reveals itself fully. Here, as if by a miracle, are raucous purples, coy yellows, prosaic blues, belligerent reds, and what the late poet Denise Levertov called ardent whites. Here are glazes thin as breath, cracks that enhance a form rather than mar it because of where they occur. Here are deposits of ash which unify, like a calligrapher's *hana* stroke, elements in a piece that previously were not well integrated. Here is a pot that raises nothing but a shrug from its maker and causes someone else to do a double take.

The pots—jars, tiles, masks, urns, torsos, bowls, faux industrial tools, water pitchers—come forth sintered, flashed, scorched, ash-decorated, swollen, fatigued, and composed. Some glazes are seen to have produced unfamiliar colors, other glazes to have weeped across a piece like colored rain. As the pieces come from the kiln they're arranged on large tables where a milling crowd of potters and their families and everyone's friends can examine them at leisure, lifting, comparing, appraising. Meaning bursts through in disjointed ways in some pieces that are technically flawed. Other work shows exceptional technical skill but no strong vision. Classic pieces contrast with kitsch, the whimsical with the romantic.

Gradually exposed to light, the interior of the kiln appears tomblike. Beneath one sideport a large jar sits bunked in ashes, seemingly the dust of centuries. At another sideport a cluster of tumble-stacked, unglazed cups looks like a nest of dinosaur eggs. Pots that have buckled may have destroyed stronger pots alongside them. Dripping glazes may have glued some pots to the shelves. (They can often be tapped free using a wooden mallet, a loosening achieved not by direct blows but by setting up a harmonic vibration.) On the surface of pots from the front of the kiln you can read the generational and evolutionary phases of the firing, the layering up of ash. Pieces clink now. Glaze and clay have become glass and stone.

What Jack calls "successful" is any pot that offers good evidence of the anagama process. It might not in itself be a beautiful object. I asked him once what a potter means at an unloading by referring to a pot as "a failure." Is it a failure because it cracked or was otherwise distorted by the heat and temperature? Or was it an aesthetic failure because the color was unappealing?

After a moment he asked, "What's the difference?"

The ceramics historian Daniel Rhodes has written, "Often the kiln confers graces on the pots which exceed even the potter's dreams. The greatest pots are those one meets coming from the kiln as strong objects; they may seem in texture or color quite beyond one's power to visualize or predict."

After an unloading, after everyone has departed, Jack has a frustrated and somewhat forlorn look on his face which perhaps nothing but the preparation for another firing can cure. He is left with his own pots, and perhaps the work of someone who couldn't make arrangements to get there that day.

"The best pots," he told me one evening, "make me understand something I never did before." After a pause he said, "In wood fire, what I'm involved with in myself is the part some people call 'nature.' It's an emotional thing that's grown into me through the things I have eaten and the space that I have lived in, and stuff that has seeped into me over a very long period of time. I know that. And if we separate ourselves from nature, we will never understand wood fire. We will never appreciate it in its ultimate sense."

A characteristic movement of Jack's hands is to bring two disparate things together, keeping them there side by side. Sometimes he seems like a man come from some great distance in time. One of the first things Nora told me about him was that he was "about a thousand years old."

MY CONVERSATIONS AND working days with Jack were always marked by long silences, as if we were fishing for steelhead together in the coastal rivers and not inclined to talk much because it broke our concentration on the fish. Late one night when he was stoking the front port and we were sitting together for four or five minutes at a time, Jack told me about a pot he'd placed in Tanner's River, the river the creek he lives by drains into. He told me he waded out and put it down in the current and left it there for several months, and that when he came back and pulled it out, holding it up to the light and letting the water spill down his arms, he was astonished to find he felt the same way he'd felt taking the pot out of the kiln. Jack, who is childless, never looked across at me but kept his eyes on the fire.

When he sat down again, I told him that for several years I had been walking in the current of the river by my house. In summer the current is clear, the river no deeper than three feet, and you can see the bottom on the other side more than three hundred feet away. It's a strong current, I said, but I'd learned to walk in it without a staff by not having any specific goal, no particular place I had to get to, nothing I had to do. I just wanted to be in the current. I wanted to feel it against my legs, feel it against my arms when I swept them back and forth in the cold water. I wanted the undulation of it to enter my flesh. I wanted to take the physical sensation and translate it.

"The kiln's just like the river," said Jack. "We're trying to get back inside something here."

The next morning, before I left, I walked up the creek on Jack's place to a spot where beaver had been working. They'd built a series of dams, and the water there was so calm I could follow the convolution of clouds in its surface. Ravens called around me, that complicated raw cry and pop and cluck and mutter they can make. I thought of the beaver back home on Quartz Creek, and imagined beaver all over the mountains carrying on despite all that had happened to the country they lived in. I saw their forbearance.

At the next unloading, Jack gave me one of his large pots. It was fall. I took it home and put it out in the middle of the river to overwinter.

MIDWAY THROUGH my time at the kiln, Jack had a one-person show at a local gallery. I came up for the opening on a cool, wet October night.

Jack's work was poorly displayed, the pieces not arranged to show them at any advantage. Too much of it was set against a wall, like painting. Jack had set some firewood and shanks of bark out to signal a larger causality. He'd also posted this statement on the wall in typescript:

Each pot tells a *story*. The story emerges in the process. It becomes visible in layers—layers of earth and fire, layers of emotion, ideas and change. Between the layers there seems to be a vibration—a connecting field of invisible dust, only felt, unmeasured and pointing to the unknown.

The wood-fire kiln is the window that opens into this beautiful dynamic place. Through this window I'm allowed to participate and engage in this fundamental process. Between the living layers of expression, the kiln holds me, somewhat like a rock might be held in the middle of the river's flow. We're both looking for possibilities on our journey to the sea. Maybe I could compare it to a burning star, held in the center of this vibrating space, waiting to burn out.

Wherever or whatever this place is, it's where I'm happy—between the layers of ash, floating, swirling, bouncing along like some lucky, created fool. Enjoy the pottery and thank you for coming to take a look.

People mill through the gallery for an hour before Jack begins a formal slide presentation. The crowd is an admixture of university professors, art critics from Portland, potters from inside and outside the Dragon Kiln community, local environmentalists, some of Jack's logging and farming neighbors, and a three-man crew he's been working with at a paying job aboard a National Marine Fisheries Service boat.

His presentation is disarmingly open, unpretentious. He begins by saying that, starting out, he wanted to make pots that reflected "what I grew up around" and that he liked "unpredictable energy." Because he "didn't have a lot of money," he took "whatever materials were available to me and tried to make it work." He became fascinated with flame patterns and with the way his pots were warping and bending, revealing the space around them. He started "looking more closely at living textures" in the woods and tide pools. He began melting local rock into his pots. "This kind of thing," he says, "got me out of my studio." When he saw the way salt ate into some of his vessels, it occurred to him "that there was a new way to make an opening in a pot."

He says he wanted to make pottery "to express where we live," and glances around at the audience, as much as to say that he realizes this is a kind of unorthodox idea, but is wondering what could be saner.

He became interested, he continues, in the design of anagama kilns after a cave kiln he built in a hillside behind his house suggested a way to bring wood fire more directly into play. He shows slides of the Dragon Kiln in various stages of development, and then begins showing examples of the work of everyone in the community that's grown up around the kiln, as if everyone there in the audience understands that no one can manage such a thing by himself. He speaks knowledgeably about other people's work, offering praise only for what he truly admires. He says he likes one man's work (radically different from his own) because "it's coming from somewhere, a real place [the industrial belt of the Midwest], and that's what he's about." He says of another person's work that he "always leaves room for the wood to be involved."

Toward the end of his presentation Jack is depicting things integral to his work, but the connection is lost on some of the audience. He's showing slides of a recent fishing trip to Alaska, of the people he works with and their boat, and of his neighbors at work in the woods.

The last few slides are of slash burning on clearcuts in the Coast Range. He says that fire, like the felling of trees, is an expression of the human activity of logging, making clear that his own vision has also been shaped by the years he worked for Crown Zellerbach.

By the end of the show, Jack's allegiance to his community, his regard for physical labor, and his preoccupation with the processes rather than the objects of life have been reiterated on several levels. It's apparent he works every idea he has through the filter of local materials, local geography, local people. No artist I've ever met flies so completely in the face of a tradition of the elite, or so completely ignores elitism as a worthy or desirable goal. What he is looking for, he makes clear, is a reintegration of "man" and "nature," something like the conformity between a river and its bed. And in this he is as unconscious and striking a protégé of Thoreau as possibly exists in the world of American art.

Jack closes with two questions for the audience. First, he asks, how do you relate to natural materials? What do they mean to you, and what is the history of your relationship with those materials? Second, what are the possibilities for wood fire? What are the possibilities for human wood-firing?

I bought one of Jack's large pots for a friend in California and milled among the crowd until it thinned and only Jack and a few friends were left. It was suggested we all go somewhere for coffee, but it was late and Jack wanted to get home. A couple of weeks before, Jack had quoted a passage to me from Jiro Hirada's

A Glimpse of Japanese Ideals. "The essence of real beauty," wrote Hirada, "may be gathered from the commonplace, from what lies close around us in life. By learning to appreciate this truth, our lives will doubtless be enriched and ennobled."

"These words," Jack wrote later, "personify the mind of the Dragon." They relate to "the calm serenity of what may be termed a commonplace scene," two men, their backs to each other, felling black locust in a woodlot.

It takes about five hours to drive from Jack's house to mine, to cross the Coast Range, move up the Willamette Valley and then up the McKenzie into the Cascade Range. I got home from Jack's opening just before dawn and watched first light rise in the woods and infuse a stream of river fog. I heard birds calling out repeatedly as the day began to brighten. I was relieved to be home. I went down to the riverbank and sat, weary from the drive, wanting the refreshment of cool air in my lungs and on my face. In that morning stillness, the hesitation of breath that bridges night and day, I heard a characteristic river sound, a sound that can be unsettling at night and which in daylight is often dismissed as something else. It is a shifting on the cobble bottom of the river, a muffled thud coming from a place where the current has prized a rock loose and wedged it differently in the bed.

10

THE WHALEBOAT

THIS MANY PAGES into the book, I can feel it in the small of my back. A congressional report, four pounds twelve ounces, dead across my thighs as a paving stone. I am reading it closely in an overstuffed chair in the fifteen-foot-square, second-story room in which I've worked for nearly thirty years. Aside, the bare floor of shiplapped Douglas fir is dappled with moving shadow, sunlight blinking through the limbs of a forest beyond the glass windows. Birdsong passes through the glass—robins, guttural ravens, rasping Steller's jays. Once in a while the staccato cry of a pileated woodpecker, the whistle of an osprey. The Doppler rise and fall of passing cars on the road along the river occasionally distracts me from the description of human tragedy braced on my legs.

The book, a focus of my research for a book, is General

Adolphus Greely's *Report on the Proceedings of the United States Expedition to Lady Franklin Bay, Grinnell Land.* Published in 1888, this first of the two volumes is 545 pages long, bound in sheepskin of a light fawn color, grained to look like calf and blind-tooled with a scorching iron. Greely's salient subject here is the disaster that befell him and his party on tiny Pim Island in the Canadian high Arctic in 1883–1884. Of the group of twenty-five men who overwintered, sixteen perished from exposure and starvation. Another man drowned, an eighteenth was executed. The living stole one another's food and ate the dead. On an overcast August morning in 1987 I visited the ruins of their wretched encampment, a site by a small pond from which they were rescued after the most callous government delays. For several hours that day I perambulated the low stone walls of their roofless hut, picking my way around scraps of abandoned clothing, rusted cans, and wind-thrown squares of boat canvas. I stood on a nearby rise, head bowed like a tardy preacher before a neat row of sagging depressions, the graves of the first to die.

This morning, reading Greely's book and recalling the visit, I make notes on a yellow pad. I review in my mind the exact contour of rock and soil the general refers to when he writes, "just to the east of our hut . . ."; but, too, I know what it would look like if one approached from the other side, came at it from the east, so that it lay "just to the west . . ." I've gone there to see.

Reading assiduously in this chair every day I'm sometimes distracted by a movement, a sound nearby—the tick of wood grain in the house as it adjusts to warming air, a flash of sunlight outside in the leaf crown of wind-burst alders, the *whirr-buzz* of a hummingbird hanging briefly at a windowpane. Notes on the desk flutter and skid in a breeze and I'm drawn, just now, from the brutality of Greely's winter quarters into a more insistent reality, one here in the room, another out past the windows. Two separate realities, inside and out, but they elide subtly. I know this room, well enough to work its layout in the dark, to reach within a book or two of the right title on shelves holding hundreds of books, or land a crooked toss in the wastebasket. I could round the drop-leaf table of Honduran mahogany in front of me, upon which is stacked research for the work of which Greely's narrative is a part, step around this furniture here in darkness, and not clip a thigh. Yet, each day I spot something in the room too long unremembered, or see it as if for the first time; and then if I'm not careful whatever it is will pull me off the task at hand—Greely's anxious men, now, struggling to get a whaleboat upturned on the walls of their stone hut to create shelter and make a ridgeline for stretched canvas. My gaze has left the sentence and holds now on the wooden model of a whaleboat across the room, a dry fly landing on a trout pool.

I saw the model for the first time in 1988, in a store in Camden, Maine, with a friend, the painter Alan Magee. It was a stunning piece of handwork, but I wanted to think about it for a few weeks. I finally wrote my friend and asked if he could locate the store again, purchase it for me, and have the store send it on along with the name of the model maker. The urge to possess the boat grew out of my desire to scrutinize it. The fashioning of its parts and their assembly showed such exacting attentiveness to detail, the model was didactic. I could sit with it and a work like Willits Ansel's *The Whaleboat: A Study of Design, Construction and Use from 1850 to 1970* and, using both, plumb the reality. The gaff rigging of the sails, the placement of the tubs of whale line between the thwarts, the shape of the lion's tongue, the arrangement of the first and second irons in a crotch on the starboard wale—all these things could be clarified for me in three dimensions.

I purchased the model because it was beautiful, vivid, and correct, and because it bore so well an elaborate and arcane history of human encounter with the wild. Like many objects in this room, once fixed upon it gushed.

The boat, ten inches long, its mast rising seven inches above the keel, was built on a scale of ⅓" = 1' by Harry McCreery, Bangor, Maine. Shortly after I purchased the boat I wrote to ask him which woods he'd used in its construction, and whether his model was based on the New Bedford whaleboat of about 1860. It was, he wrote back. And the many hand-carved pieces, he explained, were all of basswood, but he'd stained them differently to mimic the contrasts between the dozen types of wood to be seen in an unpainted, full-scale boat. Whaleboats utilized white oak in the keel, spruce for thwarts, and were floored with pine. The exterior planking was rot-resistant cedar, the oars ash, the loggerhead (around which the whale line was belayed) was made of hickory, the bow chocks of lignum vitae.

In the years when the construction of this boat was routine work, boatwrights possessed a sophisticated knowledge of the properties of various species of wood, knowledge so rarefied a man could build a boat that exceeded his ability to reason. By combining portability (lightness), strength (resistance to rack and torsion), and propellability in such a canny way, American whaleboat builders brought to perfection a nautical design descendant from European shallops, on the one hand, and Algonquin oceangoing canoes. In the mid-nineteenth century this durable "surf boat" could be found at work in every corner of the world, from the Mozambique Channel to the Beaufort Sea, from the Azores to Tasmania. It was simple to construct (meaning easy to repair), its materials were relatively inexpensive, and even with slight men at the oars it was quick and maneuverable on the water. The joinery and bracing employed in it and the varying degree of flexibility in the woods used in its construction left it rigid but still supple. It successfully resisted the forces that threatened its integrity at the same time that it gave in to them.

I like to glance at the model when I'm working. I don't know a hundredth of what Mr. McCreery knows, or Mr. Ansel, but that day in Camden I saw perfection, and now I have it before me. The boat's a reminder of a kind of intelligence I respect.

Looking up from Greely's tome, I have become aware of a knot in my lower back. I twist sideways and arch my spine to relieve tension. My eyes drift from the boat, positioned in a glass case atop a tall oak filing cabinet, pass over a paulownia wood *tansu* in which I store manuscripts, traverse a set of birch-veneer shelves full of books and mementos of travel, and exit a set of three double-hung windows framed in unpainted pine in the south wall.

Beyond the windows, past the combination of incandescent lamplight and tree-filtered sunlight in this room, beyond the tidiness of my quarters, stands an unmanaged wood. The dark, tall trunks contrast sharply this morning with sheets of sunlight. Fronds of Western red cedar bob and gyrate in a light breeze. Leaves of Indian plum shaped like lanceolate blades and the palmate leaves of maples obscure and flick sunshine. The pigments of green among these trees alone—emerald on to celadon—are difficult to be definitive about. The cedar and yew greens are darker than those of Indian plum, hazelnut, and maple; but where light and shadow intervene, matte and gloss shift the hues' intensity. Too, the delicate structure of a cedar frond holds color less firmly than the broad leaf of a maple.

Beyond the first picket of well-formed trunks by the house a space drops, a deep well of air that opens above a clearing. (I can't see the floor of the clearing from my chair. The house stands above it on an old riverbank which slopes down twenty feet.) Past the clearing, a buffer of the same species of trees fronts a two-lane highway parallel to the south wall of windows. On the other side of the road, about a hundred and fifty feet away, a last wall of trees rises, the same species again, but here mixed with Oregon ash, black cottonwood, and vine maple.

Outside the last forest plane the McKenzie River flows westward at a brisk four knots, fed by snow and glacier melt, groundwater, and cold artesian springs in the Cascades. The river is about three hundred and fifty feet wide here and three or four feet deep. Its piebald bottom of cobble rock is visible nearly all the way across. On the far side, a mountain bears up steeply through oldgrowth forest for about six hundred feet. The land there has never been mined, logged, homesteaded, or otherwise disturbed by human enterprise, except for the dozing of a dirt road which parallels the river.

When I stand in front of the windows and look out I recognize these components, but do not see all of them at once. It depends on the light, which is to say on the season, the hour of the day, and conditions in the sky. On a clear winter morning, with deciduous trees shut of their leaves, I see more of the ridgeline above the south bank of the river and more of the river itself. On a day like today, an April morning, the ridgeline is masked by the thickening of the woods that comes with spring. I locate the ridge now by connecting a trend: the lower edge of patches of blue.

Any scrutiny of these woods, of the clearing and the river, made from these windows through curtains of sunshine, moonlight, snowfall, or wind current is rewarded. Species of trees are seen to be differentiated, for example, not just by the relative smoothness of their bark, but by the angle at which limbs leave the trunks, by the type of moss that clings to them, the sorts of birds that favor them for nests and roosts, the way their crowns flex differently on the same breeze, the soil they choose, the plants that crowd them. All these variations in cellular structure, in arboreal architecture and the corralling of light make for different sorts of wood for lumber. Harry McCreery would grasp it right away.

The world outside these windows, in front of which I've written for years at a draftsman's table, passes through a greater range of temperature in any given day than I experience inside, is more affected by wind, is richer in sound and odor. On this side the woods have been domesticated into cabinets and furniture. The air is still, less robust. A spider in its ceiling-corner web scuttles after a moth too large to be subdued entirely by entrapment. A carpenter ant taps its antennae across the floor, a sightless man with a cane. Dust motes do not swirl in the shaft of sunlight that pins the shadow of my desk chair to the floor. I imagine these the quarters of one Ishmael; here, the mind of a person who, looking out upon nature, wishes to understand the inscrutable visage of that force against which Ahab wants to act. In Ishmael, the rumination, in Ahab the doing.

From the pointillistic murmur of cedar and Douglas fir limbs bright out the windows, my eye slings back to the basswood model, to its white mainsail and jib, motionless in the windless interior of the glass case. Its harpoons booted motionless in the boat crotch. Its shadow on the white wall so distorted the craft looks lanteen-rigged, a fifteenth-century dhow. In boats like this men chased down and killed the largest creatures human beings have ever confronted. In the modern era, launched from a pelagic vessel manned by men often unknown to one another at the start of a two-year voyage, its employment marked a shift from a community-based to a corporate-based technology designed to exploit nature. Its advent marked the beginning of the late Holocene die-off of nonhuman life. Ishmael, with his modern ironies about the "all-grasping Western world" and man "the money-making animal," worked here, pulling second oar in Starbuck's boat, the most skilled position after Queequeg's, Starbuck's harpooner and boat steerer. In that seat he felt the "white ash breeze" of the recovery stroke as he and his companions strained after the descried whale. From that forward thwart he heard the strike of the harpoon, and from there he spoke to the reader of wrenching death, "the speechlessly quick, chaotic bundling of a man into Eternity."

Once, sitting here at the draftsman's table, it occurred to me that, ablaze like a ribbon of manganese in a late afternoon sun-strike, the river presented an open field, a clearing. There was no reason I could not stroll in it if I dressed warmly and braced myself against its current. I went down from the house in that hour, wearing the wet suit I use for tropical diving, took for a staff a cottonwood limb peeled of its bark by beaver, and waded out. My movements no longer restricted by brush and tree trunks, I experienced a fresh sensation, like laying down the initial brush stroke on a blank canvas. Since that day I have walked in the river in all seasons except late fall, winter, and early spring, when the water is too high and fast. I've walked up and down in it on moonlit nights, and on nights of the new moon when the only light falling in the woods has come from the bulb left burning above my desk, that and photons from the stars above, the suns Ishmael imagined as islands in a "continentless," continuous sea.

Crabbing upcurrent some evenings, feeling the force of the water on my legs and a night breeze in my face, I often think of myself as passing the house offshore. Up there in that room, as I see it, is the reading and the thinking-through, a theory of rivers, of trees moving, of falling light. Here on the river, as I lurch against a freshening in the current, is the practice of rivers. In navigating by the glow of the Milky Way, the practice of light. In steadying up with a staff, the practice of wood.

To walk the river is to become inculcated in horizontal movement. From the windows of my room I watch the river's breadth undulate and heave past, tens of thousands of shards of light clattering through the trees. Between the window and the river passes the highway, with its horizontal traffic. Some nights I see a vehicle diddering along the dirt road on the south side of the river, its light poke yet another horizontal emphasis. Through breaks in the trees I follow the flat flight of great blue herons over the river, harlequin ducks, common mergansers, and Canada geese. This through-line, square-bounded by window frames, cuts boldly across a vertical strike of tall hemlock, cedar, and fir boles. At noon on a summer day the river vibrates like a simmering ingot beyond a backlit woods; at dusk on a winter afternoon, the paved road by the river is almost as bright, a long deep gloss of rainwater glowing silver in the sharp rays of the setting sun.

Little vertical line or movement contradicts the horizontal impression of these two-dimensional scenes. Falling snow and rain, maple seed cases helicoptering toward the ground, the dry descending leaves of autumn. The scene alters suddenly, however, if one throws up a window and leans out. More blue sky is immediately apparent, more forest floor (and, so, the natural vertical tension these two create). More subtle is the effect of entering the sonic landscape of the woods. The scrape of branches, birdsong and wind shear, the purl and roar of the farther-off river all impart spatial volume to the air. You step into the space you've been looking at.

Some months after I moved into this room, with fall coming on, I had to decide whether to close the three windows in the south wall. Standing open, they admitted bats, moths, bees, errant winds, and the redolence of the woods. Left open, they would admit winter rain and snowstorms across my writing table. I decided to shut two of the three, to leave the middle window open an inch or so. I've done this ever since. The part of my table that abuts this window's sill periodically needs to be cleared of fir needles, spider silk, moth wings, bird feathers, cottonwood seeds, maple leaves, dustings of pollen, and assorted insects borne in on the breeze.

I gain such a strong sense of the outer world through that slit of open window, I believe closing it would mean not only a loss of knowledge but a loss of air, loss of a breathable medium necessary to the experience of the room. If it were closed, I believe the occupant would eventually suffocate.

From where I sit now in the aquamarine armchair, I can study something subtle through the slot between the window sash and sill, a delicate shimmering not apparent when viewed through the minor distortion of the windowpane: sunlight, ricocheting from the moving surface of the river, illuminates the undersides of leaves suspended stone-still in the air. From years of looking, I know nothing I see out there is as complex as the play of sunlight. And I know a perplexing thing: the three dimensions of that space all too easily slide toward two. I view this world sometimes like a dazed man, as layers seriatim. Losing, just for a moment, depth of field and scale, I don't know whether a brilliant shudder of light is coming from the roll of the river over its bed, from a scuffle of wind on its surface, or from lofting spider silk or a dip of leaves close or far. Or any of these things overlaid. Without intent concentration my eye can't sort it, perhaps because my eye is entrained too tightly with my mind.

My eyes hold on the boat. Its lines are as pleasing to me as the proportions of a salmon. I like to study paintings or to examine pieces of sculpture where the artist has been so sensitive that the form—line alone—carries much of the content. Mr. McCreery's model is carvel-built, its exterior planks butted squarely against each other instead of overlapped (clinker-built). The smooth lines of his model—a fairly strong sheer, the hard turn of its bilge, the curve of its spoon bow, the short dead-rise—accentuate a feature characteristic of such double-ended boats. Roughly five times as long as they were wide, they were tapered to give them a narrow or "fine" entrance in the water and a long "run" aft. Even an untrained eye recognizes in a good model the meaning in this gathering of lines: smooth, fast, quiet.

Two cedar benches stand amid wild hawthorn, bearberry, and huckleberry brush on the river's near bank. Their flat backs fold down on contoured seats, so the benches' pale, weathered profiles are easily missed in a casual glance from road or river. I walk to the benches nearly every day to sit and watch. The position I take up down there is not unlike the one I hold behind the typewriter. Sitting on the bench, I'm ensconced in a riparian zone closed in by trees and tall bushes. I gaze on an expanse of the river's back. Up in my room I sit squarely at a worktable, looking out on a thick and chaotic wood through glass. From those benches I regularly study ospreys hunting, chinook salmon migrating, common nighthawks swooping, caddis flies hatching, and an array of watercraft. On a single summer afternoon as many as a hundred boats may pass—McKenzie River drift boats, kayaks, and rubber rafts. Their human occupants are often drifting in bliss on this relatively calm stretch of water, or casting for cutthroat trout, or paddling on eagerly to a set of riffles just downriver called Cook's Rapids.

Sunlight flexes too rapidly, too complexly, on the river's skin for the eye to spot a recurrent pattern in it, from bench or window, but I believe one is there. It's not anything I feel compelled to find, I don't believe I must know its meaning. I know that the design inherent in such things is orderly according to some logic other than the ones I know. It is akin, I think, to the logic that makes one's life morally consistent despite certain lapses of judgment.

Gazing every day like this upon the "face" of nature, Ishmael sensed confounding lacunae, gaps in the logic of that natural order. He called them "vacancies." Ahab, of course, was irritated by these same uncertainties, places in nature that made "no sense" to him. By dint of will he meant to dominate and subdue them. Again, I think of the boat. The regular stroke of five men at the oars propels it, the mate at the steering oar gives it direction. It is an object full of purpose, a hunter's boat, a killer's platform.

Once the iron is struck and the Nantucket sleigh ride begins, neither Ishmael's status as the contemplative outsider looking in nor Ahab's as the man of action counts for anything. Both are at the mercy of the cantle of nature they've struck. Repeatedly surviving this experience Ishmael feels redeemed, Ahab triumphant. To either, the creature Ishmael describes as "faceless" is dead.

After the strike, the exhaustion of the whale's attempt to flee, and the fatal lancing, the long tow of the buoyant carcass ensues, followed by the rendering of its blubber, oil that will light, Ishmael bitterly observes, the patrician houses of shipowners and their captains. The beauty and perfection of this whaleboat, we maintain, is not compromised by the use to which it may be put. It is merely a tool with which we confront and force the inexplicable in nature.

From the overstuffed chair where I hold Greely's report open on my lap, I see the forest stirring in the morning's light. I know if I stand up and scrutinize the scene a strand of memories will unfurl, because the mysterious nature of light suspended beyond the windows will flare—a mystery Eva Figes grappled with in a novel she wrote in Monet's voice; a mystery the American painter Jennifer Bartlett pondered every day, day after day, in the same Tuscany garden; and which Goethe wrote anti-Newtonian theory about. I have long been in amazement at the flux and clarity of light, its tint, harmonics, and hue on the arctic tundra, for example, or in the Namib Desert, places where if the landscape were viewed as a two-dimensional painting one would say that the middle ground falls away, that the eye is left with the near and the far only, the horizon and the immediate surface upon which the feet stand. I recall these things at random—Figes's *Light*, the sun rising on the city of Punta Arenas on the Strait of Magellan, the sunshine I once saw falling briefly on a Vermeer painting as it was being moved in the Frick Collection in New York. I entreat friends like Alan Magee to speak about light even as we walk the very cobbled Maine beaches he paints, even while we stand stunned by McCreery's boat in a Camden shop.

A string of memories about light as I observe it daily from this room, racing past in the mind's corridors, would bind certain images. In the field below the house, a complicated splay of greens occurs more or less in the same ground plane: Himalaya blackberry, sword fern, wood sorrel, meadow rue, bracken fern, wild pea, tall blue lettuce, huckleberry, false Solomon seal, wild iris, curly dock, wild bleeding heart, sweet cicely. The leaves and fronds of all these plants rotate so slowly through the day, tracking the sun through the forest canopy, the turning does not register as a movement. It registers as a shift in the gamut of green.

Or consider how a rainstorm changes color and contrast in the forest by weighing it down. Water suspended on branches and individual leaves bends trees and plants to point at a sharper angle to the ground. When the water drains or evaporates, limbs rebound and shades of green on the ground become stronger as bare patches of the dark earth are slowly eclipsed. Undrooped, the limbs admit more light, and the somber darkness of the forest floor gives way to deeper color. Cleansed of natural dust, these greens gleam as they have not gleamed in days.

Or consider that light from a sun-shot sky flooding the canopy of a maple tree may be mistaken for a sheen brilliant on its leaves, the leaves in that moment mimicking the sky. And that in this configuration a greater volume of space surrounds the tree than if it is seen in the usual way, a dark-leafed tree against a pale sky.

Or consider how the dark grooves and runnels in Douglas fir bark slice vertically through an identical horizontal pattern created by silver light lambent on the river. Or how light surging back and forth on leaves tethered to a limb contrasts with shards and streamers of light that appear to be rafting off downriver. Or how different sections of a windblown forest move in different time, an asynchronous syncopation.

Often I've looked through the trees to the river from this room and, despite reason and familiarity, not known what I was looking at. The angle and intensity of light, in concert with chaotic movements of the air, make another landscape of the same scene, day after day. The glint on a hummingbird's eye at the open window, rain-sheen on a sprig of red cedar, light roiled in the branches of an ash tree, and the "shook foil" of the river carry the eye from the near reach of the fingertips to the far reaches of what is readable. In a split second what is perceived as real snaps. It becomes the illumination of another wood, revealed within the wood previously known.

I could not give up either of these worlds, neither the book I am holding nor the gleaming forest, though I've told you almost nothing of what Greely has said here on his grim pages, from the sentences of which I've conjured images of a bleak site on Pim Island years ago. Here in the room, I suppose, is to be found the interior world of the book; but it opens upon a world beyond the windows, where no event has been collapsed into syntax, where the vocabulary, it seems, is infinite. The indispensable connection for me lies with the open space that lets the breath of every winter storm, the ripping wind and its pelting rain, enter this room.

And what of the boat, where my glance still hangs? I imagine the six men in it in pursuit of something huge, confounding, haunting. Perhaps a goon like Flask is at the tiller, or a man as good as Starbuck is making the quick decisions. I envision cooperation in the matched stroke of their oars and nobility in this hunter's legacy, even if it represented a financial boon for but a few, as it did; and then with the advent of electricity, a change in women's fashions, the capital shifted elsewhere. The decimation of whale life that commerce initiated, seen through the scaling lens of history, does not destroy the dignity of ordinary men in the fishery, their effort to work, to survive, to provide. It only instructs us in the infernal paradoxes of life.

When I look at Mr. McCreery's boat, when I imagine the oar blades plunged in the green transparency of a storm-raked sea, the boat cranking off a wave crest, six men straining in drenched motley wool and oilskins, their mouths agape, I know that life is wild, dangerous, beautiful.

A glance at the boat, a stretch of my cramped back, a look out the window at the run of the wind in the trees on an April morning, and I return to Greely's narrative.

PART THREE

Remembrance

II

REPLACING MEMORY

1
Manhattan, 1976

THE HOURS OF COOLNESS in the morning just before
my mother died I remember for their relief. It was July
and it had been warm and humid in New York City for
several days, temperatures in the high eighties, the air motionless
and heavy with the threat of rain.

I awoke early that morning. It was also my wife's thirtieth
birthday, but our celebration would be wan. My mother was in
her last days, and the lives of all of us in the family were con-
torted by grief and tension—and by a flaring of anger at her cancer. We were exhausted.

I felt the coolness of the air immediately when I awoke. I

walked the length of the fourth-floor apartment, opened one side of a tall casement window in the living room, and looked at the sky. Cumulus clouds, moving to the southeast on a steady wind. Ten degrees cooler than yesterday's dawn, by the small tin thermometer. I leaned forward to rest my arms on the sill and began taking in details of movement in the street's pale light, the city's stirring.

In the six years I had lived in this apartment as a boy, from 1956 until 1962, I had spent cumulative months at this window. At the time, the Murray Hill section of Manhattan was mostly a neighborhood of decorous living and brownstone row houses, many of them not yet converted to apartments. East Thirty-fifth Street for me, a child newly arrived from California, presented an enchanting pattern of human life. Foot-beat policemen began their regular patrol at eight. The delivery of residential mail occurred around nine and was followed about ten by the emergence of women on shopping errands. Young men came and went the whole day on three-wheel grocery cart bikes, either struggling with a full load up the moderate rise of Murray Hill from Gristede's down on Third Avenue, or hurtling back the other way, driving no-hands against light traffic, cartons of empty bottles clattering explosively as the bikes' solid tires nicked potholes.

In the afternoon a dozen young girls in private-school uniforms swirled in glee and posed with exaggerated emotion across the street, waiting to be taken home. By dinnertime the street was almost empty of people; then, around eleven, it was briefly animated again with couples returning from the theater or some other entertainment. Until dawn, the pattern of glinting chrome and color in the two rows of curbed automobiles remained unchanged. And from night to night that pattern hardly varied.

Overlaying the street's regular, diurnal rhythm was a more chaotic pattern of events, an unpredictability I would watch with unquenchable fascination for hours at a time. (A jog in the wall of The Advertising Club of New York next door made it impossible for me to see very far to the west on Thirty-fifth Street. But if I leaned out as far as I dared, I could see all the way to the East River in the other direction.) I would study the flow of vehicles below: an aggressive insinuation of yellow taxis, the casual slalom of a motorcycle through lines of stalled traffic, the obstreperous lumbering of large trucks. The sidewalks, with an occasional imposing stoop jutting out, were rarely crowded, for there were neither shops nor businesses here, and few tourists. But with Yeshiva University down at the corner of Lexington, the Thirty-fourth Street Armory a block away, a Swedenborgian church midblock, and Thirty-fourth Precinct police headquarters just up from Third Avenue, I still saw a fair array of dress and captivating expressions of human bearing. The tortoise pace of elderly women in drab hats paralleled the peeved ambling of a middle-aged man anxious to locate a cab. A naïf, loose-jointed in trajectory down the sidewalk, with wide-flung strides. A buttonhooking young woman, intently scanning door lintels and surreptitiously watching a building superintendent leaning sullenly against a service entrance. Two men in vested suits in conversation on the corner where, rotund and oblivious, they were a disruption, like a boulder in a creek. A boy running through red-lighted traffic with a large bouquet in his hand, held forth like a bowsprit.

All these gaits together with their kindred modulations seemed mysteriously revealing to me. Lingering couples embraced, separated with resolve, then embraced once more. People halted and turned toward each other in hilarious laughter. I watched as though I would never see such things again—screaming arguments, the otherworldly navigations of the deranged, and the haughty stride of single men dressed meticulously in evening clothes.

This pattern of traffic and people, an overlay of personality and idiosyncrasy on the day's fixed events, fed me in a wordless way. My eyes would drift up from these patterns to follow the sky over lower Manhattan, a flock of house sparrows, scudding clouds, a distant airplane approaching La Guardia or Idlewild with impossible slowness.

Another sort of animation drew me regularly to this window: weather. The sound of thunder. Or a rising hiss over the sound of automobiles that meant the streets were wet from a silent rain. The barely audible rattle of dozens of panes of glass in the window's leadwork—a freshening wind. A sudden dimming of sunshine in the living room. Whatever I was doing, these signals would pull me away. At night, in the isolating light cone of a street lamp, I could see the slant, the density, and sometimes the exact size of raindrops. (None of this could I learn with my bare hands outstretched, in the penumbral dark under the building's cornices.) I watched rainwater course east in sheets down the calico-patched street in the wake of a storm; and cascades of snow, floating and wind-driven, as varied in their character as falls of rain, pile up in the streets. I watched the darkness between buildings burst with lightning, and I studied intently the rattle-drum of hail on car roofs.

The weather I watched from this window, no matter how wild, was always comforting. My back was to rooms secured by family life. East and west, the room shared its walls with people I imagined little different from myself. And from this window I could see a marvel as imbued with meaning for me then as a minaret— the Empire State Building. The high windows of its east wall gleamed imperially in the first rays of dawn, before the light flared down Thirty-fifth Street, glinting in bits of mica in the façades of brownstones. Beneath the hammer of winter storms, the building seemed courageous and adamantine.

THE MORNING THAT my mother would die I rested my forearms on the sill of the window, glad for the change of weather. I could see more of the wind, moving gray clouds, than I could feel; but I knew the walk to the subway later that morning, and the short walk up Seventy-seventh Street to Lenox Hill Hospital, would be cooler.

I had been daydreaming at the window for perhaps an hour when my father came downstairs. The faint odors in the street's air—the dampness of basements, the acrid fragrance of ailanthus trees, the aromatics in roof tar—had drawn me off into a dozen memories. My father paused, speechless, at the foot of the stairs by the dining table. As determined as he was to lead a normal life around Mother's last days, he was at the beck and call of her disease almost as much as she was. With a high salute of his right hand, meant to demonstrate confidence, and an ironic grimace, he went out the door. Downstairs he would meet my brother, who worked with him, and together they would take a cab up to the hospital. My brother, three years younger, was worn out by these marathon days but uncomplaining, almost always calm. He and my father would eat breakfast together at the hospital and sit with Mother until Sandra and I arrived, then leave for work.

I wanted an undisturbed morning, the luxury of that kind of time, in which to give Sandra her birthday presents, to have a conversation not shrouded by death. I made breakfast and took it into the bedroom. While we sipped coffee I offered her what I had gotten. Among other things, a fossil trilobite, symbol of longevity. But we could not break the rind of oppression this terminal disease had created.

While Sandra showered, I dressed and returned to the window. I stood there with my hands in my pockets staring at the weathered surface of the window's wood frame, with its peeling black paint. I took in details in the pitted surface of the sandstone ledge and at its boundary, where the ledge met the color of buildings across the street. I saw the stillness of the ledge against the sluggish flow of early morning traffic and a stream of pedestrians in summer clothing below. The air above the street was a little warmer now. The wind continued to blow steadily, briskly moving cloud banks out over Brooklyn.

I felt a great affection for the city, for its tight Joseph's coat of buildings, the vitality of its people, the enduring grace of its plane trees, and the layers of its history, all of it washed by a great tide of weather under maritime skies. Standing at the window I felt the insistence and the assurance of the city, and how I was woven in here through memory and affection.

Sandra touched my shoulder. It was time we were gone, up-town. But something stayed me. I leaned out, bracing my left palm against the window's mullion. The color I saw in people's clothes was now muted. Traffic and pedestrians, the start-up of myriad businesses, had stirred the night's dust. The air was more rank with exhaust. A flock of pigeons came down the corridor of the street toward me, piebald, dove gray, white, brindled ginger, ash black—thirty or more of them. They were turning the bot-tom of a long parabolic arc, from which they shot up suddenly, out over Park Avenue. They reached a high, stalling apex, rolled over it, and fell off to the south, where they were cut from view by a building. A few moments later they emerged much smaller, wings pounding over brownstones below Thirty-fourth Street, on a course parallel to the wind's.

I left, leaving the window open.

When Sandra and I emerged a half hour later from the hospi-tal elevator, my brother was waiting to meet us. I could see by the high, wistful cast of his face that she was gone.

II

Arizona, 1954

OUR TRAIN ARRIVED at Grand Canyon Village on the South Rim late on a summer afternoon. With my brother, Dennis, and a friend of my mother, a young woman named Ann, I had come up on the Santa Fe spur line from Williams, a town about thirty miles west of Flagstaff. We had left Los Angeles the evening before, making a rail crossing of the Sonoran Desert so magical I had fallen silent before it.

The train itself was spellbinding. I do not remember falling asleep as we crossed the desert, but I know that I must have. I only remember sitting alone in a large seat in the darkened obser-vation car, looking at the stars and feeling nearly out of breath with fortune—being able to wander up and down the aisles of the streaking train, sitting in this observation car hour by hour staring at the desert's sheer plain, the silhouettes of isolated mountain ranges, and, above, the huge swath of the Milky Way.

Near midnight we stopped for a few minutes in Needles, a railroad town on the lower Colorado across the river from the Fort Mojave Indian Reservation. The scene on the platform was dreamlike, increasing my sense of blessing. The temperature was over one hundred degrees, but it was a dry heat, pleasant. I had never been up this late at night. Twenty or thirty Indians—I didn't know then, but they would have been Chemuwevis as well as Mohaves, and also Navajos, who worked on many of the Santa Fe repair crews—craned their necks, looking for disembarking passengers or cars to board. Mexican families stood tightly together, stolid, shy, and alert. The way darkness crowded the platform's pale lamplight, the way the smoky light gleamed on silver bracelets and corn-blossom necklaces, leaving its sheen on the heavy raven hair of so many women—all this so late in the heated night made Needles seem very foreign. I wanted to stay. I could have spent all the time I had been offered at Grand Canyon right here.

But we left. I returned to my seat in the now completely empty observation car. I am sure I fell asleep shortly after we crossed the river, on the way to Kingman.

John, Ann's husband of only a few months and a seasonal ranger at the park, met the train at the canyon. My brother and I were to have two weeks with them before Mother came up to join us. (The three of them taught together in the secondary school system in southern California's San Fernando Valley.)

On the way up from Williams, the train had climbed through piñon and juniper savannah. As I descended the train car's steps, I saw fully for the first time the largest trees I had ever looked at—ponderosa pines. In the same moment, their fragrance came to me on the warm air, a sweet odor, less sharp than that of other pines.

John embraced Ann fiercely and said, "I will never be separated from you, ever again, for this long." Their passion and his words seemed wondrous to me, profound and almost unfathomable. I stared at the huge ponderosas, which I wanted to touch.

During those two weeks, Denny and I traveled the South and East Rims of the canyon with Ann while John lectured daily to visitors. The four of us lived in a small log cabin with a high-pitched roof. Sometimes I rose early, before the sun, and went outside. I would just stand in the trees or wander nearby in the first light. I could not believe the stillness.

A short distance from the cabin was a one-room museum with an office. I spent hours there, looking at pinned insects, stuffed birds, and small animals. Some of these creatures seemed incredibly exotic to me, like the Kaibab squirrel with its tufted ears—perhaps a made-up animal.

I read pamphlets about the geology of the canyon and its Indian history, and I went with my brother to some of John's lectures. The most entrancing was one in which he described the succession of limestones, sandstones, and shales that make up the visible canyon walls. The precision and orderliness of his perception, the names he gave so easily to these thousands of feet of wild, unclimbable, and completely outsize walls, seemed inspired, a way to *grasp* it all. I think this was the first such litany I committed to memory:

> Kaibab, Toroweap,
> Coconiño, Hermit;
> Supai, Redwall,
> Temple, Muav.
> Bright Angel.
> Tapeats.

On John's days off we drove out to picnic at Shoshone Point, a place on the East Rim set aside by the Park Service for its employees. Here, far from the pressing streams of visitor traffic, the silence within the canyon reverberated like silence in the nave of a large cathedral. The small clearing with its few picnic tables was a kind of mecca, a place where the otherwise terrifying falloff of the canyon seemed to comfort or redeem. I saw a mountain lion there one afternoon. It leaped the narrow road in one long bound, its head strangely small, its long tail strangely thick, a creature the color of Coconiño sandstone.

I DID NOT GO back to the canyon after that summer for twenty-six years. In the spring of 1980, I joined several other writers and editors at a workshop there in the Park Service's Albright Training Center. I arrived at night by plane, so did not see much until the next morning. I got up early, just after sunrise, thinking I would walk over to the El Tovar Lodge on the rim of the canyon for breakfast. The walk, I thought, would be a way to reenter the landscape, alone and quietly, before the activities of the workshop caught me up in a flow of ideas and in protracted discussions.

I didn't remember the area well enough that morning to know where I was, relative to the cabin we'd stayed in, but I set off through the woods toward what felt like the canyon's rim. The gentle roll of the land, the sponginess of ponderosa needles beneath my feet, familiar but nameless odors in the air, the soft twitter of chickadees up ahead—all this rounded into a pattern my body remembered.

At a certain point I emerged from the trees onto a paved road, which seemed the one to take to the lodge. I'd not gone more than a few yards, however, before I was transfixed by the sight of a small building. It was boarded up, but it had once been the museum. An image of its interior formed vividly in my mind— the smooth, glass-topped display stands with bird eggs and prehistoric tools, the cabinets and drawers full of vials of seeds and insect trays.

I walked on, elated and curiously composed. I would come back.

At the foot of the road was a wide opening in the trees. Once it might have been a parking lot. I was only partway across when I realized that the young pines growing here were actually coming up between train rails. Again I stood transfixed. It was here, all those years ago, that I had gotten off the train. I held tightly to that moment and began stepping eastward along the tracks, looking up every few steps to pure stands of ponderosa growing a hundred feet away to the south. Then I recognized a pattern in the trees, the way a dozen of the untapered, cinnamon-colored trunks stood together on a shallow slope. It had been here exactly that I had stepped off. I stared at them for many minutes, wondering more than anything at the way memory, given so little, could surge so unerringly.

I walked up to the trees and put my fingers on the bark, the large flat plates of small, concave scales. Far above, the narrow crowns were still against the bluing sky.

On the other side of the tracks I walked past the entrance to the lodge and stood at the edge of the canyon before a low, broad wall of stone. The moment my knees touched the wall, my unbounded view was shot with another memory—the feel of this stone angle against my belly when I was nine, and had had to hoist myself up onto the wall in order to see deep into the canyon. Now, I stood there long after the desire to gaze at the canyon had passed. I recalled suddenly how young ponderosas, bruised, smell like oranges. I waited, anxious, for memories that came like bursts of light: the mountain lion in its leap; the odor and jingle of harness mules and saddle horses in the hot sun at the top of Bright Angel Trail; my brother, light-footed as a doe, at the wall of an Anasazi ruin. These images brought with them, even in their randomness, a reassurance about time, about the unbroken duration and continuous meaning of a single human life. With that came a sense of joy, which I took with me to breakfast.

III

Bear River, Idaho, 1991

CORT BOUGHT a potted sulfur buckwheat in the Albertson's in Jackson and he and John and I left for Idaho by way of Afton, Wyoming, passing through Montpelier and then Paris, Idaho. We turned off the main road there, drove west through Mink Creek and then Preston, and swung north on U.S. 91, crossing the bridge over Bear Creek, where we pulled off.

Cort had been here before. Neither John nor I had, but I had wanted to see the place for a long time. In this river bottom, rising away from me to the Bannock Range in the northwest and, more precipitously, to the Bear River Range behind me in the southeast, several hundred people had been violently killed on a bitter cold morning in January 1863. This obscure incident on the Bear River, once commonly called a "battle" by Western historians, has more often been referred to in recent years as a massacre, an unnecessary killing. Twenty-two men of the Second Cavalry and the Third Infantry, California Volunteers, under the command of a Colonel Patrick Connor, were shot dead by Northern Shoshone. No one knows how many Shoshone were killed, but most estimate it was well over three hundred—more Indians than were killed in any other massacre in the West, including those at Sand Creek, Colorado (1864), Washita, Oklahoma (1868), or Wounded Knee, South Dakota (1890).

Connor's stated reason for bringing three hundred troops north from Salt Lake City that winter on a forced march was to protect the Overland Mail Route. The incident that triggered his decision was the death of a white miner in a skirmish involving several miners and Indians near Preston, a few days after Christmas, 1862. In his official report, Connor said he meant to "chastise" the Shoshone. He permitted a federal marshal to accompany him, carrying arrest warrants for three Shoshone men reputedly involved in the fatal incident with the miners, but Connor told the marshal it was not his intent to take any prisoners.

The Shoshone, four hundred to four hundred fifty of them, were camped in willow thickets at the mouth of a ravine formed by Beaver Creek, several hundred yards short of its confluence with the Bear River. The spot was a traditional winter campsite, well protected from a prevailing north wind, with hot springs and with winter grazing for about two hundred horses. The night before the massacre, a man named Bear Hunter was in the nearby village of Franklin with his family, purchasing and loading sacks of wheat. He saw Connor's troops arriving, surmised their real purpose, and brought word back to the encampment.

Early the following morning, realizing he had lost the advantage of surprise, Connor massed his cavalry openly on the south side of the river, across from the Indian camp. The temperature was probably in the low teens. Connor then waited impatiently for his infantry, which had bogged in heavy snow on the road out of Franklin.

The Shoshone were by now all awake and digging in, for Connor's intentions had become plain. (Connor, of course, had no evidence that these particular Shoshone people had done anything wrong, only the suspicion that the men the U.S. marshal wanted were among them.) One of the Shoshone men shouted out in perfect English, "Come on you California sons-of-bitches. We're ready for you." Provoked by the remark, Connor surged across the icy river and ordered the cavalry to charge. Fourteen of his soldiers were cut down almost instantly. Connor retreated to regroup and to help his foot soldiers, now arriving, get across the river.

Once they were over, Connor divided his forces, sending one column up the west slope of the ravine and another up the east slope, achieving a double flanking of the Indian camp. From these elevated positions the soldiers raked the camp with a furious, enfilading fire. The Shoshone, lightly armed, fought back with sporadic shots and in hand-to-hand combat for three or four hours, until late in the morning, by which time most of them were dead. Connor ordered his troops to kill every wounded Indian and to set fire to all seventy tepees, scattering, burning, or fouling all the food they could find as they did so. (Historians believe as many as sixty Shoshone might have escaped, most of them by swimming the partly frozen river.) In the final stages of the fight, Shoshone women were raped. Bear Hunter was tortured to death with a white-hot bayonet.

Connor reported two hundred twenty-four Indians killed. Residents of Franklin, six miles away, riding through the smoldering camp and into the willow thickets the next morning, counted many more dead, including nearly one hundred women and children. They took a few survivors back, housing them and treating their injuries. Connor, who returned immediately to Salt Lake City, denounced the Mormon people of Franklin in his official report as unhelpful and ungrateful. For their part, the Mormons may only have been heedful of Brigham Young's official policy: it was better to feed Indians than to fight with them.

JOHN AND CORT AND I read in silence the historical plaques on a stone obelisk at the roadside. I felt more grief than outrage, looking across at the mouth of what is no longer called Beaver Creek but Battle Creek. An interpretive sign, erected in October 1990 by the Idaho Historical Society, seeks to correct the assumption that the fight here was a battle. It calls the encounter "a military disaster unmatched in Western history." A 1990 National Park Service plaque, designating the undistinguished ravine across the river bottom as a National Historical Landmark, says with no apparent irony that the spot "possesses national significance in communicating the history of the United States of America."

We left the highway, drove up a dirt road, and parked at the site of the encampment, which is not signed or marked. Where the Shoshone tepees once stood, in fact, the creek is now clogged with debris and refuse—a school locker, a refrigerator, a mattress, scorched magazines and tin cans, lawn furniture riddled with bullet holes. Violet green swallows swooped the muddy water, only eight or ten feet across. On what is today called Cedar Bluff—the west side of the ravine—an iron-wheel combine and a walking-beam plow stood inert in sage and buckbrush. Overhead we heard the mewing of Franklin's gulls. From bottom flats near the river came the lowing of beef cattle.

Cort took the sulfur buckwheat from the truck, and the three of us started up the east side of the creek. The ravine, crisscrossed with horse and cattle tracks, was badly eroded. A variety of exotic grasses barely held in place a fine, pale tan, friable soil. Suddenly we saw a red fox. Then a muskrat in the water. Then the first of nine beaver dams, each built with marginal materials—teasel stalks and shreds of buckbrush, along with willow sticks and a few locust limbs. As we moved farther up the creek we heard yellow-headed blackbirds and mourning doves. In the slack water behind each succeeding dam, the water appeared heavier—silt was settling out before the water flowed on to the next dam, a hundred feet or so downstream. The beaver were clarifying the watercourse.

We finally found a small, open point of land near the creek. Cort put the buckwheat down and began to dig. He meant the planting as a simple gesture of respect. When he finished, I filled a boot with water and came back up the steep embankment. I poured it through my fingers, slowly, watching the small yellow flowers teeter in the warm air. Cort had gone on up the creek, but I met John's eye. He raised his eyebrow in acknowledgment, but he was preoccupied with his own thoughts and stepped away.

I climbed to the top of the ravine on the east side and walked north until I came to a high bluff above the creek where hundreds of bank swallows were nesting. I sat watching them while I waited for my friends to emerge from the willow thickets below. A few months before, Cort had lent me his copy of Newall Hart's scarce history, *The Bear River Massacre,* which contains reproductions of military reports and other primary materials. He recommended I read Brigham Madsen's *The Shoshoni Frontier and the Bear River Massacre.* Cort himself had written about the incident in his *Idaho for the Curious.* When he and John joined me, Cort said he wanted to cross the creek and look over a section of Cedar Bluff he'd not walked on an earlier visit. I wanted to watch the swallows a while longer. John essayed another plan, and we each went our way again.

I worked back south along the creek bottom, pausing for long moments to watch for beaver, which I did not see. Frogs croaked.

I came on mule-deer tracks. The warm air, laced with creek-bottom odors, was making me drowsy. I climbed back to the top of the ravine at the place where we had planted the buckwheat. A road there paralleled the creek, and its two tracks were littered with spent 12-gauge shotgun shells, empty boxes of .308 Winchester ammunition, and broken lengths of PVC pipe. I followed a barbed-wire fence past a bathtub stock tank to the place where we'd parked.

I opened Hart's book on the hood of the truck. Tipped against the back endsheet is a large, folded plat map of the "Connor Battle Field," made in 1926 by W. K. Aiken, the surveyor of Franklin County, Idaho. I oriented it in front of me and began matching its detail to the landscape—Aiken's elevations, the sketchy suggestion of an early road to Montana, and a spot to the south where Aiken thought Connor had caught his first glimpse of the Shoshone encampment that morning. In the upper-right corner of his map Mr. Aiken had written, not so cryptically, "Not a Sparrow Falls."

The river's meander had since carried it nearly three quarters of a mile to the south side of its floodplain. Otherwise the land—ranched and planted mostly to hay crops, dotted with farmhouses and outbuildings, and divided by wire fences—did not, I thought, look so very different. You could see the cattle, and you could smell pigs faintly in the air.

John came back. He took a bird guide out of the truck and began slowly to page through it. Cort returned with the lower jaw of a young mule deer, which we took as a souvenir. We drove back out to the road and headed north for Pocatello.

IV

Southern California, 1988

SANDRA AND I WERE in Whittier, California, for a ceremony at the town's college. It was the sort of day one rarely sees in the Los Angeles basin anymore: the air gin-clear, with fresh, balmy winds swirling through the eucalyptus trees, trailing their aromatic odor. The transparency of the air, with a trace of the Pacific in it, was intoxicating.

As we left the campus, Sandra said she could understand now what I meant about the sunlight, the clear air of my childhood.

"Yes," I answered. "It was like this often in the spring, after the rains in February. Back then—well, it was a long time ago. Thirty years, thirty-five years ago."

It was obvious anyway, she said, how this kind of light had affected the way I saw things.

I told her something Wallace Stegner wrote: whatever landscape a child is exposed to early on, that will be the sort of gauze through which he or she will see all the world afterward. I said I thought it was emotional sight, not strictly a physical thing.

The spanking freshness of the afternoon encouraged a long drive. I asked Sandra if she wanted to go out to Reseda, where our family had lived in several houses, starting in 1948.

IN NOVEMBER 1985 I had come down to Los Angeles from my home in Oregon. I was meeting a photographer who lived there, and with whom I was working on a story about the California desert for *National Geographic*. Flying into Los Angeles usually made me melancholy—and indignant. What I remembered from my childhood here, especially a rural countryside of farms and orchards out toward Canoga Park and Granada Hills, was not merely "gone." It had been obliterated, as if by a kind of warfare, and the remnant earth dimmed beneath a hideous pall of brown air.

A conversation with people in Los Angeles about these changes never soothes anyone. It only leaves a kind of sourness and creates impedance between people, like radio static. On the way to eat dinner with my friend, ruminating nevertheless in a silent funk about the place, I suddenly and vividly saw a photograph in my mind. It was of a young boy, riding the cantilevered support of a mailbox like a horse. On the side of the mailbox was

"5837." I wrote the numerals down on the edge of a newspaper in my lap. I was not sure what they meant, but I recognized the boy as myself.

During dinner, I just as suddenly remembered the words "Wilbur Avenue," a street in Reseda. We had lived in three different houses in that town, the last one on Calvert Street. I had visited it several times in the intervening years, but hadn't been able to remember where the other two houses were.

The next day I rented a car and drove out to the Calvert Street home. Some thirty citrus and fruit trees my brother and I had planted in the mid-1950s had been dug out, and the lot had been divided to accommodate a second house, but parts of the lawn we had so diligently watered and weeded were still growing. I had raised pigeons here, and had had my first dog, a Kerry blue terrier.

I inquired at a gas station on Victory Boulevard and found I was only a few blocks from crossing Wilbur Avenue. I made the turn there but saw the house numbers were in the six thousands and climbing; coming back the other way, I pulled up tentatively in front of 5837. I got out slowly, stared at the ranch-style house, and was suffused with a feeling, more emotion than knowledge, that this had been my home. Oleander bushes that had once shielded the house from the road were gone, along with a white rail fence and about fifteen feet of the front yard. In the late forties, before flood-control projects altered the drainage of this part of the San Fernando Valley, Wilbur Avenue had been a two-lane road with high, paved berms meant to channel floodwater north to the Los Angeles River. In those days it also served as a corridor for sheep being moved to pasture. Now it was four lanes wide, with modest curbs.

One walnut tree remained in the yard, and a grapefruit tree closer to the house. I glimpsed part of the backyard through a breezeway but kept moving toward the front door, to knock and introduce myself.

There was no answer. I waited awhile and knocked again. When no one answered I walked around to the breezeway, where there was a kitchen door. I nearly collided with a small, elderly woman whose hands flew up involuntarily in defense. I quickly gave my name, explaining I had grown up here, that I only wished to look around a little, if I could. Fright still gripped her face.

"Do you know," I said to her, "how, from the family room, you have to take that odd step up to the hallway, where the bedrooms are?"

Her face relaxed. She waved off her anxiousness, seemingly chagrined. She explained that the owner of the house, a woman named Mrs. Little, was inside dying of cancer. I remembered the name. She had lived out near Palmdale when we rented the house. I said that I was sorry, that there was no need for me to go inside.

"Well, please, have a look around," she said. She was relaxed now, serene, acting as though we were distant relatives. She walked into the backyard with me. At nearly each step, having difficulty stemming the pressure of memories, I blurted something—about a tree, about a cinder-block wall (still unfinished) around a patio. I pointed to some aging apricot and grapefruit trees, and to a massive walnut tree. We were standing on a concrete path, where I squatted down to peer at a column of ants going in and out of a crack. I had watched ants in this same crack almost forty years before. These were their progeny, still gathering food here. The mystery of their life, which had once transfixed me, seemed in no way to have diminished. I felt tears brim under my eyes and spill onto my cheeks. The woman touched my forearm deliberately but lightly, and walked away.

The horse stalls, a barn, and a row of chicken coops were gone, but I found scraps of green rolled roofing and splinters of framing lumber from them in the tall grass. I remembered mischief I had created here as a five-year-old. And then, like a series of sudden inflorescences, came memories first of the texture of tomatoes I had raised in a garden beside the chicken coops, and then of the sound of bees—how my friends and I had dared one another to walk past a hive of feral honeybees behind the barn where it ran close to the back fence.

Tempted to pick apricots and a grapefruit, I decided I had no right to do so. I said good-bye to the woman and asked her to convey my good wishes to Mrs. Little, who I could not think would remember me.

Driving straight from the house to Anza-Borrego Desert State Park in the western Sonoran Desert, a hundred and fifty miles away, I felt a transcendent calm. I promised myself I would return and try to find the first house, the location of which was lost to me.

SANDRA AND I CAME over from Whittier on the freeways, turning north off the Ventura onto Reseda Boulevard, then cutting over to Wilbur, which ran parallel. The house could not hold for her what it held for me, and I felt selfish using our time like this. But I wanted to share the good feeling I had had. The neighborhood still has about it something of the atmosphere of a much older San Fernando Valley—a bit run-down, but with no large housing developments, no landscaped and overwatered lawns. I drove past the house and had to turn and come back. The mailbox with its numbers was gone. The lot was empty: the house and all the trees had been razed; the bare, packed, red-brown earth had been swept clean. Only the tread marks of a single tractor were apparent, where it had turned on soft ground.

I got out of the car and walked back and forth across the lot, silently. On the ground near a neighbor's cinder-block fence I saw an apricot pit. I put it in my pocket.

"I've been thinking," I said to Sandra, once I was standing beside the car again. "The first house may have been way out on Wilbur, toward the Santa Susanas." She looked off that way.

"Would you mind driving? That way I could look. I might get the pattern of something, the way it looked."

"Yes," she said. "Certainly."

We turned around and headed north on Wilbur, windows open to the fresh breeze. We drove past the house where my friend Leon had lived, where I had first bitten into the flesh of a pomegranate, and then slowly past other places that I knew but which I could not recognize. The air all around was brilliant.

12

A PASSAGE OF THE HANDS

M Y HANDS WERE BORN breech in the winter of 1945, two hours before sunrise. Sitting with them today, two thousand miles and more from that spot, turning each one slowly in bright sunshine, watching the incisive light raise short, pale lines from old cuts, and seeing the odd cant of the left ring finger, I know they have a history, though I cannot remember where it starts. As they began, they gripped whatever might hold me upright, surely caressed and kneaded my mother's breasts, yanked at the restrictions of pajamas. And then they learned to work buttons, to tie shoelaces and lift the milk glass, to work together.

The pressure and friction of a pencil as I labored down the spelling of words right-handed raised the oldest permanent mark, a callus on the third joint of the middle finger. I remember no trying accident to either hand in these early years, though there must have been glass cuts, thorn punctures, spider bites, nails torn to the cuticle, scrapes from bicycle falls, pin blisters from kitchen grease, splinters, nails blackened from door pinches, pain lingering from having all four fingers forced backward at once, and the first true weariness, coming from work with lumber and stones, with tools made for larger hands.

It is from these first years, five and six and seven, that I am able to remember so well, or perhaps the hands themselves remember, a great range of texture—the subtle corrugation of cardboard boxes, the slickness of the oilcloth on the kitchen table, the shuddering bend of a horse's short-haired belly, the even give in warm wax, the raised oak grain in my school-desk top, the fuzziness of dead bumblebees, the coarseness of sheaves immediate to the polished silk of unhusked corn, the burnish of rake handles and bucket bails, the rigidness of the bony crest rising beneath the skin of a dog's head, the tackiness of flypaper, the sharpness of saws and ice picks.

It is impossible to determine where in any such specific memory, of course, texture gives way to heft, to shape, to temperature. The coolness of a camellia petal seems inseparable from that texture, warmth from the velvet rub of a horse's nose, heft from a brick's dry burr. And what can be said, as the hand recalls the earliest touch and exploration, of how texture changes with depth? Not alone the press of the palm on a dog's head or fingers boring to the roots of wool on a sheep's flank, but of, say, what happens with an orange: the hands work in concert to disassemble the fruit, running a thumb over the beaded surface of the skin, plying the soft white flay of the interior, the string net of fiber clinging to the translucent skin cases, dividing the yielding grain of the flesh beneath, with its hard, wrinkled seeds. And, further, how is one to separate these textures from a memory of the burst of fragrance as the skin is torn, or from the sound of the sections being parted—to say nothing of the taste, juice dripping from the chin, or the urge to devour, then, even the astringent skin, all initiated by the curiosity of the hands?

Looking back, it's easy to see that the education of the hands (and so the person) begins like a language: a gathering of simple words, the assembly of simple sentences, all this leading eventually to the forging of instructive metaphors. Afterward nothing can truly be separated, to stand alone in the hands' tactile memory. Taking the lay of the dog's fur, the slow petting of the loved dog is the increasingly complicated heart speaking with the hand.

Still, because of an occasional, surprising flair of the hands, the insistence of their scarred surfaces, it is possible for me to sustain the illusion that they have a history independent of the mind's perception, the heart's passion; a history of gathering what appeals, of expressing exasperation with their own stupidity, of faith in the accrual of brute work. If my hands began to explore complex knowledge by seeking and sorting texture—I am compelled to believe this—then the first names my memory truly embraced came from the hands' differentiating among fruits and woven fabrics.

GROWING ON FARMS and in orchards and truck gardens around our home in rural California was a chaos of fruit: navel and Valencia oranges, tangerines, red and yellow grapefruit, pomegranates, lemons, pomelos, greengage and damson plums, freestone and cling peaches, apricots, figs, tangelos, Concord and muscadine grapes. Nectarines, Crenshaw, casaba, and honeydew melons, watermelons, and cantaloupes. My boyish hands knew the planting, the pruning, the picking, and the packing of some of these fruits, the force and the touch required. I sought them all out for the resilience of their ripeness and knew the different sensation of each—pips, radius, cleavage. I ate even tart pomegranates with ardor, from melons I dug gobs of succulent meat with mouth and fingers. Slicing open a cantaloupe or a melon with a knife, I would hesitate always at the sight of the cleft fistula of seeds. It unsettled me, as if it were the fruit's knowing brain.

The fabrics were my mother's. They were stacked in bolts catawampus on open shelves and in a closet in a room in our small house where she both slept and sewed, where she laid out skirts, suits, and dresses for her customers. Lawn, organdy, batiste, and other fine cottons; cambric and gingham; silks—moiré, crepe de chine, taffeta; handkerchief and other weights of linen; light wools like gabardine; silk and cotton damasks; silk and rayon satins; cotton and wool twills; velvet; netted cloths like tulle. These fabrics differed not only in their texture and weave, in the fineness of their threads, but in the way they passed or reflected light, in their drape, and, most obviously from a distance, in their color and pattern.

I handled these fabrics as though they were animal skins, opening out bolts on the couch when Mother was working, holding them against the window light, raking them with my nails, crumpling them in my fist, then furling them as neatly as I could. Decades later, reading "samite of Ethnise" and "uncut rolls of brocade of Tabronit" in a paperback translation of Wolfram von Eschenbach's *Parzival*, I watched my free hand rise up to welcome the touch of these cloths.

It embarrassed and confounded me that other boys knew so little of cloth, and mocked the knowledge; but growing up with orchards and groves and vine fields, we shared a conventional, peculiar intimacy with fruit. We pelted one another with rotten plums and the green husks of walnuts. We flipped gourds and rolled melons into the paths of oncoming, unsuspecting cars. This prank of the hand—throwing, rolling, flipping—meant nothing without the close companionship of the eye. The eye measured the distance, the crossing or closing speed of the object, and then the hand—the wrist snapping, the fingers' tips guiding to the last—decided upon a single trajectory, measured force, and then a rotten plum hit someone square in the back or sailed wide, or the melon exploded beneath a tire or rolled cleanly to the far side of the road. And we clapped in glee and wiped our hands on our pants.

In these early years—eight and nine and ten—the hands became attuned to each other. They began to slide the hafts of pitchforks and pry bars smoothly, to be more aware of each other's placement for leverage and of the slight difference in strength. It would be three or four more years before, playing the infield in baseball, I would sense the spatial and temporal depth of awareness my hands had of each other, would feel, short-hopping a sharp grounder blind in front of third base, flicking the ball from gloved-left to bare-right hand, making the cross-body throw, that balletic poise of the still fingers after the release, would sense how mindless the beauty of it was.

I do not remember the ascendancy of the right hand. It was the one I was forced to write with, though by that time the right hand could already have asserted itself, reaching always first for a hammer or a peach. As I began to be judged according to the per-formance of my right hand alone—how well it imitated the Palmer cursive, how legibly it totaled mathematical figures—perhaps here is where the hands first realized how complicated their relationship would become. I remember a furious nun grab-bing my six-year-old hands in prayer and wrenching the right thumb from under the left. Right over left, she insisted. *Right over left.* Right over left in praying to God.

In these early years my hands were frequently folded in prayer. They, too, collected chickens' eggs, contended with the neat assembly of plastic fighter planes, picked knots from bale twine, clapped chalkboard erasers, took trout off baited hooks, and trenched flower beds. They harbored and applauded homing pigeons. When I was eleven, my mother married again and we moved east to New York. The same hands took on new city tasks, struggled more often with coins and with tying the full Windsor knot. Also, now, they pursued a more diligent and precise comb-ing of my hair. And were in anxious anticipation of touching a girl. And that caress having been given, one hand confirmed the memory later with the other in exuberant disbelief. They over-hauled and pulled at each other like puppies.

I remember from these years—fourteen and fifteen and six-teen—marveling at the dexterity of my hands. In games of catch, one hand tipped the falling ball to the other, to be seized firmly in the same instant the body crashed to the ground. Or the hands changed effortlessly on the dribble at the start of a fast break in basketball. I remember disassembling, cleaning, and reassembling a two-barrel carburetor, knowing the memory of where all the parts fit was within my hands. I can recall the baton reversal of a pencil as I wrote then erased, wrote then erased, composing sentences on a sheet of paper. And I remember how the hands, so clever with a ball, so deft with a pair of needle-nose pliers, fumbled attaching a cymbidium orchid so close to a girl's body, so near the mysterious breast.

By now, sixteen or so, my hands were as accustomed to books, to magazines, newspapers, and typing paper, as they were to mechanic's tools and baseballs. A blade in my pocketknife was a shape my fingers had experienced years earlier as an oleander leaf. The shape of my fountain pen I knew first as a eucalyptus twig, drawing make-believe roads in wet ground. As my hands had once strained to bring small bluegills to shore, now they reeled striped bass from the Atlantic's surf. As they had once entwined horses' manes, now they twirled girls' ponytails. I had stripped them in those years of manure, paint, axle grease, animal gore, plaster, soap suds, and machine oil; I had cleaned them of sap and tar and putty, of pond scum and potting soil, of fish scales and grass stains. The gashes and cuts had healed smoothly. They were lithe, strenuous. The unimpeded reach of the fingers away from one another in three planes, their extreme effective span, was a subtle source of confidence and wonder. They showed succinctly the physical intelligence of the body. They expressed so unmistakably the vulnerability in sexual desire. They drew so deliberately the curtains of my privacy.

One July afternoon I stood at an ocean breakwater with a friend, firing stones one after another in long, beautiful arcs a hundred feet to the edge of the water. We threw for accuracy, aiming to hit small breaking waves with cutting *thwips*. My friend tired of the game and lay down on his towel. A few moments later I turned and threw in a single motion just as he leaped to his feet. The stone caught him full in the side of the head. He was in the hospital a month with a fractured skull, unable to speak clearly until he was operated on. The following summer we were playing baseball together again, but I could not throw hard or accurately for months after the accident, and I shied away completely from a growing desire to be a pitcher.

My hands lost innocence or gained humanity that day, as they had another day when I was pulled off my first dog, screaming, my hands grasping feebly in the air, after he'd been run over and killed in the road. Lying awake at night I sometimes remember throwing the near deadly stone, or punching a neighbor's horse with my adolescent fist, or heedlessly swinging a 16-gauge shotgun, leading quail—if I hadn't forgotten to switch off the trigger safety, I would have shot an uncle in the head. My hands lay silent at my sides those nights. No memory of their grace or benediction could change their melancholy stillness.

While I was in college I worked two summers at a ranch in Wyoming. My hands got the feel of new tools—foot nips, frog pick, fence pliers, skiving knife. I began to see that the invention, dexterity, and quickness of the hands could take many directions in a man's life; and that a man should be attentive to what his hands loved to do, and so learn not only what he might be good at for a long time but what would make him happy. It pleased me to smooth every wrinkle from a saddle blanket before I settled a saddle squarely on a horse's back. And I liked, too, to turn the thin pages of a Latin edition of the *Aeneid* as I slowly accomplished them that first summer, feeling the impression of the type. It was strengthening to work with my hands, with ropes and bridles and hay bales, with double-bitted axes and bow saws, currying horses, scooping grain, adding my hands' oil to wooden door latches in the barn, calming horses at the foot of a loading ramp, adjusting my hat against the sun, buckling my chaps on a frosty morning. I'd watch the same hand lay a book lovingly on a night table and reach for the lamp's pull cord.

I had never learned to type, but by that second summer, at nineteen, I was writing out the first few stories longhand in pencil. I liked the sound and the sight of the writing going on, the back pressure through my hand. When I had erased and crossed out and rewritten a story all the way through, I would type it out slowly with two or sometimes four fingers, my right thumb on the space bar, as I do to this day. Certain keys and a spot on the space bar are worn through to metal on my typewriters from the oblique angles at which my fingernails strike them.

HAD I BEEN ABLE to grasp it during those summers in Wyoming, I might have seen that I couldn't get far from writing stories and physical work, either activity, and remain happy. It proved true that in these two movements my hands found their chief joy, aside from the touching of other human beings. But I could not see it then. My hands only sought out and gave in to the pleasures.

I began to travel extensively while I was in college. Eventually I visited many places, staying with different sorts of people. Most worked some substantial part of the day with their hands. I gravitated toward the company of cowboys and farmers both, to the work of loggers and orchardists, but mostly toward the company of field biologists, college-educated men and women who worked long days open to the weather, studying the lives of wild animals. In their presence, sometimes for weeks at a time, occasionally in stupefying cold or under significant physical strain, I helped wherever I could and wrote in my journal what had happened and, sometimes, what I thought of what had happened. In this way my hands came to know the prick and compression of syringes, the wiring and soldering of radio collars, the arming of anesthetizing guns, the setting of traps and snares, the deployment of otter trawls and plankton tows, the operation of calipers and tripod scales, and the manipulation of various kinds of sieves and packages used to sort and store parts of dead animals, parts created with the use of skinning and butchering knives, with bone saws, teasing needles, tweezers, poultry shears, and hemostatic clamps. My hands were in a dozen kinds of blood, including my own.

Everywhere I journeyed I marveled at the hands of other creatures, at how their palms and digits revealed history, at how well they performed tasks, at the elegant and incontrovertible beauty of their design. I cradled the paws of wolves and polar bears, the hooves of caribou, the forefeet of marine iguanas, the foreflippers of ringed seals and sperm whales, the hands of wallabies, of deer mice. Palpating the tendons, muscles, and bones beneath the skin or fur, I gained a rough understanding of the range of ability, of expression. I could feel where a broken bone had healed and see from superficial scars something of what a life must have been like. Deeper down, with mammals during a necropsy, I could see how blood vessels and layers of fat in a paw or in a flipper were arranged to either rid the creature of its metabolic heat or hoard it. I could see the evidence of arthritis in its phalanges, how that could come to me.

I have never touched a dead human, nor do I wish to. The living hands of another person, however, draw me, as strongly as the eyes. What is their history? What are their emotions? What longing is there? I can follow a cabinetmaker's hands for hours as they verify and detect, shave, fit, and rub; or a chef's hands adroitly dicing vegetables or shaping pastry. And who has not known faintness at the sight of a lover's hand? What man has not wished to take up the hands of the woman he loves and pore over them with reverence and curiosity? Who has not in reverie wished to love the lover's hands?

Years after my mother died I visited her oldest living friend. We were doing dishes together and she said, "You have your mother's hands." Was that likeness a shade of love? And if now I say out of respect for my hands I would buy only the finest tools, is that, too, not love?

The hands evolve, of course. The creases deepen and the fingers begin to move two or three together at a time. If the hands of a man are put to hard use, the fingers grow blunt. They lose dexterity and the skin calluses over like hide. Hardly a pair of man's hands known to me comes to mind without a broken or dislocated finger, a lost fingertip, a permanently crushed nail. Most women my age carry scars from kitchen and housework, drawer pinches, scalds, knife and glass cuts. We hardly notice them. Sunlight, wind, and weather obscure many of these scars, but I believe the memory of their occurrence never leaves the hands. When I awaken in the night and sense my hands cupped together under the pillow, or when I sit somewhere on a porch, idly watching wind crossing a ripening field, and look down to see my hands nested in my lap as if asleep like two old dogs, it is not hard for me to believe they know. They remember all they have done, all that has happened to them, the ways in which they have been surprised or worked themselves free of desperate trouble, or lost their grip and so caused harm. It's not hard to believe they remember the heads patted, the hands shaken, the apples peeled, the hair braided, the wood split, the gears shifted, the flesh gripped and stroked, and that they convey their feelings to each other.

In recent years my hands have sometimes been very cold for long stretches. It takes little cold now to entirely numb thumbs and forefingers. They cease to speak what they know. When I was thirty-one, I accidentally cut the base of my left thumb, severing nerves, leaving the thumb confused about what was cold, what was hot, and whether or not it was touching something or only thought so. When I was thirty-six, I was helping a friend butcher a whale. We'd been up for many hours under twenty-four-hour arctic daylight and were tired. He glanced away and without thinking drove the knife into my wrist. It was a clean wound, easy to close, but with it I lost the nerves to the right thumb. Over the years each thumb has regained some sensitivity, and I believe the hands are more sympathetic to each other because of their similar wounds. The only obvious difference lies with the left hand. A broken metacarpal forced a rerouting of tendons to the middle and ring fingers as it healed and raised a boss of carpal bone tissue on the back of the hand.

At the base of the right thumb is a scar from a climbing accident. On the other thumb, a scar the same length from the jagged edge of a fuel-barrel pump. In strong sunlight, when there is a certain tension in the skin, as I have said, I can stare at my hands for a while, turning them slowly, and remember with them the days, the weather, the people present when some things happened that left scars behind. It brings forth affection for my hands. I recall how, long ago, they learned to differentiate between cotton and raw silk, between husks of the casaba and the honeydew melon, and how they thrilled to the wire bristle of a hog's back, how they clipped the water's surface in swimming-pool fights, how they painstakingly arranged bouquets, how they swung and lifted children. I have begun to wish they would speak to me, tell me stories I have forgotten.

I sit in a chair and look at the scars, the uneven cut of the nails, and reminisce. With them before me I grin as though we held something secret, remembering bad times that left no trace. I cut firewood for my parents once, winter in Alabama, swamping out dry, leafless vines to do so. Not until the next day did I realize the vines were poison ivy. The blisters grew so close and tight my hands straightened like paddles. I had to have them lanced to continue a cross-country trip, to dress and feed myself. And there have been days when my hands stiffened with cold so that I had to quit the work being done, sit it out and whimper with pain as they came slowly back to life. But these moments are inconsequential. I have looked at the pale, wrinkled hands of a drowned boy, and I have seen handless wrists.

If there were a way to speak directly to the hands, to allow them a language of their own, what I would most wish to hear is what they recall of human touch, of the first exploration of the body of another, the caresses, the cradling of breast, of head, of buttock. Does it seem to them as to me that we keep learning, even when the caressed body has been known for years? How do daydreams of an idealized body, one's own or another's, affect the hands' first tentative inquiry? Is the hand purely empirical? Does it apply an imagination? Does it retain a man's shyness, a boy's clumsiness? Do the hands anguish if there is no one to touch?

Tomorrow I shall pull blackberry vines and load a trailer with rotten timber. I will call on my hands to help me dress, to turn the spigot for water for coffee, to pull the newspaper from its tube. I will put my hands in the river and lift water where the sunlight is brightest, a playing with fractured light I never tire of. I will turn the pages of a book about the history of fire in Australia. I will sit at the typewriter, working through a story about a trip to Matagorda Island in Texas. I will ask my hands to undress me. Before I turn out the light, I will fold and set my reading glasses aside. Then I will cup my hands, the left in the right, and slide them under the pillow beneath my head, where they will speculate, as will I, about what we shall handle the next day, and dream, a spooling of their time we might later remember together and I, so slightly separated from them, might recognize.

13

LEARNING TO SEE

I N JUNE 1989, I received a puzzling letter from the Amon Carter Museum in Fort Worth, Texas, an invitation to speak at the opening of a retrospective of the work of Robert Adams. The show, "To Make It Home: Photographs of the American West, 1965–1985," had been organized by the Philadelphia Museum of Art and would travel to the Los Angeles County Museum and the Corcoran Gallery of Art in Washington, D.C., before being installed at the Amon Carter, an institution renowned for its photographic collections, in the spring of 1990.

Robert Adams, an un-self-promoting man who has published no commercially prominent book of photographs, is routinely referred to as one of the most important landscape photographers in America, by both art critics and his colleagues. His black-and-white images are intelligently composed and morally engaged. They're also hopeful, despite their sometimes depressing subject matter—brutalized landscapes and the venality of the American Dream as revealed in suburban life. Adams doesn't hold himself apart from what he indicts. He photographs with compassion and he doesn't scold. His pictures are also accessible, to such a degree that many of them seem casual. In 1981 he published *Beauty in Photography: Essays in Defense of Traditional Values,* one of the clearest statements of artistic responsibility ever written by a photographer.

If there is such a thing as an ideal of stance, technique, vision, and social contribution toward which young photographers might aspire, it's embodied in this man.

I suspected the Amon Carter had inadvertently invited the wrong person to speak. I'd no knowledge of the history of American photography sufficient to situate Robert Adams in it. I couldn't speak to the technical perfection of his prints. I'd no credentials as an art critic. As an admirer of the work, of course, I'd have something to say, but it could only be that, the words of an amateur who admired Adams's accomplishment.

I wondered for days what prompted the invitation. For about fifteen years, before putting my cameras down on September 13, 1981, never to pick them up again, I'd worked as a landscape photographer, but it was unlikely anyone at the Amon Carter knew this. I'd visited the museum in the fall of 1986 to see some of their luminist paintings and had met several of the curators, but our conversations could not have left anyone with the impression that I had the background to speak about Adams's work.

I finally decided to say yes. I wrote and told the person coordinating the program, Mary Lampe, that though I didn't feel qualified to speak I admired Mr. Adams's work, and further, I presumed an affinity with his pursuits and ideals as set forth in *Beauty in Photography.* And I told her I intended to go back and study the work of Paul Strand, Wynn Bullock, Minor White, Harry Callahan, and others who'd been an influence on my own work and thought, in order to prepare my lecture.

Months later, when I arrived at the museum, I asked Ms. Lampe how they had come to invite me and not someone more qualified. She said Mr. Adams had asked them to do so. I sensed she believed Robert Adams and I were good friends and I had to tell her I didn't know him at all. We'd never met, never corresponded, had not spoken on the phone. I was unaware, even, that it was "Bob" Adams, as Ms. Lampe called him.

"But why did you agree to come?" she asked.

"Out of respect for the work," I said. "Out of enthusiasm for the work." I also explained that I was intimidated by the prospect, and that sometimes I felt it was good to act on things like that.

Ms. Lampe subsequently sent Robert Adams a tape of my talk. He and I later met and we now correspond and speak on the phone regularly. He set the course of our friendship in the first sentence of a letter he wrote me after hearing my presentation. "Your willingness to speak in my behalf," he wrote, "confirms my belief in the community of artists."

He believed from work of mine that he'd read that we shared a sensibility, that we asked similar questions about the relationship between culture and landscape, and that our ethical leanings and our sense of an artist's social responsibility were similar. He later told me that for these reasons he'd given my name, hopefully but somewhat facetiously, to Ms. Lampe, not knowing the curators and I were acquainted and that they would write me.

I'VE LONG BEEN attracted to the way visual artists like Robert Adams imagine the world. The emotional impact of their composition of space and light is as clarifying for me as immersion in a beautifully made story. As with the work of a small group of poets I read regularly—Robert Hass, Pattiann Rogers, Garrett Hongo—I find healing in their expressions. I find reasons not to give up.

Though I no longer photograph, I have maintained since 1981 a connection with photographers and I keep up a sort of running conversation with several of them. We talk about the fate of photography in the United States, where of course art is increasingly more commodified and where, with the advent of computer manipulation, photography is the art most likely to mislead. Its history as a purveyor of objective reality, the idea that "the camera never lies," is specious, certainly; but with some artistic endeavors, say those of Cartier-Bresson, Aaron Siskind, or W. Eugene Smith, and in the fields of documentary photography, which would include some news photography, and nature photography, one can assert that the authority of the image lies with the subject. With the modern emphasis on the genius of the individual artist, however, and with the arrival of computer imaging, authority in these areas now more often lies with the photographer. This has become true to such an extent that the reversal that's occurred—the photographer, not the subject, is in charge—has caused the rules of evidence to be changed in courts of law; and it has foisted upon an unwitting public a steady stream, for example, of fabricated images of wildlife.

As a beginning photographer I was most attracted to color and form, to the emotional consequence of line. It is no wonder, looking back now, that I pored over the images of someone like Edward Weston, or that I felt isolated in some of my pursuits because at the time few serious photographers outside Ernst Haas and Eliot Porter worked as I did in color. I wanted to photograph the streaming of light. For a long while it made no difference whether that light was falling down the stone walls of a building in New York or lambent on the corrugations of a wheat field. Ansel Adams was suggested to me early on as a model, but he seemed to my eye inclined to overstate. I wanted the sort of subtlety I would later come to admire in Bob Adams's work and in the aerial photographs of Emmet Gowin.

The more I gravitated as a writer toward landscape as a context in which to work out what I was thinking as a young man about issues like justice, tolerance, ambiguity, and compassion, the more I came to concentrate on landforms as a photographer. I valued in particular the work of one or two wildlife photographers shooting *in situ,* in the bush. (I remember enthusiastically

contacting friends about John Dominis's groundbreaking portfolio of African cat photographs, which appeared in three succes-
sive issues of *Life* in January 1967.) But I was not inclined toward
mastering the kind of technical skill it took to make such photographs. More fundamentally, I had misgivings about what I
regarded as invasions of the privacy of wild animals. The latter
notion I thought so personal an idea I kept it mostly to myself;
today, of course, it's a central concern of wildlife photographers,
especially for a contingent that includes Frans Lanting, the late
Michio Hoshino, Gary Braasch, Tui De Roy, and the team of
Susan Middleton and David Liittschwager.

I began photographing in a conscientious way in the summer
of 1965. I was soon concentrating on landscapes, and in the mid-
1970s, with a small list of publication credits behind me, I made an
appointment to see Joe Scherschel, an assistant director of the
photographic staff at *National Geographic.* He told me frankly that
though my landscape portfolio was up to the standards of the
magazine, the paucity of wildlife images and human subjects
made it unlikely that he could offer me any assignments. In
response I remember thinking this was unlikely to change, for
either of us. Discouraged, I started to scale back the effort to market my photographs and to make part of my living that way. I
continued to make pictures, and I was glad that much of this
work was still effectively represented by a stock agency in New
York; but by 1978 I knew photography for me was becoming more
a conscious exercise in awareness, a technique for paying attention. It would finally turn into a sequestered exploration of light
and spatial volume.

Three events in the late 1970s changed the way I understood
myself as a photographer. One summer afternoon I left the
house for an appointment with an art director in a nearby city.
Strapped to the seat of my motorcycle was a box of photographs,
perhaps three hundred images representative of the best work I
had done. The two-lane road I traveled winds gently through
steep mountainous country. When I got to town the photographs were gone. I never found a trace of them, though I

searched every foot of the road for two days. The loss dismantled my enthusiasm for photography so thoroughly that I took it for a message to do something else.

In the summer of 1976 my mother was dying of cancer. To ease her burden, and to brighten the sterile room in Lenox Hill Hospital in New York where she lay dying, I made a set of large Cibachrome prints from some of my 35-mm Kodachrome images—a white horse standing in a field of tall wild grasses bounded by a white post-and-plank fence; a faded pink boat trailer from the 1940s, abandoned in the woods; a small copse of quaking aspen, their leaves turning bright yellow on the far side of a remote mountain swamp. It was the only set of prints I would ever make. As good as they were, the change in color balance and the loss of transparency and contrast when compared with the originals, the reduction in sharpness, created a deep doubt about ever wanting to do such a thing again. I hung the images in a few shows, then put them away. I knew if I didn't start developing and printing my own images, I wouldn't be entering any more shows.

I winced whenever I saw my photographs reproduced in magazines and books, but I made my peace with that. Time-Life Books was publishing a series then called *American Wilderness,* each volume of which was devoted to a different landscape—the Maine woods, the Cascade Mountains, the Grand Canyon. I was pleased to see my work included in these volumes, but I realized that just as the distance between what I saw and what I was able to record was huge, so was that between what I recorded and what people saw. Seeing the printed images on the page was like finding one's haiku published as nineteen-syllable poems.

The third event occurred around the first serious choice I made as a photographer to concentrate on a limited subject. The subject was always light, but I wanted to explore a single form, which turned out to be the flow of water in creeks and rivers near my home. I photographed in every season, when the water was high in February and March, when it was low in August, when it was transparent in July, when it was an opaque jade in December.

In 1980 I began to photograph moving water in moonlight, exposures of twenty-five or thirty minutes. These images suffered from reciprocity failure—the color balance in them collapsed—but they also recorded something extraordinary, a pattern of flow we cannot actually see. They revealed the organizing principle logicians would one day call a strange attractor.

The streaming of water around a rock is one of the most complex motions of which human beings are aware. The change from a laminar, more or less uniform flow to turbulent flow around a single rock is so abstruse a transition mathematically that even the most sophisticated Cray computer cannot make it through to a satisfactory description.

Aesthetically, of course, no such difficulty exists. The eye dotes on the shift, delights in the scintillating sheeting, the roll-off of light around a rock, like hair responding to the stroke of a brush. Sometimes I photographed the flow of water in sunshine at 1/2000 of a second and then later I'd photograph the same rock in moonlight. Putting the photos side by side, I could see something hidden beneath the dazzle of the high-speed image that compared with our renderings of the Milky Way from space: the random pin-dot infernos of our own and every other sun form a spiraling, geometrical shape motionless to our eyes. In the moonlit photographs, the stray streaks from errant water splashes were eliminated (in light that weak, they occur too quickly to be recorded); what was etched on the film instead were orderly, fundamental lines of flow, created by particle after illuminated particle of gleaming water, as if each were a tracer bullet. (Years later, reading *Chaos,* James Gleick's lucid report on chaos theory, I would sit bolt upright in my chair. What I'd photographed was the deep pattern in turbulence, the clothing, as it were, of the strange attractor.)

In the months I worked at making these photographs, I came to realize I actually had two subjects as a photographer. First, these still images of a moving thing, a living thing—as close as I would probably ever come to fully photographing an animal. Second, natural light falling on orchards, images of a subject routinely understood as a still life. The orchards near me were mostly filbert orchards. In their change of color and form through the seasons, in the rain and snow that fell through them, in crows that sat on their winter branches, in leaves accumulated under them on bare dark ground, in the wind that coursed them, in the labyrinths of their limbs, ramulose within the imposed order of the orchard plot, I saw the same profundity of life I found in literature.

This was all work I was eager to do, but I would never get to it.

In September 1981 I was working in the Beaufort Sea off the north coast of Alaska with several marine biologists. We were conducting a food-chain survey intended to provide baseline data to guide offshore oil drilling, an impulsive and politically motivated development program funded by the Bureau of Land Management and pushed hard at the time by the Reagan government. On September 12, three of us rendezvoused at Point Barrow with a National Oceanic and Atmospheric Administration research vessel, the *Oceanographer*. They hoisted us, our gear, and our twenty-foot Boston Whaler aboard and we sailed west into pack ice in the northern Chukchi Sea.

Scientific field research is sometimes a literally bloody business. In our study we were trying to determine the flow of energy through various "levels" (artificially determined) of the marine food web. To gather data we retrieved plankton and caught fish with different sorts of traps and trawls, and we examined the contents of bearded seal, ringed seal, and spotted seal stomachs. To accomplish the latter, we shot and killed the animals. Shooting seals located us squarely in the moral dilemma of our work, and it occasioned talk aboard the *Oceanographer* about the barbarousness of science. The irony here was that without these data creatures like the ringed seal could not be afforded legal protection against oil development. The killings were a manifestation of the perversions in our age, our Kafkaesque predicaments.

I was disturbed by the fatal aspects of our work, as were my companions, but I willingly participated. I would later write an essay about the killing, but something else happened during that trip, less dramatic and more profound in its consequences for me.

Late one afternoon, working our way back to the *Oceanographer* through a snow squall, the three of us came upon a polar bear. We decided to follow him for a few minutes and I got out my cameras. The bear, swimming through loose pack ice, was clearly annoyed by our presence, though in our view we were maintaining a reasonable distance. He very soon climbed out on an ice floe, crossed it, and dropped into open water on the far side. We had to go the long way around in the workboat, but we caught up. He hissed at us and otherwise conveyed his irritation, but we continued idling along beside him.

Eventually we backed off. The bear disappeared in gauze curtains of blowing snow. We returned to the *Oceanographer,* to a warm meal and dry clothes.

Once the boat was secure and our scientific samples squared away in the lab, I went to my cabin. I dropped my pack on the floor, stripped off my heavy clothes, showered, and lay down in my bunk. I tried to recall every detail of the encounter with the bear. What had he been doing when we first saw him? Did he change direction then? How had he proceeded? Exactly how did he climb out of the water onto the ice floe? What were the mechanics of it? When he shook off seawater, how was it different from a dog shucking water? When he hissed, what color was the inside of his mouth?

I don't know how long I lay there, a half hour perhaps, but when I was through, when I'd answered these questions and was satisfied that I'd recalled the sequence of events precisely and in sufficient detail, I got up, dressed, and went to dinner. Remembering what happened in an encounter was crucial to my work as a writer, and attending to my cameras during our time with the bear had altered and shrunk my memory of it. While the polar bear was doing something, I was checking f-stops and attempting to frame and focus from a moving boat.

I regarded the meeting as a warning to me as a writer. Having successfully recovered details from each minute, I believed, of that encounter, having disciplined myself to do that, I sensed I wouldn't pick up a camera ever again.

It was not solely contact with this lone bear a hundred miles off the northwest coast of Alaska, of course, that ended my active involvement with photography. The change had been coming for a while. The power of the polar bear's presence, his emergence from the snow squall and his subsequent disappearance, had created an atmosphere in which I could grasp more easily a complex misgiving that had been building in me. I view any encounter with a wild animal in its own territory as a gift, an opportunity to sense the real animal, not the zoo creature, the TV creature, the advertising creature. But this gift had been more overwhelming. In some way the bear had grabbed me by the shirtfront and said, Think about this. Think about what these cameras in your hands are doing.

Years later, I'm still thinking about it. Some of what culminated for me that day is easy to understand. As a writer, I had begun to feel I was missing critical details in situations such as this one because I was distracted. I was also starting to feel uncomfortable about the way photographs tend to collapse events into a single moment, about how much they leave out. (Archeologists face a similar problem when they save only what they recognize from a dig. Years afterward, the context long having been destroyed, the archeologist might wonder what was present that he or she didn't recognize at the time. So begins a reevaluation of the meaning of the entire site.)

I was also disturbed about how nature and landscape photographs, my own and others', were coming to be used, not in advertising where you took your chances (some photographers at that time began labeling their images explicitly: NO TOBACCO, NO ALCOHOL), but in the editorial pages of national magazines. It is a polite fiction of our era that the average person, including the average art director, is more informed about natural history than an educated person was in Columbus's age. Because this is not true, the majority of nature photographers who work out in the field have felt a peculiar burden to record accurately the great range of habitat and animal behavior they see, including nature's "dark" side. (Photographers accepted the fact back then that magazines in the United States, generally speaking, were not interested in photographs of mating animals—unless they were chaste or cute—or in predatory encounters if they were bloody or harrowing, as many were.)

What happened as a result of this convention was that people looking at magazines in the 1970s increasingly came to think of wild animals as vivacious and decorative in the natural world. Promoted as elegant, brave, graceful, sinister, wise, etc., according to their species, animals were deprived of personality and the capacity to be innovative. Every wildlife photographer I know can recount a story of confrontation with an art director in which he or she argued unsuccessfully for an image that told a fuller or a truer story about a particular species of animal in a layout. It was the noble lion, the thieving hyena, and the mischievous monkey, however, who routinely triumphed. A female wolf killing one of her pups, or a male bonobo approaching a female with a prominent erection, was not anything magazine editors were comfortable with.

In the late seventies, I asked around among several publishers to see whether they might have any interest in a series of disturbing photographs made in a zoo by a woman named Ilya. She'd taken them on assignment for *Life*, but very few of them were ever published because she'd concentrated on depicting animals apparently driven insane by their incarceration. I remember as particularly unsettling the look of psychosis in the face of a male lion, its mane twisted into knots. I could develop no interest in publishing her work. An eccentric view, people felt. Too distressing.

So, along with a growing political awareness of endangered landscapes and their indigenous animals in the 1970s came, ironically, a more and more dazzling presentation of those creatures in incomplete and prejudicial ways. Photo editors made them look not like what they were but the way editors wanted them to appear—well-groomed, appropriate to stereotype, and living safely apart from the machinations of human enterprise. To my mind there was little difference then between a *Playboy* calendar and a wildlife calendar. Both celebrated the conventionally gorgeous, the overly endowed, the seductive. I and many other photographers at the time were apprehensive about the implications of this trend.

Another concern I had that September afternoon, a more complicated one, was what was happening to memory in my generation. The advertising injunction to preserve family memories by taking photographs had become so shrill a demand, and the practice had become so compulsive, that recording the event was more important for some than participating in it. The inculcated rationale which grew up around this practice was that to take and preserve family photos was to act in a socially responsible way. The assumption seemed specious to me. My generation was the first to have ready access to inexpensive tape recorders and cameras. Far from recording memories of these talks and events, what we seemed to be doing was storing memories that would never be retrieved, that would never form a coherent narrative. In the same way that our desk drawers and cabinet shelves slowly filled with these "personal" sounds and images, we were beginning, it seemed to me, to live our lives in dissociated bits and pieces. The narrative spine of an individual life was disappearing. The order of events was becoming increasingly meaningless.

This worry, together with the increasingly commercial use to which the work of photographers like myself was being put and the preference for an entertaining but not necessarily coherent landscape of wild animals (images that essentially lied to children), made me more and more reluctant to stay involved. Some of the contemporary photographers I most respect—Lanting, Hoshino, Braasch, De Roy, Jim Brandenburg, Flip Nicklin, Sam Abell, Nick Nichols, Galen Rowell—have managed through the strength of their work and their personal integrity to overcome some of these problems, which are part and parcel of working in a world dominated more and more by commercial interests pursuing business strategies. But I knew I had no gift here to persevere. That realization, and my reluctance to photograph animals in the first place, may have precipitated my decision that day in the Chukchi.

As a writer, I had yet other concerns, peculiar to that discipline. I had begun to wonder whether my searching for the telling photographic image in a situation was beginning to interfere with my writing about what happened. I was someone who took a long time to let a story settle. I'd begun to suspect that the photographs made while I was in a note-taking stage were starting to lock my words into a pattern, and that the pattern was being determined too early. Photographs, in some way, were introducing preconceptions into a process I wanted to keep fluid. I often have no clear idea of what I'm doing. I just act. I pitch in, I try to stay alert to everything around me. I don't want to stop and focus on a finished image, which I'm inclined to do as a photographer. I want, instead, to see a sentence fragment scrawled in my notebook, smeared by rain. I don't want the clean, fixed image right away.

An attentive mind, I'm sure, can see the flaws in my reasoning. Some photographers are doing no more than taking notes when they click the shutter. It's only after a shoot that they discover what the story is. But by trying to both photograph and write, I'd begun to feel I was attempting to create two parallel but independent stories. The effort had become confusing and draining. I let go of photography partly because its defining process, to my mind, was less congruent with the way I wanted to work.

On June 16, 1979, forty-one sperm whales beached themselves at the mouth of the Siuslaw River on the Oregon coast, about one hundred miles from my home. I wrote a long essay about the stranding but didn't start work on it until after I'd spent two days photographing the eclipse of these beasts' lives and the aftermath of their deaths. That was the last time I attempted to do both things.

Perhaps the most rarefied of my concerns about photography that day in the Chukchi was one that lay for me at the heart of photography: recording a fleeting pattern of light in a defined volume of space. Light always attracted me. Indeed, twenty-five years after the fact, I can still vividly recall the light falling at dusk on a windbreak of trees in Mitchell, Oregon. It rendered me speechless when I saw it, and by some magic I managed to get it down on film. The problem of rendering volume in photography, however, was one I never solved beyond employing the conventional solutions of perspective and depth of field. I could recognize spatial volume successfully addressed in the work of other photographers—in Adams's work, for example, partly because so many of his photographs do not have an object as a subject. Finding some way myself to render volume successfully in a photograph would mean, I believed, walking too far away from my work as a writer. And, ultimately, it was as a writer that I felt more comfortable.

I MISS MAKING photographs. A short while ago I received a call from a curator at the Whitney Museum in New York named May Castleberry. She had just mounted a show called "Perpetual Mirage: Photographic Narratives of the Desert West" and I had been able to provide some minor assistance with it. She was calling now to pursue a conversation we'd begun at the time about Rockwell Kent, an illustrator, painter, and socialist widely known in the thirties, forties, and fifties. She wanted to hang a selection of his "nocturnes," prints and drawings Kent had made of people under starlit night skies. She was calling to see what I could suggest about his motivation.

Given Kent's leanings toward Nordic myth and legend and his espousal of Teddy Roosevelt's "strenuous life," it seemed obvious to me that he would want to portray his heroic (mostly male) figures against the vault of the heavens. But there were at least two other things at work here, I believed. First, Kent was strongly drawn to high latitudes, like Greenland, where in winter one can view the deep night sky for weeks on end. It was not really the "night" sky, however, he was drawing; it was the sunless sky of a winter day. Quotidian life assumes mythic proportions here not because it's heroic, but because it's carried out beneath the stars.

Secondly, I conjectured, because Kent was an artist working on flat surfaces, he sought, like every such artist, ways to suggest volume, to make the third dimension apparent. Beyond what clouds provide, the daytime sky has no depth; it's the night sky that gives an artist volume. While it takes an extraordinary person—the light and space artist James Turrell, say—to make the celestial vault visible in sunshine, many artists have successfully conveyed a sense of the sky's volume by painting it at night.

THE CONCEIT CAN easily grow up in a photographer that he or she has pretty much seen all the large things—the range of possible emotion to be evoked with light, the contrasts to be made by arranging objects in different scales, problems in the third and fourth dimension. But every serious photographer, I believe, has encountered at some point ideas unanticipated and dumbfounding. The shock causes you to reexamine all you've assumed about your own work and the work of others, especially the work of people you've never particularly understood. This happened most recently for me in seeing the photography of Linda Connor. While working on a story about international air freight, I became so disoriented, flying every day from one spot on the globe to another thousands of miles away, I did not know what time I was living in. Whatever time it was, it was out of phase with the sun, a time not to be dialed up on a watch, mine or anyone else's.

At a pause in this international hurtling, during a six-hour layover in Cape Town, I went for a ride with an acquaintance. He drove us out to Clifton Bay on the west side of Table Mountain. I was so dazed by my abuse of time that I was open to thoughts I might otherwise never have had. One of those thoughts was that I could recognize the physicality of time. We can discern the physical nature of space in a picture, grasp the way, for example, Robert Adams is able to photograph the air itself, making it visible like a plein air painter. In Cape Town that day I saw what I came to call indigenous time. It clung to the flanks of Table Mountain. It resisted being absorbed into my helter-skelter time. It seemed not yet to have been subjugated by Dutch and British colonial expansion, as the physical landscape so clearly had been. It was time apparent to the senses, palpable. What made me believe I was correct in this perception was that, only a month before, I'd examined a collection of Linda Connor's work, a book called *Luminance.* I realized there at Table Mountain that she'd photographed what I was looking at. She'd photographed indigenous time.

I'd grasped Ms. Connor's photographs in some fashion after an initial pass, but I hadn't sensed their depth, their power, what Gerard Manley Hopkins called "the achieve of the thing." With this new insight I wrote her an excited note, an attempt to thank her for work that opened the door to a room I'd never explored.

One of the great blessings of our modern age, a kind of redemption for its cruelties and unmitigated greed, is that one can walk down to a corner bookstore and find a copy of Ms. Connor's book. Or of Robert Adams's *What We Brought: The New World,* or Frans Lanting's *Bonobo: The Forgotten Ape,* or, say, Mary Peck's *Chaco Canyon: A Center and Its World,* and then be knocked across the room by a truth one had not, until that moment, clearly discerned.

It is more than illumination, though, more than a confirmation of one's intuition, aesthetics, or beliefs that comes out of the perusal of such a photographer's images. It's regaining the feeling that one is not cut off from the wellsprings of intelligence and goodwill, of sympathy for human plight.

I do not know, of course, why the photographers I admire, even the ones I know, photograph, but I am acutely aware that without the infusion of their images hope would wither in me. I feel an allegiance to their work more as a writer than as someone who once tried to see in this way, perhaps because I presume we share certain principles related to the effort to imagine or explain.

It is correct, I think, as Robert Adams wrote me that day, to believe in a community of artists stimulated by and respectful of one another's work. But it's also true that without an audience (of which we're all a part) the work remains unfinished, unfulfilled. A photographer seeks intimacy with the world and then endeavors to share it. Inherent in that desire to share is a love of humanity. In different media, and from time to time, we have succeeded, I believe, in helping one another understand what is going on. We have come to see that, in some way, this is our purpose with each other.

PART FOUR

An Opening Quartet

14

DEATH

M Y MOTHER WAS bitten by a black widow on the train from Birmingham to Mobile when she was a girl. She held a potted geranium in her lap, a gift for her aunt, and the spider crawled from its leaves and bit her on the finger. She flung the pot away in the aisle and lapsed into a sweating fright with troubled breathing, the passengers solicitous around her. A man in a light-colored seersucker suit, she remembered, stamped the spider out on the floor, steadying himself against the rhythmic sway of the car with a hand on her seat.

I saw a black widow in our garage, a one-car garage narrow as a hallway, built for slender cars of the thirties, with a dirt floor. In the kitchen she shouted, Don't go near it, do you understand me? Don't go near it. Not until she could get someone to kill it. I didn't. I hunkered a few feet from its web, a boy with a flashlight craning his head to see the red hourglass, a chalice of poison it seemed.

I was spanked hysterically when she found me fascinated as a bird over a reflection in water. Another man came and killed the black widow, swatting at it with a board, missing and missing, the spider running away, the man shouting at my mother to get back, get back. I watched through a living-room window shrouded in curtains.

He said he killed it. He showed her and left.

On a shelf at the rear of the garage I found boxes of checks, some filled in with my mother's cursive. Inside another were checks with no handwriting. We're rich, Packard, I told my closest friend. You write in whatever you want. I had seen it time and again at the grocery, at the hardware store. I had Packard's wonder. You can even, I said, write in a hundred dollars. More, a thousand, and go to the bank. They give it to you.

He said yes, his voice carrying an image of the horizon over the ocean.

Yes, I said. We just write in these spaces, copying the words from the other checks. *One Thousand Dollars and No Cents.*

We put the checks back on the shelf. We had to make a plan. We had to pack the bags that we would tie to the seats and handlebars of our freshly oiled bikes.

On a July afternoon with a wind riding up the skirts of long-leaved eucalyptus, swirling the leaves and clusters of seed buttons, a sound that by hiding and then revealing the tree, hiding and revealing, made me flush with expectations I could not explain, three men in a convertible ran over my dog. His life ended abruptly, a painting cut open. I rocked his head in my lap and crooned, as if I had the power to give life. Would a bowl of water change it, a bowl of food? And who were these men in the lime green car, a species known to every southern California boy, 1949 Ford, idling now in the middle of the road, top down, brake lights lit up, the three of them looking back over the seats? They

got out and walked back, leaving both doors ajar, walked beneath the towering eucalyptus in their neat khakis and short-sleeved white shirts. Navy boys. Mother had a hand on my shoulder but I couldn't hear her words, every sound but the wind in the trees shut out. The men closed on us slowly, their eyes on the dog. I pulled more of him across my lap. Another man, a neighbor, floated in. They took the dog from me.

Afterward I sat in the shade underneath the eucalyptus, a space emptied by the absence of the dog, looking at the spot in the road where we had been. I did not find him. No one I asked said. I did not know where the dog was. Ever.

I THOUGHT IT WAS a shirt in the water wrapping itself around my legs in the bubbling surf, languid as wash in a bucket, until the punctures began. I lost my balance, fell over shrieking in the wavelets on a flat beach in inches of water. A stinging like nettles closed on my calves and ankles, my hands still moving toward it curiously as I fell, the bursts like a lash of hot pins up one thigh and across my back. I fell into the cool water shrieking, the clouds spinning away and away. I curled up like a shrimp in the wet sand until someone came, shrieking.

Portuguese man-of-war they told my mother, who could not be consoled, who mashed my hair with her stroking. Weeping, cradling, possessing me until the ambulance came. I remember lying down inside, relief in the purity of the refrigerated sheets, crying in the humiliation of my vomit.

PACKARD'S PARENTS were away. We pelted the trunks of peach trees in the orchard with fallen fruit, ground the peaches in each other's face, smeared each other's hair with the slime, then kicking and beating each other's temples with our fists we fought in earnest, wrenching buttons off, one taunting, the other charging the taunter, a flailing outcry at the misshapen stupidity that now made our friendship.

I lay still on my back, redolent of peaches, bruised, not interested now in the pursuit of anger, forgetting what it had been about—a touch in the wrong place, spitting the pulp at each other, so funny at first. I heard *thwack,* a while, then *thwack* again. Then *thwack.* Packard, throwing pitches hard in the driveway. A space opened up, a room to step into, the possibility of an apology. We would be the same again. The misunderstanding, so dumb.

Packard held a kitten by its tail, winding it overhead like a stone in a sling before firing it at the garage door, where it struck the planks above another crawling slowly in a circle.

INTO THE BAG I put one pair of socks, my collection of bird feathers wrapped in toilet paper, two candy bars, and five of the white checks from the box. In my wallet I had only the one check, written out after many tries in imitation of my mother's hand with her fountain pen, my name and the money. I tied the bag to the handlebars of the bicycle with string and rode away down the street under the eucalyptus trees. Tomorrow, my mother had said, we would get another dog.

15

MURDER

*I*N JUNE OF 1965 I left a friend's home in Santa Fe at dawn, drove north through Abiquiu, where Georgia O'Keeffe was then living, passed slowly through a lovely valley high in the San Juans that holds the town of Chama, and turned west for Durango. I crossed the Utah border west of Dove Creek, and ate lunch in the Mormon stillness of Monticello.

I was twenty, headed for Wyoming to work the summer on a friend's ranch, wrangling horses. And I was innocently in love, as perhaps you can only be at that age. The young woman lived in Salt Lake City. Anticipating each encounter—with her, beginning that night in Salt Lake, and the months afterward working with horses in Jackson Hole—made the sense of covering miles quickly in good weather an exquisite pleasure.

The highway north from Monticello runs ribbon-smooth

through bleak, wild country. When I left the cafe I fell back into a rhythm with it. The performance of the car, the torque curves through all four gears and so the right moment to shift, was well-known to me. Flying down U.S. 191 and double-clutching out of the turns eased the irritation that had grown in me in Monticello, under the stares of cafe patrons. "No, sir, we don't serve any coffee," the waitress had said. And, "No, sir, we don't have any ashtrays. We don't smoke here."

I rifled over the road course, holding a steady seventy through the turns and rises. The only traffic was a pickup or a car, sometimes a tractor-trailer rig, every six or eight minutes. I had a Ruger Single-Six .22 magnum pistol under the seat. In a leather case in the trunk was a rifle. In those days in that country a young man traveled with guns as a matter of course, with no criminal intent.

The two-lane highway passed clean beneath the hiss of new tires. Wind coming through the windows vibrated softly in the interior of the car. I remember the sight of the chrome tachometer, fitted to the steering column, gleaming in the sunshine, the spotless black nap of the floor carpets. I can recall the feel of the rolled seat covers under my thighs. In the seat opposite me sat my dog, a mongrel coyote I'd caught in the woods of southern Michigan as a pup. We'd driven the country for days at a time together, trips to New York City, to Helena, to Louisiana, the wind roaring at the windows, the tires whispering and thudding over rain-slicked concrete roads, the V-8 engine with its four-barrel carburetor, guttering through straight exhaust pipes.

A small, nondescript hill rises just south of Moab. The road climbs its gentle southern slope for several hundred yards and then falls off so abruptly a driver headed north confronts for a moment a blind spot. I hit the hill at probably eighty, imagining details of the evening ahead with Jan in Salt Lake. I saw a police car making a K-turn in the road a hundred yards in front of me as I came over the rise. The steering wheel seemed to stiffen, to resist in that moment, but that is likely a false memory. I never touched the horn, there was no time, no point. I focused on missing him, as he continued to back up slowly across the midstripe. I hurtled past on the left, going off the road in a spray of sand and dirt and whacking sagebrush with the rear fender as I tried to pull the car back on the road. It being the police, I thought it best just to keep going. His barn-size stupidity was a flat trade-off, I figured, with my speeding. I got the skidding car back up on the road and drove on to Moab at a touch under the legal sixty, with the police cruiser right behind me.

I slowed to the designated thirty-five at the city limit and a few blocks into town turned in to an A&W Root Beer stand. The police car went by. I tried to detect from the corner of my eye without turning my head whether he was turning his and staring at me through his sunglasses. He was. I continued to study the hand-scripted legend on the menu board in front of me. When the waitress came over I ordered a hamburger and what many people then called a black cow, a root beer float.

The air beneath the awning where I was parked was still and cool. I could feel the sweat drying on the back of my thighs. I got out and took the dog without a leash to a patch of dry grass and weeds in the harsh light at the edge of the parking lot. I noticed two young women there while I waited, sitting in a black 1960 Thunderbird backed up against a fence.

I ate my lunch slowly, scanning my Utah map and scrutinizing its detailed diagram of the streets of Salt Lake. I had the radio on. From time to time I glanced over at the two women in the Thunderbird. They had a child with them, a boy just a few years old. The women and I made eye contact once or twice. I smiled.

It occurred to me the cop would have had a tough time trying to force a ticket on me for speeding.

The sound of a door closing made me look up. One of the women in the Thunderbird, the one on the passenger side, had gotten out and was walking over. She looked seventeen or eighteen. She was very pregnant. My dog sat still in her seat as the woman approached the window. She leaned down and looked in, but didn't say anything. I reached for the dog and at my touch she turned and stepped nimbly into the backseat. Without a word the woman opened the door and got in.

"Hi," I said, conscious of being very casual.

"You live around here?" she asked.

"No. I'm coming from Indiana, from school there."

"Where're you going?"

"Wyoming."

She stared ahead in silence. I remember seeing the sweat beaded up on her small hands, her stout fingers, the maternity blouse billowing in a pink-and-white pattern over her lap.

"What do you think you might do for a woman?"

"What's that?"

"For a woman that might be in trouble, might have lots of trouble."

In the cool air under the metal awning, out of the glaring desert light, her language seemed dreary, detached.

"What kind of trouble is that?"

"Family trouble."

"You need money?"

"Would you kill my husband?"

The ebb of my nonchalance in this conversation was now complete. I sensed a border I did not know.

"I've got a gun over there in that car. He's in a garage outside of town, working on his car. All you have to do is walk in there, walk right up to him, and shoot him. He won't know you. There's no one else there. No one could hear."

I stared at her, her pallid cheeks, her full breasts.

"I'm not a liar. He's there. And I want to kill him."

She turned halfway to me, for the first time, no longer speaking to the windshield. Her milky blue eyes were both desperate and distant.

"He's working on his car. He doesn't care." She inclined her head. "That woman over there? Her sister's gonna have his kid too. I'd kill him myself, but I can't. I'd screw up. He'd beat me up so bad, I'd lose the baby."

I was afraid to say anything, make any movement. Her voice edged on hysteria, on laughter.

After a few moments of my silence her hand went to the door handle. "If you want to do it, no one would know. You could throw the gun away. I wouldn't say anything. I don't even know your name."

When the stillness hung on she said, "Well, forget it. Just forget it. Forget I even got in here." She got out, closed the door firmly, and walked away, reaching across to her right temple with her left hand in a prolonged, deliberate movement to sweep her blonde hair off her face, a movement that carried her across the sunlit lot to the Thunderbird. She sat there sullen and tight-lipped. When the boy came to her from the backseat she shoved him away, as if he were a younger brother she had to baby-sit.

I paid for my lunch and left. The peculiar tone of muscle in my young body, the quickness of my hand reflexes that made driving seem so natural, so complete a skill, was gone. I drove slowly north through town. The same officer sat austerely in the same car, parked just past the bridge over the Colorado River at the edge of town. I drove under the speed limit for more than an hour. I passed one or two buildings that could have been garages, but there was no sign of life.

I crossed the Green River and turned north for Price on U.S. 6. After a bit I pulled over and let the dog out. She bounded with exuberance through the sage and, a time or two, stood poised, looking back at me. I leaned against the car, smoking a cigarette. I couldn't remember if I'd loaded the pistol the night before when I was putting things in my car in Santa Fe. I thought of being with Jan that night and, suddenly impatient, whistled for the dog with exasperation.

16

SPEED

THE AIR WRITHED in scarfs of heat. I felt the heat of the engine on my bare feet through the fire wall, the sun beating on my head, the heat-helmet of my black hair. The tar-slurry patches in the road broadcast heat against the door, against the left side of my face. The streets, this far into an August afternoon, sagged in potholes at the intersection. The breath I drew was the heat of the sun, heat-glare of enamel, heat of motor block, fetid exhaust of the engine.

The light changed. I eased the clutch and moving air began to strip the heat. My head cooled until only my eyes still burned behind sunglasses. Second gear and a vacuum began to develop around the car, sucking heat out of the pool of heat and noise we'd been sitting in. I shifted to third at just under sixty in a forty-mile-per-hour zone between lights, downshifting to second to meet the broken stagger of red lights, then to first, engine braking up to the yellow crosswalk, the back hammer of the dual exhaust system one more anger in the anger of heat. Idling on the red. The car fills again with heat.

We surge and lay up like this from light to light, through metal and pavement and glass corridors that heat the heat. We cross burning gangs of steel rail, factory sidings, the road widening as it enters the old industrial core, a battalion of brick buildings disgorging steel bearings and brake drums into yards stacked with pig iron and volcanic slag, ranks of channel iron on rusty flatbeds.

A half mile. Two more lights. The insouciance of cows. Pasture and white board fences break down the brick flanks. At eighty I ease into fourth and the manic heat, ripped silk now, tatters away as if caught on the fences, the concertina wire around town.

Behind us, that's what we're thinking. Women in open sandals and damp shorts slumped on their arms at sorting tables in airless Laundromats. People pushing carts from air-conditioned malls raising an arm to ward off the incessant light which glints from mica chips in the griddle sidewalk. Their hands jump back from the door handles of their cars. They recoil from the sting of Naugahyde upholstery and gasp for air in these broilers.

Summer in northern Indiana, the pale light of the dog days, the smolder of towns like South Bend. We were pulling away at over a hundred.

I'd borrowed my younger brother's car, a two-seat convertible. The open country roads between South Bend and Shipshewana, fifty miles to the east, held some promise of relief in the rush of wind. I drove south on Indiana 331 for Wakarusa, way out of the way, so we wouldn't have to go through Elkhart, stagger through its impertinent traffic lights in lines of soft-boiled sedans and irritated drivers, not in this car.

We turned east on Indiana 4 and hurtled toward Wakarusa at an illegal and dangerous speed. We could not hear ourselves talk over the wind blast unless we shouted. We smiled at each other. My brother's taste in those days ran to Corvettes, and this was the most powerful one he had ever purchased. Chevrolet made no bigger stock engine and its Corvette assembly line squeezed no more dynamic force out of a motor block: 430 horsepower at 5200 rpm. "Four hundred and thirty-five pounds of torque at forty-four grand," in the argot of our youth.

My brother and I had grown up in southern California, where in the 1950s Detroit's production automobiles were reinvented. What Detroit lifted from all the retooling and fabrication done by teenagers and young men in home garages in the fifties and sixties in California, and what it later borrowed from Europe in the way of steering and suspension systems, became Detroit's "new" production cars of the late sixties and early seventies. Or we thought that. The Corvette, we maintained, came of age in California, inspired by our fathers and older brothers reboring, tinkering, and improvising with Detroit's timid creations. It was America's sole production sports car. What it lacked in finesse (suspension, steering, cornering ability) it made up for in raw power. The car grew out of a drag-strip, not a road-racing mentality. Models like the one I was driving carried even more of that California heritage in a Detroit chassis and body: its standard carburetion system and its shift linkage were designed by California outfits, Holly and Hurst.

California loomed big for us in Indiana in August because we could forget Indiana's long brutal winters during those flaccid, mercurial days. We could almost imagine California freeways, not Indiana toll roads, and a night run to Barstow holding a steady hundred over the Mojave, not these short six-mile runs between towns. Young men in Indiana pitied the basketball skill and acumen of players from California. So did we with California history shake our heads at what passed for a hot automobile with Indiana men.

Highway 331 rolled past broad-field farmsteads bounded by oak and maple and sycamore copses. The Corvette, set up on wide-tread racing tires, handled smoothly here and the two of us shared a sense of abandon. We had no way then, of course, 1968, to appreciate how little gas cost: thirty-one cents a gallon. But the rip of the wind made us forget the heat and we knew that out here the police rarely turned up. The radar traps were on the Indiana Toll Road and on the main highways west for Gary and south to Indianapolis. I drove with impunity. Our hair vibrated in the slipstream that boiled over the windshield like river rapids.

My father had some experience with race cars, roadsters like a K-2 Allard that he owned when he met my mother, and which he claimed once to have driven from Montclair, New Jersey, to Los Angeles in three days. When I came of age he took me out on back roads in Ocean County, New Jersey, and showed me how to drive, how to pull out of a skid, how to shift, how to use a tachometer. I gained confidence from these lessons, though I didn't know how deeply ingrained they were, if they were down there in my unconscious solid as a shovel, ready to serve in an emergency. I drove with enthusiasm but not recklessly, a distinction corroborated for me in the detachment and ease apparent in my companion sitting buckled in the other seat. In those days, on the verge of adulthood, courting such danger was a source of our vigor. We were pressed by few responsibilities. We drove aggressively and affected a languid attitude at the steering wheel. Except for the racket from the tuned exhaust system hammering the air as I downshifted into turns, we seemed to draw no one's attention. Two boys in white T-shirts driving a black convertible very fast on a dry road on a blistering day.

In Wakarusa the face of the law sat in a patrol car at the single light. He nodded his approval as I came to a proper stop and waited calmly on the red, then, glancing both ways for errant traffic, departed slowly at the green, radiating a sense of responsibility and shifting into second gear at about fifteen. I nodded to the cop. Who was fooled?

From Wakarusa we dropped down to Indiana 119, for Goshen, and then headed east and north toward Shipshewana. Shipshewana stood at the center of a Mennonite community. My friend, a filmmaker, wanted to find out about a stock auction that took place there regularly. So we said, asking directions. What he really wanted was to scout locations and to discover how the Amish here might take to his desire to document their auction.

We pulled up in Goshen for gas, but also to show off, to parade ourselves and the vehicle. We were full of pretending we were driving in from California, though we were both in school in South Bend. And, sure, there were other 427 'Vettes around, pal, but not ones like this one. My brother had made it even more intimidating (only to a certain class of people, of course—we were oblivious) by stripping it of ornament. The chrome body trim and manufacturer's symbols had been removed. The black fiberglass body showed no panel seams. The magnesium wheels were dull gray, the tires black sidewalls with black-on-black lettering. The seats and interior were black. The faces of some of the dashboard instruments showed the only bits of bright color. The floor mats were red.

At the gas station we responded with laconic detachment to the curiosity of the attendant, using an arcane jargon indispensable to this kind of conversation.

"Jesus, some car."

"Yeah."

"Three-ninety?"

"Four-twenty-seven."

"What's the compression?"

"Twelve."

"Jesus. You got deuces in there or a four-barrel?"

"Holly four. The exhaust is tuned. The lakers are for real."

"You got Iskindarian cams?"

"Yeah."

We bantered like lawyers before a trial. The only way the attendant could win was to know more about the car and the engine than I did. The tank was full before I ran out of esoteric information about the transmission and rear end. I left a discrete *chirp* of burning rubber in second gear as I pulled away into traffic.

He hadn't mentioned the heat. If we'd been driving a Plymouth sedan, that would have been his opener. When I told him we were from California, he glanced into the car and told me it was illegal to drive barefoot in Indiana.

We cruised slowly around town in Shipshewana, looking for somebody to introduce ourselves to. It was apparent right away that the car carried no weight at all here. These people preferred buttons on their pants to zippers and they had little truck with electricity. We felt one kind of authority—horsepower—slip away and a second emerge: we were on a professional quest. We acted more intent now, even solemn, though merely sitting in such a car, a high-strung horse all a-jitter in a small corral, made it difficult to regard ourselves in a serious light.

We parked—the only car—near a large barn where we speculated the auction probably took place and got out. There was no one around. Barefoot in Levi's and T-shirts, our long hair tied back but wind-ravaged at the edges, we tried to appear in need of assistance. No one came. We walked up to the barn and peered in. No one. The bare ground in front of the building had been hoof-beaten to dust the consistency of flour and was pilled with desiccated crumbles of horse manure. In the stillness only one sound came to us, the rising drone of cicadas from elms growing beside a building that could be a store.

No one in there either. Was it Sunday? No.

We got back in the car and pulled out on the highway. We'd go out to one of the farmhouses we could see. In the rearview mirror I spotted a man in dark trousers and suspenders watching us from the shade of the elms. I thought to turn around, but by then Don and I shared a sense that we were so out of place we might as well have been pulling into some town in Mongolia.

I passed a horse-drawn buggy. I began to distinguish men working in outlying fields and stepping through barn doors. And to notice horses standing head down in the heat. We pulled into a yard. A man in a dark hat wearing dark trousers and with his white shirt buttoned to the throat came over to my side of the car. I didn't want to shut the engine off, to indicate we assumed we could stay. We'd be moving right along. He and Don tried to converse over the *ba-bam-bam-buh-bam-buh-buh-bam* of the exhaust. I was so chagrined by our outlandish appearance I didn't pay attention to the conversation. It was cordial and succinct. The man showed no sign of finding us strange or presumptuous. Yes, there was a stock auction coming up in a week. People from all around in Lagrange and Elkhart Counties and from Michigan would be bidding, mostly on draft and carriage horses. And pigs. I realized as they spoke that the air was pungent with the odors of fresh-cut grass and pig manure. And that the air was a bit cooler here and not so hazy as it was in South Bend.

He told us to see a Mr. Huster and gave us directions. We thanked him sincerely, with all the politeness we could muster without seeming to be false. I let in the oversize eleven-inch clutch slowly and pulled away as quietly as possible. While the man was talking with Don, I'd been looking sidelong at his hands, suspended at the level of my face. Large, calm, deliberate hands.

Don asked if I'd brought any shoes. If Mr. Huster was at home he wanted to get out of the car, get away from the car, to inquire about the auction. Yes, I had. We stopped on a swath of golden field stubble at the side of the road and I fished them out from behind the seat.

Don began to laugh. He made an exaggerated sound like an idling engine's and crossed his eyes and leered in self-mockery at the foolishness we must have represented to the other man, ignorant as North Side Chicago VISTA volunteers on the Navajo Reservation.

Mr. Huster was home. Don raised a finger to signal me from his front porch, where someone had answered Don's knock, to indicate success. He disappeared behind a closing screen door. My interest in his film had ebbed, and it was too hot to sit in the car waiting. I walked over to a fence in a windbreak of poplars and stood in the cooler air. There were Belgian draft horses in the paddock. White fetlocks, blazed faces. Flaxen manes and docked tails. And Percherons, a darker chestnut than the Belgians and smaller headed. Both breeds, stout as bridge timbers, were huge, even-tempered animals.

There were six Belgians, four Percherons. I studied them to see if I could tell which might be matched pairs. Ants moved along the whitewashed fence rail. The light-blue sky was empty of birds. Only the rising, strident chorus of cicadas and the movement of grazing horses, the streaming of the ants, broke up the stillness, the insistence of the heat.

When Don came back to the car, he had the perplexed look of someone at odds with many things.

"How'd you do?"

"Fine. This guy sort of runs the auction. It's all right with him to film. I think. Not really sure."

We stood facing each other on opposite sides of the car.

"Look at these horses," I said.

"Yeah, what are they, Clydesdales?"

"The light ones are Belgians. The others are Percherons. Same deal."

"This guy Huster sells horses. Maybe these here are for sale."

"How much? He say how much?"

A woman was approaching us from the house with a tray. It bore a large stoneware pitcher and two glasses with ice. She was petite. She wore no makeup. Maybe she was twenty. The hemline of her gray jumper broke at her shins. Underneath it, she wore a plain, high-collared blouse with long sleeves. She held the tray out with a demure smile and spoke not a word.

We nodded politely and took the glasses as silently. We drank the ice water in that *uh-gluck, uh-gluck, uh-gluck* rhythm that is to drink without tasting. She held the tray out for our glasses and poured them full again. We drank again, half a glass each.

"Thanks very much," I said. "It's very thoughtful. Appreciate it."

She smiled and squinted at us with her head tilted, teetering between her world and ours, as though half-convinced we weren't there. No one spoke. She walked away with an air of having satisfied herself.

"You want to drive back to the barn? Is that where they have the auction?"

"Yeah, let's go by there. I want to see the situation inside, where we can set up."

We drove section-line roads back to Indiana 5, the highway on which the barn stood. I sensed the authority of the car again, and took some sort of reassurance from the slickness with which I shifted.

"I'll be out in a minute," said Don. He stepped through a side door into the barn.

I looked around for the man I'd seen under the trees before. After a while I got out and walked over to the circles of shade cast by the elms growing next to the building I thought was a store. The rear of the building was open, like a stable shed. The man I'd seen was sitting astride a backless chair with a sickle cupped in his arm like a violin. He was stroking it with a foot-long sharpening stone. He smiled and acknowledged me with a slight movement of his head. Hand tools and small farm implements—harrow rakes and plow bottoms—sat in orderly piles on the ground all around him. Blacksmith, I thought. In spite of his apparent cordiality, I sensed no opening for a conversation. I stood watching as though the scene before me were a diorama.

"Where you boys from?" he said in an even voice, but suddenly.

"South Bend. We're in school over there. We're thinking about making a movie here."

"Oh!"

"We just want to check the lighting in the barn over there."

He ceased stroking the sickle blade and looked up, but said nothing. He was in his thirties. He looked as though he were regarding a painting in a gallery that had no meaning for him.

"Well," I said, turning away, "we're just going to be here a minute. Sorry if we disturbed you."

He didn't watch me leave. It wasn't rudeness I felt as much as a sense that, for him, what I was speaking about was impractical, remote from the task then in his hands. Perhaps it would have been different if it hadn't been so hot, if the air under the elms hadn't felt so staggered.

"We going somewhere else?" I asked Don as he got in the car.

He shrugged. "Let's go up to Michigan, up to Three Rivers and eat dinner."

I pulled out on Indiana 5 and headed north. We passed the ranks of orderly Amish fields, the neat two-story frame houses and carriage buildings. Towheaded boys and girls stood still in front yards staring, midgame, looking like children from an N. C. Wyeth drawing in that famous edition of *Tom Sawyer*.

"Gene Stratton Porter is buried around here somewhere," I said.

"Who?"

"She wrote about waifs and orphans. Like James Oliver Curwood, Rider Haggard, that vein. The stories hold together pretty good when you're young, then they feel stranger, like zoo animals."

I slowed at the T-junction with Indiana 120. No traffic. I turned left. Thunderheads building in the west. An afternoon cloudburst to come.

"So, you going to make a movie?"

Don shrugged and leaned down to take my sneakers off. "Yeah. I think so. I want to break through all that . . . what? Understatement?"

"You mean how reserved, how noncommittal they all are?"

"Yeah. That."

We were shouting now over the sound of the car's acceleration. I shifted to third so smoothly the steady line of the Corvette's hood rose just slightly. We knew what we were doing. I hit fourth doing nearly ninety.

17

THEFT

I N T H E C O O L Georgia morning under dogwoods my
uncle's Mercury Marquis possessed animal-like qualities, like
a workhorse taken from a shaded stall at dawn, sleek and
quivering. Later, under the match strike of the summer sun, the
car would be too hot to touch, and in the humid air my legs
would stick to the leather seats. With the thud of the big doors
just then, though, I only felt class coming to attention, the
teacher taking his seat.

My uncle Gordon lit a Panatella cigar and headed us south out
of Thomaston. We were driving to a farm in Macon County, a
quarter-section of land on the east bank of the Flint River owned
by a man named Arthur Drewpierce. The Drewpierces, my uncle
told me, had been in that part of Macon County since before
cotton, seven generations or more. He and Mr. Drewpierce had

business to discuss that morning, he made clear as we drove along, gesturing occasionally with his cigar hand at a distant barn, offering a few lines of history or an anecdote. I knew when he asked me to accompany him, though, that he had a separate reason and thought it not likely that it was solely to meet Mr. Drewpierce. It was Gordon's way quietly to set a problem before me. He was then the Upson County superintendent of schools as well as the superintendent of schools in the county seat of Thomaston, but he had taught high school for many years and some at Auburn University, his alma mater. He was as devoted to the idea of a formal education as other men were to the pursuit of financial profit.

I lived hundreds of miles from his home, in an apartment in Manhattan with my younger brother and my parents. Whenever my brother and I came for a visit, Gordon would impress on us the need to understand the family's history, the incidents in our slow migration from the Delaware Water Gap in 1725 through Virginia to Georgia and Alabama. He would emphasize our obligations to the integrity and honor of that family, no matter what we may have heard from others of horse thievery or disinheritance.

He was neither obsessive about family history nor overbearing about integrity, only direct and serious. And because he undermined the gravity of these concerns with wit or humor he seemed neither pedantic nor sanctimonious. He appeared to suggest, however, that there was something debilitating that haunted human society. He implied that the knowledge he conveyed was crucial to survival, that Armageddons loomed for us, always. The threats he saw to civilization were vague. They had to do with the failure to remember, which explained some of his devotion to the study of history, and the failure to honor. The high polish of his shoes, the careful routine of his days, the deliberation with which he spoke, like his library and the perfectly maintained car, were his proofs against such menace.

We rolled south in the big Mercury. I sat with my elbow out the window in the car's slipstream. In the summer of my twelfth year I could almost manage this naturally.

Gordon was being promoted by businessmen and state educa-tors for the House of Representatives. I understood that his driv-ing out to see Mr. Drewpierce had something to do with this, that he wanted Mr. Drewpierce's views. I was staring at a feral wall of kudzu vine festooned in the roadside trees, wondering what he had in mind for me, when he began to speak of Indians.

I'd heard some of these stories from him before, about the Kashita and Coweta, and about Andrew Jackson's fight with the Creeks at Horseshoe Bend on the Tallapoosa. His recountings seemed exotic; I knew no one else in Georgia who referred to local Indians. He lined out their histories with the same knowl-edge and authority he brought to discussions of what he called the War Between the States. I knew no other adult who took his-tory as seriously. I listened attentively, knowing this was a pre-lude, that he was leading me someplace.

His language tended to be formal and dramatic and was sometimes biblical in its cadence; his views he decanted in slow measure. The sentences sounded rehearsed, but they weren't. The Creeks, he was saying, were a confederacy of tribes, the most powerful of which were the Muskogee. The ceremonies of a farming people held them to the earth, in particular *boskita,* an eight-day celebration built around the ripening of the last corn plants. (We drove a macadam network of backcountry roads with no signs as he spoke, passing isolated clapboard shacks elevated on stone pilings and weathered gray, passing the spindle-lattice of picked cotton fields and fields thick with sorghum and ripening corn, passing Herefords slow-grazing pastures in the awakening light.)

"But long before that . . ." He was pausing now, gathering the documents in his mind. ". . . long before the Muskogee, it might have been Aztecs who were here. Before that culture had either name or notoriety among the Spaniards, before they were a hor-ror for the Mixtecs to behold, they might have been living right here on these creeks, tending their gardens, worshiping the sun."

He looked at me, to see how I was taking it in, gauging his next remark.

"A man named Whittier, from the university up at Athens, has been down to see Mr. Drewpierce. He wants to excavate along the river there at the edge of his fields. He believes Aztecs once camped there. Now, Mr. Drewpierce, he has no strong feelings about this yet—either way. It's in a state of negotiation for him. Mr. Drewpierce reads his Bible closely on this and other matters though, so Mr. Whittier, you see, might not be able to dig there. We may or may not learn anything more of this campsite beyond what Mr. Drewpierce's man Otis found last fall, a few bits of pottery. He may decide to take a six-bottom plow to it, you understand."

I nodded yes. Yes I would not bring up the subject in Mr. Drewpierce's presence; and, yessir, if Mr. Drewpierce brought it up and suggested I go down to the site while you talked together I would go (and this, certainly, was why my uncle had brought me here). And, yessir, I wouldn't touch or take anything.

"Do they teach you these things in school?"

"Yessir."

"About the Aztecs?"

"Yes, I've heard of it, heard of them."

"I don't remember it well, just that the Aztecs came in from the north and conquered the Mixtecs and others, and then the Spaniards slaughtered them."

"And they had a great empire."

"Yes, they did. They were great builders and mathematicians. When you walk along the river, think about these people, how they started out on these creeks. Mr. Whittier is impassioned to prove his point, you understand, which could be a mistake— archeologically and with Mr. Drewpierce."

He looked at me with an amused smile. I basked in the level of his confidence in me.

MR. DREWPIERCE WAS a tall man and I thought him disdainful at first. He wore a clean white shirt under a fresh-laundered pair of Union bib overalls and greeted us in a quiet voice. He steered us to a gather of green-and-white metal lawn chairs on his porch and called to his wife to bring us some lemonade.

I drank my lemonade in silence while the two men spoke, a light conversation of gossip, weather, and anecdote which I knew often preceded serious conversation in such a setting.

"Boy, I believe I know where you might interest yourself for an hour or two," said Mr. Drewpierce.

I glanced across at his long face, not meaning to stare at the way his dark eyebrows rolled down into the corners of his eye sockets.

"Yessir?"

"You see that fence running yonder?"

"Yessir."

"Well, you go out there and follow that fence down to the river, and then you walk on up there about five hundred yards, to where the river comes on a bend, and right there in the crook of it is some mighty interesting things washing out of the sand."

I looked to Gordon, who nodded approval of a plan he was pleased to have helped fashion.

The morning heat and humidity had now become oppressive. Crossing the fields and walking the fence I began to sweat, a scent attractive to mosquitoes and, I suspected, chiggers. Canebrake rattlers lay in the field rows here and cottonmouth water moccasins were in the river. The country seethed with the threat of violence from small animals. I watched anxiously, too, for poison ivy. I was relieved when the banks of the river appeared at the end of the fence and I felt a faint, fitful breeze off the water.

I found the bend with no trouble, and saw the first potsherds before I'd walked a dozen feet. I squatted down on my haunches to study them: gray and reddish shards, some incised with stylized patterns resembling the impression of leaf fronds, some looking blackened by fire. I brought my fingers hesitantly into contact with their gritty edges protruding from the soil. *Aztecs.* I stood and walked farther along the curving bank. I discovered concentrations of potsherds in two more places, and nearby found glistening flakes of quartz, a sign of worked stone. I began a diligent search for arrowheads. That I would take nothing from this place had been my faith, but I felt now a need beyond all restraint and thought. I could not understand how taking a single arrowhead might matter at all.

I searched for nearly an hour, looking for any object that suggested weaponry or adversity. I found nothing. Disappointed, I instead pulled two potsherds from the soil to examine more closely. One looked as if it had been broken away from the smooth rim of a bowl or jar. The other was intricately hatched with fine lines. I washed the sandy red soil off both in the river. They glistened like fish in my hands, and now seemed very valuable. I pushed them deliberately into the pockets of my shorts. What Aztecs had once held, I now held. The thought worked on me that the confluence here was preordained, a cabalistic power was inherent in this simple act. In taking possession of these two pieces of pottery, I had transcended the intrusive nuisance of insects and heat, the threat of snakes and poisonous plants. I felt ownership.

I walked back along the fence to the Drewpierce place. My eyes cooled when I rested them in the pine-straw shadows of a loblolly copse, the Drewpierce woodlot. The light on the muddy surface of the river had been fierce, predatory.

They were still talking. I sat on the ground beneath a weeping willow, studying how the fabric of my shorts might disguise the shape of what was in my pockets. I hated having to wear shorts, that I was not old enough for pants.

The men talked on. I felt hungry. I began to imagine how I would explain what I'd found to my brother, tell him how I, myself, had located this obscure site, had discovered what once had belonged to Aztecs, and had carefully removed only these two pieces of pottery. If he reacted with jealousy I would offer him one. Or maybe just give him one on his birthday, anyway.

My uncle hailed me to the porch, and we said good-bye before Mr. Drewpierce would feel obliged to invite us for lunch. We drove east in the big car with the wind blowing through the open windows. We stopped at a family cafe in Marshallville for lunch.

They all knew him. They called him Mr. Holstun when we walked in.

My uncle asked if I'd had a good time, but he did not ask what I had seen. Sitting there at the Formica table, I could not fit the desire to share my excitement to any story I might confidently tell. Riding in the car I felt a piece of pottery, its outline clearly visible, stabbing me in the leg. When I showed no inclination to discuss the site or Mr. Whittier's ideas, I felt sure Gordon knew I'd stolen something.

On the way home Gordon said the river site might not be Aztecan. He said he respected Mr. Whittier's views and hoped Mr. Drewpierce would allow Mr. Whittier to carefully examine what was there, but he believed the pieces of pottery now sitting on the Drewpierce mantlepiece would prove to be Mayan. The Mayans traded vigorously and extensively north of their homes in the Yucatán Peninsula, he said. Some of their pottery, he told me, had been found in sites as far north as New York State.

"These are all theories," he concluded. "Just speculation. Someday men will have the tools to confirm what they believe happened here"—he gestured out the window—"before we came along. And then in another time they will talk about us, about what we did, or what we might have believed. We make sense of ourselves as a people through history. That is why we should make no modifications in records of the past, you see, but only speculate."

On the long ride back to Thomaston I searched beyond his words for the power that had been undeniable and true on the riverbank. An angry silence, for me, grew up between us, as if he had ruined something.

That night I lay wide awake, succumbing finally to shame and stupidity. The boyish fascination with notoriety that makes being any kind of outlaw attractive was gone now. I felt the false step, the bad faith, that ultimately makes the outlaw an out-cast among his own people. I couldn't continue to deny it with bravado. If the house had not been asleep, I would have gone upstairs and asked Gordon not for absolution but to listen to my explanation, to the intelligence I had arrived at on my own

through shame. I knew that night that I was on the verge of the territory of adults.

In the morning, my thoughts were jumbled and I said nothing to him. The act was ineradicable and I lived with it.

GORDON DID NOT enter the race for a congressional seat, although he seemed assured of winning it. He didn't want it. I continued to see him once a year or so after that, until he died in 1976. We enjoyed many fine and complicated discussions while I was in college, and in some ways I came to reflect his sense of values. The incident at the river, though we never referred to it, formed part of our understanding of each other.

Twenty-five years after that day on the Flint River, walking in a remote area on the west rim of Marble Canyon in northern Arizona with two archeologists, I came upon the ruins of an Anasazi dwelling, a structure about eight hundred years old. Scattered all around it in the dust were hundreds of potsherds, some beautifully decorated with red-on-black designs, others finely incised with a fingernail to accentuate a corrugated pattern in the clay. With the permission of the archeologists I moved several of these shards to photograph them against a background of sunlit canyon walls and white cumulus clouds floating in a bright blue sky. When I was finished I returned each piece to its cradle of dust.

It occurred to me, of course, to take a potsherd as a memento, but I had no such desire. I agreed with my companions that the shards formed part of a historical record, that they should be left for some other mind to come upon and to interpret after we are gone. I had no desire to take anything, either, because of the esteem I had for my companions, my regard for their profession and for our friendship. I couldn't shake a feeling, though, which had clung to me since I'd moved the potsherds, that something was wrong. Something was unfinished.

That evening I sat on my sleeping bag working up the day's notes by the light of a fire. Across from me one of my companions, Bob Euler, was cleaning our dinner dishes. He was older

than me by about twenty years, a professor of archeology, a former university president.

"Bob?" I said. He looked up. "I want you to know that even though I picked up those potsherds back there to photograph, I didn't pocket them. I haven't picked up anything on these sites. I just want to tell you that plainly. I don't do that."

"Yes," he said, "I noticed."

Acknowledgments

I<small>T IS CUSTOMARY</small> in a book like this, which brings recent essays and new work together, for the writer to thank the editors with whom he or she has collaborated. I want to do this here in an explicit way because skilled and sympathetic editors play a pivotal role in a writer's work over the years. I do not mean solely by offering a pat on the back or by a willingness to support a writer in the exploration of a place or an event that takes hold of his imagination. The editors who influence me most put the story itself and the reader first. They elicit from the writer greater precision, a more eloquent language, and a more concise narrative to achieve that end. In the search for clarity, it takes a remarkable editor to protect both the spirit of the story and the reader's interests.

Over the past twenty years I've benefited from the astute editorial attention of many good people, foremost among them Lewis Lapham, Charis Conn, Janet Wondra, Robley Wilson, Chip Blake, John Rasmus, Paul Perry, and Laurie Graham, who for many years was my editor at Scribner.

When I started selecting essays and planning additional work for *About This Life,* I began a collaboration with a new editor, Robin Desser, at Knopf. I quickly learned that I was working with someone who understood, sometimes better than I did, what I was up to; her empathy made many decisions easier. I want to express my gratitude for her guidance in bringing the book and several of the essays to their final form.

Janet Wondra at *The Georgia Review* edited "Searching for Depth in Bonaire" with me. The essay is reprinted here in virtually the same form in which it appeared in the magazine. Both Sarah Ferrell and Michael Leahy at the *New York Times* worked with me on "A Short Passage in Northern Hokkaido." Robley Wilson, the editor of *The North American Review,* where I have been a contributing editor since 1977, helped sharpen "Orchids on the Volcanoes." (On this and subsequent trips to the Galápagos I received the generous and genial support of Bill Roberson of Inca Floats.) Gerry Marzorati, then at *Harper's,* took the lightest touch of a pencil to "Informed by Indifference." (It is a pleasure to thank Guy Guthridge, manager of the National Science Foundation's Artists and Writers in Antarctica Program, for his unstinting support and accommodation on several trips to Antarctica, and Peter Wilkniss, former director of the NSF's Office of Polar Programs, for his friendship and facilitation.)

Lewis Lapham and Charis Conn at *Harper's,* where I have been a contributing editor since 1984, worked on "Flight" with me. (I would like to thank Jon Austin at Northwest Airlines, who understood, as relatively few in media relations do, the level of detail some writers require in order to write the story that interests them. Also Mary Jean Olsen at Boeing, for arranging for me to see the assembly of the 747-400 freighter at Everett, Washington. Odette Fodor and Pits van der Hoeven provided assistance on KLM's international routes. Paul Omodt of the Airline Pilots Association helped at several points with important information.)

Peter Stine at *Witness* along with special-issue editor Tom Lyon edited "Apologia." John Rasmus, then at *Outside,* edited "In a Country of Light, Among Animals." Robert Atwan provided editorial guidance when I was writing "The American Geographies" for a collection of work he was editing, *Openings: Original Essays by Contemporary Soviet and American Writers* (University of Washington Press, 1990). Chip Blake and Emily Hiestand at *Orion* also helped in editing this essay. "Effleurage: The Stroke of Fire" was also edited by Charis Conn and Lewis Lapham.

Stephen Corey at *The Georgia Review* worked with me on "Replacing Memory." Mark Jannot at *Men's Journal,* with John Rasmus, edited "A Passage of the Hands." Robin Cruise at *Rocky Mountain* magazine helped with "Murder."

Other essays here benefited from the editorial attention of both Laurie Graham and Robin Desser.

Finally, I would like to thank Peter Matson, my literary agent, who for many years has offered guidance and good counsel in editorial and other matters.

TEXT ACKNOWLEDGMENTS

Some of these essays, several under different titles and in a slightly different form, originally appeared in the following publications:

"Searching for Depth in Bonaire," *The Georgia Review* (autumn 1996); "A Short Passage in Northern Hokkaido," *The New York Times Magazine, The Sophisticated Traveler* (October 5, 1986); "Orchids on the Volcanoes," *The North American Review* (June 1989); "Informed by Indifference," *Harper's* (May 1988); "Flight," *Harper's* (October 1995); "Apologia," *Witness* (winter 1989); "In a Country of Light, Among Animals," *Outside* (June/July 1981); "The American Geographies," *Orion* (autumn 1989); "Effleurage: The Stroke of Fire," *Harper's* (January 1998); "The Whaleboat," *Outside* (May 1998); "Replacing Memory," *The Georgia Review* (spring 1993); "A Passage of the Hands," *Men's Journal* (December 1996/January 1997); "Learning to See," *DoubleTake* (spring 1998); "Murder," *Rocky Mountain Magazine* (May/June 1981) and *Oregon Quarterly* (spring 1998).

ALSO BY BARRY LOPEZ

"Among the greatest twentieth-century
American nature writers."
—*San Francisco Chronicle*

CROSSING OPEN GROUND

National Book Award–winning author Barry Lopez weaves
an invigorating spell in *Crossing Open Ground*. Through his
crystalline vision, Lopez urges us toward a new attitude, a
re-enchantment with the world that is vital to our sense of
place, our well-being and our very survival.

Nonfiction/Nature/0-679-72183-5

THE REDISCOVERY OF NORTH AMERICA

Five hundred years ago an Italian named Christopher
Columbus came to America and began a process not of
discovery but of incursion—a "ruthless, angry search for
wealth"—that continues today. This provocative book draws
a direct line between the atrocities of the Spanish conquista-
dors and the ongoing pillage of our lands and waters, and
challenges us to adopt an ethic that will make further depre-
dations impossible.

History/Nature/0-679-74099-6

VINTAGE BOOKS
Available at your local bookstore, or call toll-free to order:
1-800-793-2665 (credit cards only).